The New Chinese America

The New Chinese America

CLASS, ECONOMY, AND SOCIAL HIERARCHY

XIAOJIAN ZHAO

RUTGERS UNIVERSITY PRESS

New Brunswick, New Jersey, and London

LIBRARY OF CONGRESS CATALOGING-IN-PUBLICATION DATA

Zhao, Xiaojian, 1953–
    The new Chinese America : class, economy, and social hierarchy /
Xiaojian Zhao.
        p.   cm.
    Includes bibliographical references and index.
    ISBN 978–0–8135–4691–9 (hardcover : alk. paper) —
ISBN 978–0–8135–4692–6 (pbk. : alk. paper)
    1. Chinese Americans—History.   2. Chinese Americans—Social
conditions.   3. Chinese Americans—Economic conditions.   4. Com-
munity life—United States—History.   5. Immigrants—United States—
History.   6. Social classes—United States—History.   7. Dominance
(Psychology)—United States—History.   8. United States—Ethnic
relations.   9. United States—Social conditions—Ethnic relations.   I. Title.
    E184.C5Z43123 2010
    973'.04951—dc22   2009018770

A British Cataloging-in-Publication record for this book is available
from the British Library.

Copyright © 2010 by Xiaojian Zhao

Visit our Web site: http://rutgerspress.rutgers.edu

Manufactured in the United States of America

For Sue and Hai
with love

Contents

Acknowledgments

The research of this book would not have been possible without the generous support and assistance of many individuals. I owe thanks to all the men and women who participated in this study and shared life stories that included legally sensitive details and were sometimes emotionally difficult to recount, although few of their real names will appear in the book. I am grateful to Chin Chin Chang, Julie Chuang, Katherine Gonzales, Anna Hui, Alice Stone, Henry Tai, Loretta Tse, Tony Wang, Ping Yao, and Yi Zhang for putting me in contact with many of the participants. Tsang Wai-Yin of the *Shijie zhoukan*, whose reports on new immigrants in New York led me to expand my research from California to the East Coast, not only shared with me her own research experiences but also kindly took me to Manhattan's and Flushing's Chinatowns and introduced me to many of her acquaintances. Ping Yao, Patrick Pribyl, and Elizabeth Zhang kindly hosted me when I was in Los Angeles and made their house available for me to conduct oral history interviews. I enjoyed Ping's company at employment offices and immigration firms, and her enthusiasm for my research was much needed at times when progress seemed slow. The hospitality of Maggie Gee, Ann, Alan, and Jianmin Zhao, and Feng Zheng made my trips to San Francisco Bay area pleasant.

More than two dozen Chinese American associations and churches opened their doors for my visits. Special thanks go to the staffs at the *Zhonghua huiguan* in San Francisco, New York, and Los Angeles; Chinese American Citizens Alliance in San Francisco and Los Angeles; Lee Family Association in New York; and American Fujianese Association in New York. I am especially grateful to the Changle American Association for arranging interviews and responding to many of my inquires.

I want to thank Ning Zhang, who handled immigration statistics and census data skillfully and offered tips in quantitative analysis. Raelynn

Moy helped locate many Chinese language sources, and tallied and tabled businesses listed in Chinese Yellow Pages of twelve metropolitan regions. Alvin Luo, Cathy Nguyen, and Katie Do transcribed oral history interviews, made countless library trips, compiled bibliographies, and provided technical support with computer programs. Anitra Grisales, Gail Tinsley, and Jason Stohler each helped edit several chapters. Gerardo Colmenar at the UCSB library provided invaluable reference assistance. I also want to thank Jiemin Bao, Raelynn Moy, Hanxiang Li, Xiaobo Lu, Alvin Luo, Pei Wang, William Wang, Jianmin Zhao, and Ming Zhang for helping to collect Chinese-language newspapers and business directories published in Houston, New York, Chicago, Seattle, Las Vegas, and San Francisco. Min Zhou has generously shared with me her own collection of Chinese-language telephone books and other sources.

Many friends, scholars, and students helped me put my research into a social context in ways they may not fully realize. I want to thank those who listened to my stories and provided their insights: Jiemin Bao, Raelynn Moy, Sucheng Chan, Amy Chang, Meimei Chang, Douglas Daniels, Bryna Goodman, Jennifer Hong, Serene Chen, Diane Fujino, Maggie Gee, Sarah Griffith, Yaping Hsu, Peter Kwong, Him Mark and Laura Lai, Pete Lew, Wei Li, Haiming Liu, Weijing Lu, John Park, Paul Spickard, Jason Stohler, De Tang, Peisu Wen, Ping Yao, Xiao-huang Yin, Judy Yung, Ning Zhang, and Min Zhou.

I am fortunate to work with many supportive colleagues at the University of California, Santa Barbara. The Department of Asian American Studies provided an intellectual forum for my study. During the three years when I chaired the department, my colleagues made a collective effort to protect my time so that I could at least make some progress in research. I thank friends and colleagues who read the manuscript and provided critical feedback. John Park read the entire manuscript more than once and demanded that I, though a historian by training, write as an Asian American Studies scholar with an interdisciplinary audience in mind. Pei-te Lien brought important documents to my attention and offered her expertise on census research. Although fully occupied with several book projects of her own, Sucheng Chan read the manuscript more carefully than anyone else could have and offered incisive and detailed suggestions. I am grateful to have her intellectual and professional guidance. Diane Fujino encouraged me to study the less privileged, and I appreciate her comments. Conversations with James Lee helped me formulate discussions on underclass Americans, and enthusiasm from Erin Ning and Celine Shimizu was very much appreciated. I also want to thank Douglas Daniels, who read chapters at various stages, and Claudine Michel, who offered sisterly support and cheer. Both Arlene Phillips, our department manager, and Elizabeth Guerrero, our undergraduate advisor, deserve special acknowledgment for their patience, their many friendly reminders of my other responsibilities, and their countless acts of kindness.

I very much appreciate the guidance of editors of Rutgers University Press. Melanie Halkias expressed an interest in the project from the very beginning. Leslie Mitchner offered her consistent encouragement and advice, and I am grateful for her patience. I also want to thank Margaret Case, who copyedited the manuscript. My book has benefited greatly from the insightful and challenging comments from the readers with the Rutgers University Press. Critical and supportive suggestions from Roger Daniels were immensely helpful.

Chapter 4 of the book originally appeared in *Chinese Americans and the Politics of Race and Culture*, edited by Sucheng Chan and Madeline Y. Hsu (Philadelphia: Temple University Press, 2008).

This book has taken much longer to complete than I anticipated, and my deepest appreciation goes to my husband Hai and my daughter Sue, who offered unwavering love and support, even though I had to spend many evenings and weekends working. Hai was available to offer encouragement and assistance whenever needed, and the exciting moments we shared catching glimpses of dolphins and whales on the Santa Barbara waterfront kept me energized regardless of pressing deadlines. Sue was the toughest critic of my manuscript. I hope she will realize how seriously I took her criticism, and how much her comments have strengthened the book.

NOTE ON TRANSLITERATION

THE TRANSLITERATION OF PERSONAL NAMES in this book is inconsistent for a number of reasons. In Chinese practice, the family name comes before the given name. Most Chinese living in the United States reverse the order, following Western practices, but this is only done in English settings. So if a person's name comes from a Chinese-language source, his or her last name appears before the first name. This applies to Chinese in Asia as well as individuals who choose not to invert their names. When the writings of scholars who have inverted their names are listed in the bibliography, a comma follows the family name. When the author's Chinese-language publications are cited, his/her name is given the way it is with no comma after the last name.

Immigrants from Taiwan or pre-1949 China transliterate their names according to the Wade-Giles system, often with a hyphen between the two characters that form a person's given name. Names of Chinese, however, are not always transliterated systematically, as some conversions are based on local dialects instead of Mandarin. The pinyin transliteration system, one that prevails in the People's Republic of China and has been adopted by most Chinese language programs in the United States, is used for all the names and terms from Chinese-language documents.

The New Chinese America

Introduction

SCHOOLS WERE IN FULL SESSION in late April. Tests were scheduled and papers and projects were due soon. But few graduating seniors with college admissions in hand would let schoolwork spoil their celebratory mood. The air was filled with a palpable excitement. The few weeks ahead would be about proms, graduations, and gatherings reaffirming friendships before bidding farewell.

Within the Chinese American community, excitement was mixed with high anxiety over the mysterious college admissions process. The success (or failure in some cases) of the soon-to-be-college students prompted many questions from parents with younger children: Why was a particular student accepted by one college but rejected by another? Why did John win a scholarship while his equally outstanding friend Larry got nothing? What exactly were the universities looking for? How much did they weigh extracurricular actives versus grades and test scores? And how should the younger high-school students prepare themselves for the upcoming challenges?

Chinese American parents' high anxiety over the college admissions process and their strong desire to push their children ahead of the game were well anticipated by ethnic educational services. No time would be wasted. Before the departure of the senior class, programs were already scheduled to engage parents of younger children. On April 26, 2008, for example, a two-day "Education Show and Seminars" program was held in Los Angeles. This event was sponsored by *Shijie ribao* (Chinese Daily News), the most popular Chinese language newspaper in the United States; the Elite Educational Institute; and several professional services. Offering eighteen lectures and thirty exhibit tables, this education fair made available bilingual information on a wide range of topics. Lack of English proficiency, however, was not the reason for those who drove for hours to Los Angeles from all over southern California to attend these seminars; most participants were well informed. They came to this event because they believed that their ethnic service providers would have more to offer than what was available from their local high schools. It was a great opportunity for strangers from similar cultural backgrounds and with the same anxieties to mingle and exchange information and knowledge with one another, using a familiar language. The lectures and materials were about American colleges and universities, but all were delivered and disseminated in a unique Chinese American style. This was apparent in the program highlights, including catchy topics such as "Realizing the Ivy League Dream: The Three Musts in College Application," "How to Ace the SAT!" and simply, "The Road to Harvard." Only those in the know were invited to speak; among them were admission officers or members of university recruitment teams, alumni of the Ivy League, and professional education consultants.[1]

In the past few decades, accompanying the rapid growth of the Chinese American population, many ethnic business districts—the new Chinatowns—have emerged in New York, Los Angeles, the San Francisco Bay Area, Houston, and other parts of the United States. Many different classes and programs are offered to both middle-class Chinese Americans and immigrant workers, and advice on education is only one of the hundreds of services provided by Chinese American entrepreneurs. This development reflects a high level of participation in the ethnic economy from a very diverse Chinese American population. There have been ups and downs in the U.S. economy in the past two decades, but even when the price of gas skyrockets and the unemployment rate peaks, a deserted parking lot is a rare scene in Chinese business districts. As many Chinese living in the United States have become Americanized, and a significant proportion of them have achieved middle-class status and become suburban dwellers, the growth of the ethnic economy and its ability to draw participants from the community as entrepreneurs, laborers, and consumers are phenomenal.

This book is not about how much the Chinese have achieved in the United States; other scholars have studied that aspect of Chinese American history.[2] This study is built upon the existing scholarship, with a clear understanding that a substantial proportion of the Chinese American population has experienced significant upward mobility. Rather than repeating or adding to what has been done, the book will approach the ethnic community from a different angle and analyze the means through which such social mobility is made possible. If as a whole the Chinese in the United States have achieved remarkable success at a faster pace than people of other ethnic backgrounds, what in their unique experience has made such a difference? What price did they pay and exactly who paid it? To this end the book explores the inner workings and internal dynamics of the community. Through discussions of demographic composition, social hierarchies, economic networks, and group organizations, it traces the threads that bring the individuals together and illuminates the relationships among various social groups.

Studying contemporary Chinese America is a challenging task for a number of reasons. First, the current Chinese population in the United States is huge compared to what it was in the late nineteenth and early twentieth centuries. There were only 77,504 Chinese residing in the United States in 1940. Two decades later the number had increased to 237,292. Since the 1965 Immigration Act abolished the racially biased quota system, the Chinese American population has doubled every decade. The 2000 census shows a record high of close to 2.9 million Chinese, even though a significantly large number of undocumented immigrants were probably left uncounted.[3]

Second, the demographic composition of contemporary Chinese America is strikingly different from that of the earlier period. The 1965 Immigration Act, with its basic provisions for family reunification and practical preferences for certain skilled labor and professionals, provides a legal framework that works to diversify the ethnic population. Unlike the immigrant laborers who originated from the Cantonese-speaking regions in southeast China, the new immigrants arrive from Hong Kong, Taiwan, various parts of the People's Republic of China, as well as Southeast Asia and other parts of the world. Their diverse regional background and their differences in former national allegiance are in sharp contrast to that of the pioneer Chinese immigrants from rural Guangdong. In today's Chinese America, several Chinese dialects are spoken along with English; some individuals cannot communicate with one another within the community due to their linguistic differences.

Third, unlike the old days, when the majority of the Chinese were restricted to segregated Chinatowns in large cities, post-World War II opportunities have dispersed the ethnic population, obscuring the geographic boundaries of the community. To a large extent, racial discrimination during the period of Chinese Exclusion (1882–1943), World War II, and the Cold War era worked to facilitate the construction of an ethnic identity, as Chinese Americans living in the ghettos reached out to each other in solidarity. Postwar geographic and social motilities, on the other hand, have fragmented the community, making organization along ethnic lines far more difficult. The heterogeneous rather than homogenous nature of Chinese Americans today poses a major question to the current study: does it still make sense, or is it feasible at all, to view all the Chinese living in the United States as belonging to one single community?[4]

Yet it is the amazing strength of ethnicity under new and ever more complex circumstances that makes studying Chinese Americans tempting. Regardless of the diversity of the population, the reduction of political pressure from the larger society, and the disappearance of confined ethnic ghettos, the Chinese have shown an unusual ability to bond to one another. Overcoming their differences in political ideologies and economic interests, individual Chinese have continued to use ethnicity as a base of personal identity and collective activities.[5] This phenomenon makes it appealing to approach Chinese American history from a cultural perspective. Elements of a culture built on shared history, sentiments, ethos, and language that can be traced back to Confucian China are not difficult to find, and memories and feelings about the past still play an important role in group affiliations.[6] But as many cultural history scholars have found, culture is not fixed and static but rather in constant flux under contestation and negotiation. The ways in which Chinese Americans practice their traditional culture through the arts, language, religion, festivals, and performance, for example, are often reflections of the changing circumstances surrounding them in America. The Chinese did not simply transplant their traditional culture in American soil; they reconstructed or reinvented it constantly.[7] A substantial number of the narratives in this book are based on conversations with individual participants. While these conversations do reveal sentiments and ethos that can be identified as related to Chinese culture, the main concern is not what is said or done, but rather the larger social context in which these individuals are embedded.

Instead of assuming that ethnicity is a given, this book traces the ways that ethnicity is utilized by a large contingent of Chinese of varying social, economic, political, and national origins to shape their fate in the United States. It explores the historical, economic, and social foundations of the Chinese American community and the ways that ethnicity is reworked in a society undergoing rapid change. The new mechanisms that work to connect Chinese Americans today developed after the decline of the organizational networks built by pioneer Chinese immigrants, and the ways in which these mechanisms pull otherwise unrelated individuals together are drastically different from those of the old days.

This book examines the internal class dynamics among individuals in contemporary Chinese America. Because hostilities and violence had halted Chinese immigration and kept the immigrants out of the mainstream job market, ethnicity more than class tended to determine social relations of the community before World War II. Racial oppression and the struggle for racial equality are central themes of scholarly writings on the early history of Chinese in the United States. Relatively few scholars have paid attention to class differences, partly because it is assumed that racial oppression against the Chinese determined the ethnic minority's low socioeconomic status during the years of exclusion.[8] In contrast, access to mainstream opportunities after exclusion seems to have allowed Chinese Americans to be transformed from a low class of worthless, excludable, unassimilable subhumans to a group of hardworking good citizens most likely to be found on college campuses, in business circles and high-tech industries, and within well-maintained suburban neighborhoods. Although many social scientists have challenged the so-called "model minority" theory by providing evidence to show that success and wealth are not shared by everyone or equally distributed, they have often attributed such discrepancies to the existence of a large immigrant population.[9] The hidden assumption is that moving up is only a matter of time for everyone who is willing to work hard, and that as a whole contemporary Chinese America is very much a middle-class community. To reduce ethnicity to class, however, is to refuse to see the relationship between ethnicity and class. If a large number of Chinese Americans have advanced in class terms and many more are on their way up, what about the ones who have failed to do so or have little hope of achieving the same goals? Does the structure of the ethnic community pave the way for success for some individuals while denying opportunities to others?

Although always important, material possessions are not the only measure of class identification. In recent decades, some social scientists have found that class is a form of social identity constructed by individuals to cement group affiliations. Because of the long history of Chinese immigration and legal restrictions, and because of the rapid historical, economic, and social changes that have taken place in both the United States and the immigrants' ancestral land, an individual's social class can be defined in a multitude of ways.[10]

This book uses class analysis to expose the other side of the Chinese American experience in the very place where the model minority was born. It shows the difficulties of everyday survival for some Chinese laborers, and reveals their positions in a new social hierarchy. The large inflow of an immigrant population has made it possible for the expansion of an ethnic economy, in which entrepreneurs can maintain a competitive edge given their access to low-cost labor; workers who do not have access to the mainstream job market due to their lack of marketability or legal restrictions can find employment and survive; and consumers can enjoy high-quality services at bargain prices. While the growth of the ethnic economy enhances ethnic bonds by increasing mutual dependencies among different groups of participants, it is hardly a win–win situation for everyone. As shown in the following pages, the economy functions to limit possibilities for disadvantaged groups, especially undocumented immigrants.

Relying on a wide range of sources, this study combines historical research with methodologies commonly used in sociological and anthropological approaches. The assessment of the scale of Chinese immigration and the size of the Chinese population is largely based on official government documents, including the U.S. census, Immigration and Naturalization Service (INS) statistics, and surveys, case reports, press releases, and special investigation files of government agencies and research institutions. Most discussions of community dynamics are based on sources produced by Chinese Americans themselves. I rely on Chinese-language newspapers to trace historical developments and community activities. The North American edition of *Shijie ribao*, the largest Chinese-language newspaper that operates through regional service branches in New York, San Francisco, Chicago, Houston, Vancouver, and Toronto, provides the most comprehensive coverage. This Taiwan-based newspaper is truly a global enterprise. With branch offices in the People's Republic of China and Hong Kong and reporters covering different parts of the world, it offers transnational links between the ethnic community and immigrants' ancestral land as well as the Chinese diaspora. I also consult more than a dozen other Chinese-language newspapers published in California, Nevada, New York, and Texas, as well as convention proceedings, special reports, newsletters, and other miscellaneous publications from more than forty Chinese American organizations, archives, cultural centers, and churches in the Los Angeles and San Francisco Bay areas, Seattle, Washington, D.C., New York, and Boston.

The profile of ethnic businesses is drawn largely from the *Chinese Consumer Reports*, the *Chinese Consumer Yellow Pages*, and the *Chinese Business Guide and Directories* published in twelve regions in the United States, including metropolitan areas of San Francisco, Los Angeles, San Diego, Las Vegas, Seattle, Chicago, Houston, New York, New Jersey, Philadelphia, Washington, D.C., and Boston. Some detailed information about certain businesses is obtained from classified advertisements in Chinese-language newspapers. Although the number of specific businesses and organizations analyzed in detail is limited, together these materials inform my discussions of the changes within Chinese America.

A large part of the research is based on oral history interviews. Using personal connections and community networks, I have been able to recruit 128 individuals to participate in this project. The fifty-eight men and seventy women I interviewed are of diverse political, socioeconomic, and immigration backgrounds, including laborers and service providers, business owners and other employers of coethnic workers, and consumers of the ethnic economy; some of them also hold leadership positions in various community organizations (see table I.1). A total of thirty-six individuals interviewed are neither employers nor employees in the Chinese American economy: their affiliations with the community are limited to being consumers or having ties to religious organizations; political, business, and intellectual circles; and informal social groups. About 90 percent (115 individuals) of those interviewed are immigrants who arrived after 1965 or are children of these immigrants; the other 10 percent (thirteen individuals) belong to the earlier immigrant generation. Of the 115 post-1965 immigrant interviewees, fifty-nine came from mainland China, thirty-four from Taiwan, and eleven from Hong Kong. Relatively few—a total of twelve—came from other parts of Asia. Fifty-two of the individuals are or were undocumented immigrants.

Working with undocumented immigrants requires additional effort because most of them could not afford to take time off from work. To get to spend time with them, I offered my own help. I accompanied non-English-speakers to medical clinics and served as an interpreter. I gave them rides and introduced them to services and English classes. Some individuals also consulted me on issues relating to their children's education or domestic disputes, and a couple of them asked me to communicate with immigration agencies on their behalf. These interactions helped me understand the everyday struggles of these men and women, which are as important as the other materials I have collected for my research.

TABLE I.1

Characteristics and Geographic Distribution of the Interview Sample

	California	New York	Other States	Total
Male/female	29/52	23/14	6/4	58/70
Pre-/post-1965 immigrants	10/71	3/34	0/10	13/115
Origins: PRC/Taiwan/ Hong Kong/Others*	32/22/8/7	20/9/2/5	6/3/1/0	58/34/11/12
Documented/undocumented	54/27	15/22	7/3	76/52
Employer/laborer/others	23/33/25	14/18/5	2/2/6	39/53/36
Individual total	81	37	10	128

NOTE: Sample size = 128. Except for occupational characteristics, individuals born in the United States are counted according to the status of their parents. Some undocumented immigrants listed had gained legal status at the time of the interviews. Occupations are determined at the time of the interviews.

*Origins of pre-1965 immigrants are not recorded.

Although formally conducted and recorded interviews offer opportunities to examine individuals through their life experiences, they do have limitations. The participants are informed in advance that their identities will not be revealed in the published work, but some still do not feel comfortable speaking freely. One business owner in her late forties, for example, agreed to an interview after we met several times. She is lively, resourceful, well connected, and willing to help. But when the tape-recorder was on, even in the comfort of her own living room, she just could not be herself. Her tone was controlled, and she brushed aside several questions. She was reluctant to touch on certain topics; many of the rich and insightful details that she offered in our previous casual conversations did not surface at all in the recorded interview.[11]

Beginning in the summer of 2004, I modified my research method. In addition to the in-depth interviews, I started to collect information in less formal settings. I continued to schedule meetings with officials or staff members while visiting a community organization. Once there, however, I would also take the time to look around, take pictures, pick up free brochures, check out news and ads on the bulletin board, and chat with other visitors. In ethnic clusters in New York, Los Angeles, San Francisco, Oakland, Boston, and other cities, I attended church services, Bible study sessions, social gatherings, and meetings of organizations. I also conducted research in employment offices, immigration firms, day-labor jobsites, dating services, bridal shops, travel agencies, beauty salons, motels, restaurants, and supermarkets (see table I.2). These field trips gave me many opportunities to observe and talk to people. In Chinese-operated motels, I talked to clerks and cleaning ladies and observed interactions between owners/managers and their employees. In Bible study sessions, I listened to the prayers of laborers and learned how these men and women justify their sufferings through their faith in God. These observations and casual conversations have helped me gain a better understanding of the workings of ethnic community and allowed me to reach out to many individuals who are largely invisible to the academic world.

Research trips to day-labor jobsites, employment agencies, and immigration firms have been most rewarding. In metropolitan areas with a highly concentrated Chinese American population, construction workers would gather on certain street corners every morning, looking

TABLE I.2

Research Sites and Locations

	California	New York	Other States	Total
Restaurants	4	1	1	6
Day-labor camps	1	1	0	2
Employment offices	2	2	0	4
Immigration services	2	0	0	2
Motels/hotels	2	2	0	4
Churches	1	1	0	2
Travel/transportation	1	2	0	3
Community organizations/events	7	4	1	12
Other business/services	3	2	0	5

for a chance to work for the day. While waiting for potential job offers, the laborers would share their tactics in dealing with their employers and let out frustrations from time to time. The ways these laborers negotiated with their potential bosses—mainly construction contractors or middle-class Chinese American homeowners—offer invaluable insights into the power relations between coethnic employees and employers. Similar negotiations are commonplace inside employment agencies, where many job seekers are women. The stories that I heard from the workers and clients gathered in the waiting rooms of immigration law firms reveal rich details of the daily struggle of many Chinese immigrants who are not as fortunate as average Americans.

I made a major effort to reveal positions of underprivileged community members who have been largely absent in existing scholarships regardless of their indispensable roles. Table I.1 shows that a relatively large number of the interviewees are laborers, many of whom are undocumented. Some of the research sites listed in table I.2 were selected because these workers often congregate there. Most businesses included in the study tend to be small or medium in size, because these are typical of the ethnic economy.

My selection of research sites and objects invites questions that must be addressed. Are the participants in the project an accurate representation of the entire Chinese American population? Why is relatively little space devoted to the most successful members of the community, the main source of ethnic pride? What can be accomplished by revealing the plight of the underprivileged, especially that of undocumented immigrants? Would the community be better off if undocumented members remained invisible? Would any discussion of these immigrants attract unwanted attention from law enforcement agencies and therefore add more sufferings to people who are already struggling at the bottom? The question of representation is important because this book addresses issues concerning the entire community rather than a particular group. It is now common knowledge that not only has a significant proportion of the Chinese living in the United States moved up to middle-class status but also an increasing number of individuals have gained upper-class membership. Then why does the book offer few details about the accomplishments of Chinese American dignitaries such as entrepreneurs from the lists of *Forbes, Fortune,* and *Money* magazines; politicians holding powerful federal or state government posts; Nobel laureates and other distinguished scientists and scholars; and star athletes, entertainers, or television personalities? I certainly have no intention to suggest that such elite members of the community are less important than the others, but their stories have been well documented in numerous scholarly works and media productions. If the book seems to give less space to the haves than the have-nots, it is partly because we know so little about the latter. But the book is not just about the underprivileged; quite a few interviewees possess considerable wealth. Moreover, stories told by laborers reveal as much about the comforts and luxuries of their employers as they do about their own struggles. Most of the domestics interviewed, for example, worked for upper-class Chinese Americans who dwell in mansions in exclusive neighborhoods, including those owned by successful business owners and prominent politicians. The ways in which these laborers are related to the well-to-do members of the community is the main focus of the book.

Would a book that brings light to undocumented immigrants direct unwanted public attention to a community that is highly concerned about its public image? I certainly hope not. As a historian I do not believe that a comprehensive understanding of contemporary Chinese America or any ethnic community is possible if a particular group of people is excluded, regardless of the pragmatic reasons behind that omission. At the same time, ignoring the undocumented has become a convenient way to make the undocumented invisible and turn a blind eye to their plight. Much has changed since the Civil Rights era. As most Chinese Americans have achieved social mobility, as more individuals have become power players in mainstream American politics, business, and academics, perhaps it is a good time to look back at the history of Chinese immigration and reconsider, as Nathan Glazer puts it, "the one great subject of inclusion or exclusion."[12] As entrepreneurs, homeowners, and consumers in general, many Chinese Americans are happy to find laborers who will work for them for less or to acquire quality service and merchandise at good bargains. How could we take advantage of the benefits offered by these laborers without being concerned about their rights and welfare? As an integral component of the community, should the undocumented immigrants also have a place in the community's ongoing struggle for civil rights and social justice?[13]

Most of the interviews were conducted in Mandarin and then translated into English. I use pseudonyms to protect the identity of the individuals who participated in the research, and in a few cases I also altered the areas of residence of the individuals involved. The real identity of an individual is revealed if the person is a public figure speaking on behalf of an organization or institution, or if the story comes from published sources.

Following this introduction, which outlines the scope, perspectives, and methodology of the project, chapter 1 provides an overview of the Chinese American population. It begins with a critical reading of the U.S. census data and immigration statistics from 1950 to 2000, arguing that the Chinese population in the United States is heavily undercounted; a significant number of Chinese immigrant laborers who have not obtained legal status are absent in the census, although many of them may have gained entry legally. Tracing the origins of various groups of post-1965 immigrants, chapter 1 illuminates the complex circumstances that gave shape to the undocumented immigrant population. It also explores the impact of gendered immigrant networks and policies of the United States on the lives of undocumented men and women.

Chapter 2 discusses the construction of class in Chinese America. The Chinese have been in the United States for more than 150 years, and the profile of the post-1965 Chinese immigrants differs from that of immigrants who had come earlier. Contemporary immigrants come from all walks of life and from many different parts of China, Taiwan, Hong Kong, Southeast Asia, and many other regions of the world. The concept of class means different things to different people, depending on their diverse geopolitical origins, socioeconomic statuses, levels of education, and immigration backgrounds; advancement in economic terms is only one of the many measures used by the Chinese to draw class distinctions. By incorporating the voices of different Chinese social groups such as American-born Chinese and immigrants, old-timers and newcomers, mainlanders and Taiwanese immigrants from elsewhere, business owners and laborers, documented and undocumented, this chapter illustrates the different criteria used by Chinese Americans to identify social classes. It also shows how the implication of class has changed over time as the processes of social mobility have unfolded.

Chapter 3 examines the development of the ethnic economy, emphasizing its role in enhancing ethnic ties. The concept of an ethnic economy has been used by scholars to describe the employment sector that involves both immigrant owners and coethnic immigrant employees.[14] In this study, however, I use the term in a broader sense to embrace economic activities in both the employment and market/service sectors that involve predominantly Chinese Americans, both immigrants and the American-born. I downplay the immigration background of the participants because it is impossible to separate the economic activities of various groups of Chinese Americans based on this criterion. A vast majority of Chinese American families consist of both American-born and foreign-born members, and most Chinese American businesses serve both immigrants and their American-born counterparts. Whereas those born in the United States and those who arrived in an earlier era are more likely than the newcomers to be the bosses, it is not unusual for American-born Chinese to find employment in companies owned by immigrants. The situation is even more complex if we take globalization into consideration. Thus I consider a business employing mostly immigrant Chinese workers part of the ethnic economy, even if the owner was born in the United States. A law firm owned by a non-Chinese attorney may also be included if most of its employees are Chinese and it serves mainly Chinese clients. On the other hand, I do not see a company founded by a Chinese immigrant such as Yahoo Inc. as part of the ethnic economy for the reason that neither its employees nor its customers can be characterized as predominantly Chinese. What makes the Chinese ethnic economy unique is not just its access to immigrant laborers (many other ethnic groups also enjoy such an advantage), but its ability to reach out to coethnic consumers. The fact that "Serve the people" (*wei renmin fuwu*), one of Mao Zedong's most frequently quoted phrases during the Chinese Cultural Revolution, is now adopted by the New York law firm of Ross and Legan as its advertising slogan, provides just one example of how businesses and service-oriented professionals try to connect with the new immigrants, most of them from mainland China. Network services, such as employment agencies and family motels that work to link immigrant newcomers with coethnic employers and feed professional service providers with potential clients, receive special attention. These services play indispensable roles in bringing together different groups of Chinese Americans and facilitate the expansion of the ethnic economy to different parts of the United States.

Focusing on one of the most energetic new regional groups of Chinese immigrants, chapter 4 explores some of the recent dynamics within the ethnic community. The Chinese were very successful in organizing themselves half a century ago. Access to mainstream opportunities after World War II, however, has made affiliation with ethnic organizations less crucial for individuals, especially those who have left the Chinatowns. Conflicting political sentiments about governments in China and Taiwan have further weakened the strength of traditional organizations and worked to erode ethnic solidarity. Despite proclaiming itself the voice of the entire Chinese American community, today's Chinese Consolidated Benevolent Association (CCBA) has little control over the diverse and dispersed ethnic population. Many affiliates of the federation (eighty-two are listed in New York) have long reduced their activities to collecting rent from their business tenants. At the same time, however, some new regional immigrant groups began to show tremendous vigor within the community. Beginning in the 1980s, Changle County (which became a city in 1994) in the Fuzhou district of Fujian, China, became a launching pad for people willing to pay any amount to come to the United States. Of an estimated 200,000 Changle immigrants living in the United States in 2001, approximately 170,000 resided in the New York–New Jersey metropolitan areas. Because some members of this regional immigrant group have been subjected to sensational mainstream media coverage, for many years the Changle people (or Fuzhou people in general) have been categorically identified as illegal immigrants and considered the lowest class in the community. Within a relatively short period of time, however, the Changle people have gathered their own resources to build extensive entrepreneurial enterprises, and their presence in New York has revitalized the city's ethnic economy. Their association has emerged as a powerful force, in sharp contrast to the declining influence of century-old establishments. A federation of twenty-six affiliated district groups, each attached to a native town or village in China, the Changle American Association is capable of putting thousands of members onto the streets at any given time, something that even the CCBA, the fountainhead of all traditional district associations, could not do any more. Such a development is impressive, especially because the relatively new association has limited financial resources; unlike established organizations, it has no control over real estate properties, and a large proportion of its members are laborers or self-employed business owners. More important than the primordial ties that originated in their native places are their common beginnings in the United States. As menial laborers and undocumented immigrants, the Changle people understand unity and mutual support to be an urgent need, and the association has worked effectively to protect the rights and interests of its members. This chapter showcases new political dynamics within Chinese America, illuminating the ways that new immigrant groups negotiate power and space with the ethnic establishment.

Undocumented immigrants are treated as an integral part of the Chinese American community in each of the above chapters. Chapter 5 goes further to analyze the relationships between immigrant laborers and their middle-class employers/service providers, and explore the positions of these two groups in a new social hierarchy. If mobility has been achieved by a large proportion of Chinese Americans, success is not shared by everyone, for poverty remains common among the post-1965 immigrants.[15] It is arguable that the expansion of the ethnic economy enhances dependencies between employers and their laborers. Many Chinese American businesses may not have been as successful without easy access to low-cost labor and the patronage of coethnic consumers; without the assistance of the ethnic economic networks it would be much harder for some immigrants to find jobs and shelter. Such dependencies, though they seem to be mutually beneficial, do not carry the same weight for each of the involved groups. While Chinese employers are able to turn their disadvantaged fellow community members into low-wage laborers and move themselves upward at a pace faster than their non-Chinese compatriots, those who labor for them, especially the undocumented, are susceptible to exploitation and abuse.[16] Moreover, long-term dependency on coethnic employers also works to prevent these laborers from gaining access to mainstream opportunities. The ethnic consumer market, which operates in more intricate ways, reveals similar realities. While the competitive edge of the ethnic economy can benefit consumers of all classes, in areas where every other door is closed entrepreneurs are allowed to conduct business on their own terms, leaving consumers/clients with neither room for bargaining nor entitlement to any protection. In this sense, the structure of the ethnic economy is also a factor that perpetuates poverty, as business owners, professional service providers, and middle-class consumers have far more to gain and far less to lose than those who are forced to play a part. In conclusion, I raise a few questions to engage future academic debate.

Although this book provides a broad picture of post-1965 Chinese America, it does not cover every aspect of the community life or experiences of every regional group. Chinese Americans in Hawaii as well as those from Southeast Asia deserve attention but are beyond the scope of the present study. The selected sketches of individuals and profiles of businesses, combined with census and other statistics, are presented here to offer just one perspective of a fast growing and highly diverse American ethnic community. Focusing on the ways that the new ethnic economy and ethnic social hierarchy are developed, this book demonstrates that Chinese Americans today are connected to one another in ways quite different from those of the pre-World War II years. Common ancestry, history, culture, language, and value systems do provide threads for group affiliations, but ethnic strength is never an assumed factor. It is the realities of Chinese in the United States as a minority group, the existence of a large number of disadvantaged immigrants, and the need to survive for some and the desire to move up for others that invigorate the ethnic economy and strengthen ethnic bonds.

CHAPTER 1

Contemporary Chinese American Population

THE DOCUMENTED AND THE INVISIBLE

YAMEI ZHU WAS BORN IN 1963 in Shanghai, China's most populous city. An only child, she was pampered by her parents. After high school, Yamei got a job at a transportation company and worked her way up to become its controller. She married an electrician in 1988 and moved in with her in-laws. "My father said that he wouldn't let me marry unless it was into a good family," recalled Yamei. "When he found out that we had to share the same room with my in-laws—a curtain was used for privacy—and there was no indoor plumbing, his eyes filled with tears." After the birth of Yamei's son, Lulu, the small room became even more crowded.[1]

In the 1990s, the Chinese government's market-oriented economic reforms injected new vitality into Shanghai. Foreign banks and insurance companies set up offices, and international retail stores appeared in the city's old and new commercial districts. The expansion of the city's industrial and trade capabilities drew business investors, tourists, and shoppers from all over the world, which provided greater opportunities for business-minded locals. Supported by her husband and her in-laws, Yamei quit her job and opened a small eatery with a girlfriend. She made more money, but after two years she and her husband still could not afford an apartment of their own. As Lulu grew older she became increasingly concerned about his future, and the thought that the teenager might not be able to get through the extremely competitive college admissions process played a big part in her decision to leave China.

Yamei flew from Shanghai to Los Angeles in early 2001. Although she had papers certifying that she was the deputy manager of a toy factory in Shanghai and a letter from an American company inviting her to inspect a new series of products, she had never been affiliated with a toy factory in Shanghai, nor was she expected by any person or corporation in Los Angeles. These false documents, obtained from an underground migration service, had used up her family's entire savings and would expire shortly, but they made it possible for her to enter the United States. The rewards would outweigh the risk, they believed, if she were successful.

At the beginning of the twenty-first century there are approximately half a million ethnic Chinese in the United States without legal status. These individuals are largely invisible to the outside world. Since the 1990s, human smuggling and the Chinese American underground have received much media coverage and academic attention.[2] But beyond that, undocumented immigrants within Chinese America are hardly addressed. The focus on smuggling activities has created false assumptions that all undocumented immigrants were smuggled into the United States, and that all of them came from the People's Republic of China. It is important to note that a significantly large number of undocumented Chinese did not jump ship; many passed border inspection using valid travel documents. It is important to include in our research not only undocumented immigrants from the PRC but also those from Taiwan, Hong Kong, and other parts of the world. After all, the study of Chinese American experience embraces ethnic Chinese from all over the world. And regardless of their socioeconomic background, native-place affiliation, and reasons for leaving their homeland, the majority of the undocumented Chinese rely on the same ethnic networks to survive. This chapter reassesses the Chinese American population by foregrounding undocumented immigrants. Contrary to existing scholarship that treats undocumented immigrants as a marginalized group associated with the ethnic underworld, it argues that these immigrants are an indispensable component of the ethnic economy and an integral part of contemporary Chinese America.

THE DOCUMENTED AND UNDOCUMENTED IN OFFICIAL GOVERNMENT RECORDS

The history of Chinese immigration to North America dates back to the late 1840s. Although the Chinese were the first Asians to come to the United States, they were outnumbered by the Japanese in 1910 and by the Filipinos in 1930. Not until the 1980 was this situation reversed. The 2000 census recorded that, with a population of approximately 2.9 million, Chinese are now the largest Asian American group in the United States. Although China has never sent more immigrants than the Philippines in any given year, the number of Chinese admitted exceeded that of Filipinos because many ethnic Chinese come from Taiwan, Hong Kong, Southeast Asian countries, and other parts of the world.

Table 1.1 clearly shows the negative impact of exclusion and legislative changes after World War II on the growth of Chinese population. Federal legislation passed in the 1870s restricted Chinese immigration, and the 1882 Chinese Exclusion Act was enacted to deny entry to all Chinese laborers. The 1882 law was amended several times in the next two decades, adding restrictions and closing loopholes each time. Not only did these harsh laws block the entry of new arrivals they also effectively prevented male Chinese already residing in the United States from establishing families here.[3] Extralegal violence also shaped immigration and settlement patterns as, from the early 1860s to the 1890s, outbreaks of anti-Chinese violence occurred throughout California. And outside the state, cases of expulsion or murder were reported from the Snake River Canyon in Idaho; Denver, Colorado; Portland, Oregon; Rock Springs, Wyoming; and Squaw Valley, Coal Creek, Black Diamond, Tacoma, Puyallup, and Seattle in Washington. Many Chinese residences were burned down, and hundreds of individuals were killed or injured. Most survivors of the mob violence retreated to cities, giving rise to ethnically exclusive Chinatowns.[4]

The ethnic community before World War II was very much a bachelor society with a skewed sex ratio. Its rate of reproduction was extremely low. As table 1.1 shows, when the exclusion laws were strictly enforced, the Chinese population had a negative growth rate. When exclusion laws were officially repealed in 1943, only 105 immigration slots per year were allotted to China.[5] But the end of exclusion allowed Chinese to take advantage of general immigration legislation. Thousands of women gained entry under the War Brides Act of 1945, and for the first time the majority of new immigrants were female.[6] As families were reunited overnight, Chinese America was no longer a bachelor society.[7] Moreover, high birth rates in the 1950s not only led to a 58 percent increase of the population during that decade but it also changed the

TABLE 1.1

Chinese Population in the United States, 1890–2000

Year	No. of Chinese	% born in the U.S.
1890	107,475	0.7
1900	118,746	9.3
1910	94,414	20.7
1920	85,202	30.1
1930	102,159	41.2
1940	106,334	51.9
1950	150,005	53.0
1960	237,292	60.5
1970	436,062	53.1
1980	812,178	36.7
1990	1,645,472	30.7
2000	2,858,219	29.1

SOURCE: Census of the United States. Chinese from Taiwan are included.

community's demographic profile. With fewer than 40 percent immigrants, by 1960 the majority of Chinese Americans were born and raised in the United States.

The immigration reform that took place in the midst of the civil rights movement opened a new chapter in Chinese American history. In 1965, President Lyndon B. Johnson signed the Immigration and Nationality Act into law in front of the Statue of Liberty. Though he claimed in public that it was not a revolutionary act, one can hardly overemphasize the historical significance of this piece of legislation. As racial criteria were removed, each nation-state was allotted an equal number of immigration slots, and the annual quota for Chinese shot from 105 to 20,000 individuals.[8] Not only were close relatives of U.S. citizens and permanent residents treated as preferred individuals, but parents, spouses, and minor children of citizens could come outside the quota limit.[9] In addition, since the mid-1980s, new measures have been developed to attract professionals from all over the world, paving the way for international students with advanced degrees from American universities to find work and establish permanent residence in the United

States. Immigration data show that students from the PRC, Taiwan, and Hong Kong in particular have taken advantage of the situation and applied for the H-1B visa to change their legal status from students to workers.[10]

The growth of the Chinese American population after 1965 also had much to do with political developments in Asia as well as relationships between the United States and governments in Asia. In 1949, the nationalist government lost control over the Chinese mainland and retreated to the island of Taiwan, but it continued to be recognized by the United States as the only legitimate Chinese government. Chinese from the People's Republic of China could not travel to America until 1979, when their government established diplomatic relations with the United States. Although official U.S.–Taiwan ties were cut due to the "one China" principle agreed upon by both China and the United States, the island was granted its own quota, a number equivalent to that of a nation. Hong Kong, a former British colony, initially received a quota of only 200 (as did other colonies), but the allotment was successively raised to 300, then 600, and 5,000 in 1987. During the run-up to its 1997 return to China, the United States increased Hong Kong's immigration quota to 10,000 in the 1990s and in the three years before 1997, to 25,600, granting admission to almost every qualified applicant. In other words, between 1979 and 1997, the quota allotment for ethnic Chinese was more than twice, and during a three-year period three times that of a single nation.[11] After 1999, immigrants from Hong Kong continued to arrive outside the Chinese quota, and residents from the former British colony have continued to enjoy visa-free access into the United States.[12]

Special historical circumstances in China also led to U.S. legislation permitting Chinese with nonimmigrant status to obtain permanent residence in the United States. Months after the 1989 Tiananmen incident, President George H. W. Bush issued Executive Order 12711, which instructed the offices of the U.S. attorney general and the secretary of state to provide protection to students from the PRC.[13] The order contravened the Chinese government's two-year home-country residence requirement for its students abroad, allowing them to find work and stay in the United States immediately after the completion of their training. The Chinese Student Protection Act passed in 1992 granted all of the PRC citizens who were in the United States between June 4, 1989, and April 11, 1990, permission to apply for permanent residency. Both measures were originally designed to protect Chinese students studying in the United States because many had participated in demonstrations in support of the Tiananmen protestors. Students and scholars who otherwise would have had to return to China after the completion of their training were able to upgrade their legal status in the United States. However, since the law did not limit the opportunities to students and scholars, it was applicable to virtually every immigrant from the PRC who was in the United States before April 1990.[14] All told, at least 50,000 Chinese seized the opportunity to become permanent residents.

Ethnic Chinese also came from the greater Chinese diaspora. Beginning in the 1960s, more relaxed U.S. immigration policies and political turmoil in Latin America and Asia, especially Cuba, Peru, Burma, the Philippines, Thailand, Malaysia, and Korea, led thousands of ethnic Chinese who had settled in these countries to remigrate to the United States. Of the approximately one million Indochinese refugees who arrived before 1990, more than 300,000 were ethnic Chinese.[15]

These changes have had a great impact on the Chinese American community. From 1970 to 2000, the ethnic population almost doubled every decade. The 2000 census recorded 2,858,291 people of Chinese ancestry, representing 1 percent of the entire U.S. population. A significant proportion of the new immigrants arrived after 1990. According to the U.S. Immigration and Naturalization Service (INS), 1,192,918 immigrants were admitted to the United States from China, Hong Kong, and Taiwan as permanent residents between 1971 and 2000. More than 44 percent of them came between 1991 and 2000 (table 1.2). Though no longer in bachelor communities, immigrants have surfaced again as the majority of the Chinese American population since 1980, and they constituted more than 70 percent of that population in 2000.

Although the 1965 immigration reform made it relatively easy for Chinese to immigrate to the United States, a large number of individuals continue to come and live in this country without legal papers. Like Yamei, these men and women have their own reasons to leave their homeland, encouraged also by the demand for entry-level workers within the Chinese American community. Filling most of the positions in the

TABLE 1.2

Chinese Immigrants Admitted to the United States, 1971–2000

Year	Number of Immigrants	Year	Number of Immigrants
1971	15,557	1991	39,890
1972	19,427	1992	46,356
1973	19,436	1993	71,801
1974	20,734	1994	70,820
1975	21,748	1995	51,811
1976	23,665	1996	62,300
1977	24,785	1997	52,330
1978	25,600	1998	48,413
1979	29,089	1999	36,112
1980	27,651	2000	49,060
1981	25,803		
1982	39,926		
1983	45,878		
1984	41,399		
1985	43,890		
1986	42,319		
1987	41,454		
1988	46,117		
1989	54,541		
1990	55,006		
Subtotal	664,025		528,893
TOTAL (1971–2000)			1,192,918

SOURCE: *Statistical Yearbook of the Immigration and Naturalization Service*, 1971–2000. The data are extracted from tables titled "Immigrants by Region and Selected Country of Last Residence." Immigrants from the PRC, Hong Kong, and Taiwan are included.

informal economic sector as restaurant servers, garment shop workers, construction laborers, and domestic care providers, these undocumented immigrants are everywhere.

Despite their ubiquity, counting these immigrants has proved challenging. Since the 1980s, the government has made some effort to estimate the undocumented population group. Most official studies are based on census data which uses a "residual method." This method subtracts the legal foreign-born population from the total foreign-born population. And the remainder or "residual" is the estimate of the unauthorized population.[16] The 1990 census estimated 70,000 undocumented residents from China. A decade later that number increased to 115,000.[17] This figure suggests that about 4 percent of the Chinese population in the United States is undocumented, which is close to the national average.

THE INVISIBLES

The method used by the Census Bureau, however, probably leaves a significant portion of the undocumented individuals uncounted for two reasons. First, the bureau counts each person on the basis of his or her "usual residence"—the place where a person lives and sleeps most of the time. In theory this would include every person residing in the United States regardless of citizenship or legal status (except for temporary visitors), but in reality the method has not been effective in counting undocumented immigrants. As the Census Bureau acknowledges, there is little difference between data collected referring to "usual residence" and that referring to "legal residence (residents with legal status)."[18] Determining the usual residence of these individuals has not been easy, as many of them have not had stable jobs and are highly mobile. Because the living conditions of these individuals do not always meet local standards and regulations, landlords are not eager to reveal their tenants' existence. Second, lack of trust in government agencies probably discourages participation by undocumented immigrants. During the 1970 census, the INS conducted raids in search of illegal aliens, which discouraged honest responses. Since 1980 the bureau has persuaded the INS to suspend raids in areas where the census takers were working, in an attempt to include as many undocumented aliens as possible. But the problem remains.[19]

The 115,000 undocumented individuals estimated on the basis of the 2000 census probably were living with legal residents, such as parents of U.S.-born children or individuals married to U.S. citizens or permanent residents. They also had probably already turned to formal institutions to fulfill special needs (parents of school-age children, for example), or were previously known to government agencies (petitioners for political asylum).[20] But many others do not have any incentives to be included in government data, and they probably do not want to have their whereabouts recorded even if there is no risk.

Current understanding of undocumented Chinese is also restricted because most studies on this topic have focused on smuggling or trafficking, and their authors have often emphasized the assistance of a third party. Overwhelming attention has been given to the ways of crossing borders, the involvement of criminal groups, and the exorbitant fees that individuals have paid in exchange for assistance.[21] This tendency has reinforced two false assumptions: that "undocumented immigrants" and "illegal immigrants" are interchangeable categories, and that all illegal immigrants came from the PRC. It is important to note that not all undocumented immigrants entered the United States illegally or used forged or illegally obtained documents; quite a large number came with genuine passports and visas for short-term visits, but they decided to stay after their visas expired. These visa overstayers could come from the PRC, Hong Kong, Taiwan, and many other parts of the world. Most researchers, however, have completely overlooked undocumented Chinese from nations and regions other than the Chinese mainland.

A good understanding of this virtually invisible group of Chinese cannot begin without knowing how many of them are out there, although the effort to estimate the undocumented population is sometimes described as quantifying "the uncountable."[22] Although getting the exact numbers is impossible, a reasonably close assessment is not entirely unattainable if all available data are evaluated using methodologies developed by demographers and immigration scholars. To estimate the undocumented Chinese population, it is necessary to take into consideration smuggled and trafficked immigrants as well as visa overstayers, and it is necessary to count individuals from the PRC as well as Hong Kong and Taiwan.

Human smuggling to the United States, which refers to border-crossing activities without inspection, has become the focal point of research on undocumented Chinese. Since the late 1980s, small and large groups of men and women from China have been smuggled into the United States by multinational collaborators running professional operations.[23] For a fee of about $20,000, which has increased to as much as $80,000 in recent years, prospective emigrants, most of them from Fujian Province, were taken by professional snakeheads (*shetou*) through

Hong Kong or Thailand before being flown to Bolivia or Panama, and then on to Mexico, to be led across the U.S. border in automobiles or on foot. After 1992, smugglers sent a number of groups to the United States by sea under miserable conditions: an estimated 20,000 people from Fujian in 1993. The *Golden Venture*, which captured American's fascination with human smuggling from China that year, carried 286 passengers. Another ship, also intercepted in 1993, had 537 people on board.[24] The business of transporting this human cargo is extremely profitable. Zheng Cuiping, a Fujianese immigrant woman who helped purchase the *Golden Venture*, made $40 million from the business operation. According to a study by the United Nations, smuggling Chinese to the United States had generated $3.5 billion by the mid-1990s.[25] The exact number of Chinese who made the crossing successfully remains unknown, and the majority of these smuggled immigrants will probably never appear on any U.S. government roll.

Trafficking, in contrast, usually refers to transporting individuals against their will. Scholars investigating early Chinese American history sometimes use the word "trafficking" to describe the ways that young Chinese women were brought to the United States for prostitution. Some researchers speculate that in recent decades, a large number of Chinese have been brought in by U.S. companies as a source of cheap labor.[26] Others argue that trafficking, like smuggling, was often organized and carried out by criminal syndicates in China, Hong Kong, Taiwan, and the United States.[27] Although such operations are very likely, few studies are able to document the direct linkage between human trafficking activities and American companies or transnational criminal organizations.

Some scholars use the term "trafficking" more broadly. They differentiate trafficking from smuggling by the presence or lack of legal documents. For them, trafficking refers to the use of legal documents often obtained illegally with the assistance of a third party to cross a border. Some scholars use this understanding of trafficking regardless of whether or not labor exploitation is an ultimate goal.[28] Like smuggling, the trafficking of Chinese sometimes involves crossing several national borders, thus requiring multinational collaboration. In the 1990s, some groups were trafficked through Thailand, where a third party provided them with fraudulent travel documents to fly to the United States. Traveling with valid documents, genuine or fake, is not as risky as illegal border crossing. For instance, Hangdong Chen, who came from Fuzhou in 1997, said that his purchased package included a phone number of a lawyer in New York. He was told to contact the lawyer only if immigration inspectors had questions about his documents.[29] So even if the travelers were caught by immigration authorities at the port of entry, they might still be able to land through proper legal procedures.

Facilitators for these relatively safe services charge higher fees than do snakeheads. By 2000, almost $60,000 was required to traffic a Chinese person to the United States. Like Yamei, some individuals obtained passports and visas using appropriated business invitations issued by American companies. Other individuals gained entry by claiming to be members of business or government delegations. Tommy Ma, a restaurant manager in southern California, came to the United States in 1997 as part of a business delegation sent by a company in Beijing. His name was added to that group by his brother, who was assigned by the company to make travel arrangements for the delegation. Tommy said he did not pay money to come, but his brother gave gifts (of up to $2,000) to the head of the delegation. Once past the inspection point in San Francisco, he disappeared from his group and was led by a friend to board an airplane to Los Angeles.[30]

Since the late 1990s, more Chinese have been trafficked than smuggled directly from China to the United States. Most of them, like Yamei and Tommy, obtained passports and visas using business invitations issued by American companies or claiming to be members of business or government delegations. Collaborations from individuals in the United States are not uncommon. Since any government or private agency, educational institution, and registered American company has the liberty to invite individuals or delegations from foreign countries, obtaining such papers need not have involved organized gangs, although a third party is often needed.

A third category of "invisible" immigrants are visa violators. Few scholars have paid much attention to temporary visitors who gained entry into the United States without the assistance of a third party. Significantly, scholars' focus on unauthorized immigrants from China has excluded these individuals. Because the U.S. tourist industry was not open to private citizens of the PRC until recently, it was very difficult for mainland Chinese to get temporary visas. However, Lili Hsu, who came with her infant son from Taiwan to escape her ex-husband, did gain entry with a genuine passport and visa as a tourist in 1989. Once her visa expired, Lili and her son became undocumented.[31]

Recognizing the complex circumstances and the diverse individual backgrounds involved in the making of an undocumented Chinese population is crucial to academic inquiries. If, as many studies have suggested, the PRC has been the major launching pad for smuggled or trafficked immigrants, then visa violators do not necessarily fit this perceived pattern.[32] As scholars, it is important to recognize the differences among these three groups. But there is also a key commonality: unless they arrive with sufficient financial resources, most undocumented Chinese immigrants, regardless of geopolitical affiliations or means of entry, have to rely on established Chinese American networks to survive, which requires scholars to see them as one group.

Government records do not have the means to keep track of illegal Chinese entrants. A 1996 report by the INS estimates that 25,000 Chinese entered the United States illegally that year, a number much lower than that of suspected illegal entrants from Mexico, El Salvador, Guatemala, Canada, Haiti, or the Philippines. According to data released by the Department of Homeland Security in 2006, only about 230,000 (about 2 percent) of the 10.5 million illegal aliens living and working in the United States in January 2005 came from China, a proportion much smaller than Mexico's and behind El Salvador's, Guatemala's, and India's.[33] Since most illegal entrants have left no trace in U.S. government records, some scholars have looked for clues in local Chinese records. Sociologist Zai Liang and his collaborators found that in 1995 alone, Fujian province sent 66,200 people (most of them irregular immigrants) to the United States, and this figure does not include short-term migrant laborers.[34] Other scholars, as well as a research group established by the White House to monitor illegal immigration from China, conclude that an average of 50,000 Chinese were smuggled or trafficked into the United States each year during the 1990s.[35] In other words, about half a million Chinese probably reached the United States illegally or with illegally obtained documents during one decade.

Counting visa overstayers is no easy task, either. Although every legal entry is recorded, the U.S. government no longer keeps track of temporary visitors. Researchers examining immigration from China or elsewhere in the late nineteenth and early twentieth centuries can compare arrival and departure records compiled by the INS. In this age of globalization, however, tracking U.S.-border-crossing activities by all foreigners has become an extremely complex matter. The expanding volume of commercial, scientific, and cultural exchanges requires that a large number of representatives from many Chinese agencies and corporations be stationed in the United States, for example, and research collaborations and partnerships between organizations in these two countries have led to frequent cross-border visits and exchanges. Since the 1980s, thousands of students have arrived from the PRC, Taiwan, and Hong Kong each year to pursue higher education in the United States, and a significantly large number of Chinese children have also enrolled in American junior high and high schools. Transnational travel has become a requirement for what was once considered a simple family gathering. Not only has the tremendous volume of daily traffic through U.S. ports of entry made accurate recordkeeping nearly impossible, but Chinese travelers may also leave or return to the United States via a third nation, making arrival and departure records, which document passenger originations and destinations, less of an indicator of Chinese immigration. Moreover, travel between the United States and China is not limited to citizens of these two nations. For all these reasons, the INS, now the Bureau of Immigration and Customs Enforcement, no longer has reliable statistics for temporary visitors. Most foreign nationals admitted with a visa for a temporary stay are required to fill out an I-94 Arrival-Departure record form at the port of entry. Immigration inspectors keep the top half of the form and the bottom half is supposed to be collected on departure. But temporary visitors admitted without visa, such as individuals from Mexico, Canada, and Hong Kong, are not required to complete an I-94 unless they request an extended stay. And not all departure forms are collected. According to a Government Accountability Office (GAO) report in 2001, 20 percent of I-94 arrival records had no matching departure record.[36]

After the World Trade Center bombing in 1993 and then the September 11 terrorist attack in 2001, the Department of Homeland Security developed a program to monitor temporary visitors; a special Immigration and Customs Enforcement unit was created to track down visa violators. The effort, however, focused mainly on individuals from areas considered a threat to U.S. security. In 2004, the government initiated a new digital screening system called US-VISIT, which uses photographs and fingerprints to identify foreign visitors. By May 2006 this system was screening arrivals at 115 airports, 15 seaports, and 154 border-crossing points, but only a dozen airports and two seaports were equipped to track down departures.[37]

The lack of a systematic tracking system of temporary visitors poses a statistical challenge for studies on visa violators. Most government estimates are based on a methodology developed by demographer Robert Warren, whose analysis of INS internal data files concludes that visa overstayers make up 41 percent of the unauthorized migrant population. But his findings show great discrepancies among different population groups. More specifically, he estimates that 16 percent of unauthorized Mexican immigrants, 27 percent of Central Americans, and 91 percent of those from other countries are visa violators. Using different databases, a GAO report suggests that the proportion of visa overstayers is between 27 and 57 percent of the total unauthorized migrant population. On the basis of these two methods, the Pew Hispanic Center estimates that between 33 and 50 percent of the unauthorized immigrant population are visa overstayers.[38] Chinese are not the main focus of these studies, but these methods suggest that the percentage of visa overstayers is very likely quite high among the undocumented Chinese.

Other methods of estimation are developed through examining the relationship between the nonimmigrant population and unauthorized immigrant population. Since the normalization of diplomatic relations between the United States and China in 1979, the number of nonimmigrant Chinese admitted increased significantly. From 1990 to 2000, between half a million to one million Chinese nonimmigrant visa holders were admitted each year, fifteen times as many as those admitted as quota and nonquota immigrants (chart 1.1). Over a period of thirty years, more than 10.7 million Chinese have come as temporary visitors; almost 8.8 million were admitted after 1986 (table 1.3). Most of these temporary visitors must have returned to their homelands as expected, but if a minuscule share of them overstayed, they would have contributed significantly to the size of undocumented population. The Pew Hispanic Center estimates that 1.7 percent of nonimmigrant visa holders from Mexico, 2.4 percent from South America, and 3.2 percent from Central

America eventually became unauthorized immigrants.[39] Applying these estimates to the Chinese, between 182,000 and 343,000 individuals would have escaped official notice by 2000. Those who arrived after the 1986 amnesty, between 149,000 and 280,000 individuals, should be included in the undocumented Chinese population in addition to the half million irregular immigrants who arrived in the 1990s. In other words, by the year of 2000, the number of Chinese who have lived in the United States without legal status is probably between 649,000 and 780,000.

ADJUSTING LEGAL STATUS

Not all undocumented immigrants remain without status forever. The INS lists five ways in which undocumented individuals can be removed from this population group: deportation, voluntary departure,

CHART 1.1

Chinese Immigrants and Nonimmigrants Admitted (1969–2000)

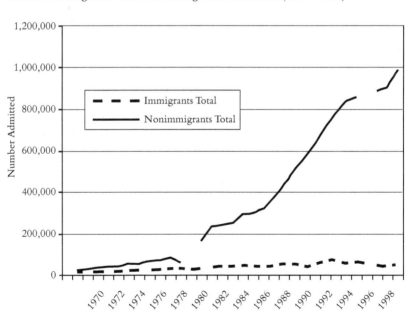

SOURCE: *Statistical Yearbook of the Immigration and Naturalization Service*, 1970–2000. Data includes individuals from PRC, Hong Kong, and Taiwan.

TABLE 1.3

Chinese Nonimmigrants Admitted to the United States, 1971–2000

Year	Number	Year	Number
1971	35,156	1987	319,000
1972	41,919	1988	368,000
1973	38,580	1989	433,000
1974	54,100	1990	505,000
1975	55,271	1991	562,000
1976	67,174	1992	626,000
1977	69,522	1993	709,000
1978	79,340	1994	772,000
1979	57,729	1995	837,000
1980	149,468*	1996	854,000
1981	158,409	1997	821,000†
1982	230,905	1998	885,000
1983	238,333	1999	904,000
1984	251,000	2000	985,000
1985	287,000		
1986	299,000		
Subtotal	1,963,438		8,759,000
TOTAL (1971–2000)			10,722,438

SOURCE: *Statistical Yearbook of the Immigration and Naturalization Service*, 1971–2000. The data are extracted from tables titled "Nonimmigrant Admitted by Selected Class of Admission and Region and Selected Country of Last Residence." Immigrants from the PRC, Hong Kong, and Taiwan are included.

*No available data for 1980. This number averages the total number of nonimmigrants admitted from 1974 to1979 and from 1980 to 1985.

†No available data for 1997. This number averages the total number of nonimmigrants admitted from 1991 to 1996 and from 1997 to 2002 (925,000 in 2001 and 709,000 in 2002).

death, status adjustment, and reentry with legal status after temporary departure.[40] Efforts to deport Chinese have not been effective because of lack of cooperation from the Chinese government.[41] Difficulties for the Chinese (especially PRC residents) to come to the United States also mean that the number of undocumented immigrants who chose to leave voluntarily is probably small. Because most of the undocumented immigrants entered before age forty (many in their twenties or early thirties), mortality rate is relatively low for those who arrived after 1986.[42] But as several government polices have paved the way for them, many undocumented immigrants have found means to adjust their status.

The biggest opportunity arrived in 1986, as the Immigration, Reform and Control Act of 1986 (IRCA) allowed immigrants to adjust their status if they had resided continuously in the United States since January 1, 1982, or were seasonal agricultural workers before 1986.[43] By May 1990, a total of 18,199 Chinese had submitted applications for legalization. More than half of the applicants—11,319 individuals—were from mainland China, while 4,449 were from Taiwan, and 2,431 were from Hong Kong. It is worth noting that only 24 percent of the petitioners (4,365 individuals) were identified as illegal entrants, and the remaining 76 percent (13,834 individuals) were visa overstayers. The 3,659 agricultural workers who adjusted their status illustrate a similar pattern: 2,630 of them, including 276 from Hong Kong and 753 from Taiwan, were visa overstayers.[44] These figures are very important to our understanding of the undocumented Chinese: they show not only the different origins of these individuals but also a very high percentage of visa overstayers.

As mentioned earlier, immigrants from the PRC had another opportunity a few years later, when the 1992 Chinese Student Protection Act permitted short-term visa holders who arrived from the PRC before 1990 to gain permanent status. Although the law was intended to provide legal protection for students and scholars, more than half the applications were neither students nor scholars, and some were undocumented at the time.[45] By the June 30, 1993, deadline, however, the INS had received only about 50,000 applications for permanent resident status, a number that was smaller than expected (there were 60,000 Chinese students/scholars in the United States at the time).[46] Some undocumented immigrants probably missed the opportunity because they had no means to prove they had been in the United States during the particular time period specified by the law.[47] Mr. Zheng, who entered without inspection in 1989, failed to take advantage of the law because he did not file taxes and could not present valid proof that he was in the United States before 1990. As a result, he worked and lived in New Jersey as an undocumented alien for almost two decades.[48]

After 1990, requesting political asylum became one of the main avenues that undocumented individuals could take to gain permanent status. Some individuals from the PRC were granted asylum by claiming to be victims of China's one-child policy in the late 1980s and early 1990s. During the Clinton administration, however, the government's generous asylum policy was condemned as a magnet for illegal Chinese entrants, and asylum petitions were subjected to more careful scrutiny. For example, only a few of the 286 passengers from the *Golden Venture* were granted asylum shortly after their arrival, and more than a hundred of them were deported. On February 3, 1997, nearly four years after the incident, the *New York Times* ran a front-page article about the passengers, pointing out that those detained by the INS would have been granted asylum had they arrived during President George H. W. Bush's administration.[49] Although they were all pardoned eleven days after the article was published, the detainees were put in a position of legal limbo and some were listed for deportation proceedings after their petitions were rejected. Only because China refused to take back asylum seekers were these individuals allowed to stay in the United States. Unless a special executive order is issued or a new law is enacted, these individuals will not be able to become permanent residents.[50]

Unlike those who were smuggled or trafficked into the United States, most visa overstayers gained entry through legitimate channels, but this does not mean easy access to legal status. National origins, paradoxically, have made a difference. The United States recognized the PRC as the only legitimate government of China in 1979 and rejected the claim by the Taiwanese government at the same time. Diplomatic gestures aside, it is no secret that the United States has continued to see China as its political opponent and Taiwan as an ally. The 1992 Chinese Student Protection Act, for example, applied only to people from the Chinese mainland. While it has been possible for undocumented Chinese from the PRC to adjust their status through asylum, that venue is not as available to aliens from non-Communist regions.

The implications of U.S. immigration policies can affect undocumented Chinese Americans of different origins in complicated ways.

Yamei came from the Chinese mainland using purchased travel documents, but once here she learned that women from the PRC had a good chance of gaining asylum if they claimed to be victims of China's one-child population control policy. An amendment to the 1996 Illegal Immigration Reform and Immigrant Responsibility Act defined forced abortions and involuntary sterilization as acts of persecution that would cause more harm to women than to men, clearing the way for female Chinese petitioners to claim that their human rights had been violated.[51] "When I first heard about the asylum program I was scared," Yamei recalled. "I was too young to have suffered much during the Cultural Revolution, and my coming to the United States was anything but political. I did not come here for myself, though. Every time we spoke on the telephone, my husband urged me to find a way to send for him and our son. I realized that [asylum] was my chance." Learning that U.S. medical experts disapproved of the use of intrauterine devices (IUDs), she was further encouraged: "I had indeed used the device—in fact I am still wearing one. If that was enough for asylum, then I was definitely a qualifier."[52]

But Yamei soon learned from her lawyer that she could improve her chance of winning asylum using a different strategy. She was told that the courts were not as sympathetic to those who claimed to be victims of the one-child policy as they had been earlier, and several petitions filed by her lawyer were rejected. She also learned that the courts seemed to be more lenient toward those who claimed to be members of Falun Gong, an anti-government religious cult banned in China. Yamei had never been part of Falun Gong; in fact she knew almost nothing about it except for the reports of its violent encounters with the police. In the end, however, she filed a petition as a Falun Gong member. She was granted asylum a year later and was able to send for her husband and son.[53]

This example shows clearly that asylum, as Alejandro Portes and Rebén G. Rumbaut put it, is not "a matter of personal choice, but of governmental decision based on a combination of legal guidelines and political expediency."[54] Whether an individual could take advantage of the asylum program is determined by the relationship between the United States and the immigrant's origin at a particular time. For this reason, it was difficult for an immigrant from the U.S. ally Taiwan, like

Lili, to take advantage of the option Yamei used to get permanent resident status. By the time Lili finally secured a divorce from her ex-husband, she and her son had been in the United States for six years. Going back as a woman without a husband and a child without a father would be hard, and she was not ready to give up the privacy that she was able to enjoy in the United States. But she needed legal status to live a normal life. She married an American citizen in 1994 hoping to adjust her status, but the marriage did not last long enough. It took Lili (a domestic care provider) sixteen years to finally gain legal status, after her employer filed a petition on her behalf claiming her as a technician with special skills needed by his company. In exchange she accepted a reduced monthly wage for two years.[55]

For a period of ten years between 1990 and 2000, more than 22,000 Chinese were counted as either granted asylum or listed for deportation. Although statistics on permanent-resident statuses given to spouses of U.S. citizens or employees of special skills are available, the government makes no effort to separate visa overstayers from new arrivals in these two categories. Assuming the number of undocumented immigrants who were able to adjust their status through marriage or employment is five to ten times greater than the asylum seekers and deportees combined, there would be still more than half a million Chinese living in the United States undocumented in 2000.

The estimate of a half million undocumented Chinese in 2000 is probably conservative, for several reasons. First, research conducted by the Pew Hispanic Center finds that unauthorized migrants account for 30 percent of a nation's foreign-born population.[56] The vast majority of the Chinese population (71 percent) was foreign-born in 2000. If the national average is applicable to the Chinese, the number of undocumented would be much bigger (over 600,000). Second, this estimate takes into consideration immigrants from the PRC, Hong Kong, and Taiwan, but still leaves out ethnic Chinese from elsewhere. Third, the government's deportation statistics reflect the number of removal decisions made rather than the actual number of departures; it is not unusual for individuals to go into hiding after receiving removal orders, although some other individuals also offered voluntary departure when threatened with deportation.[57]

Rethinking the Chinese American Population

It is extremely important to take into account the large presence of undocumented immigrants in the study of contemporary Chinese America, because it offers a different demographic profile of the community. The 2000 census includes only 115,000 of the approximately half million undocumented; the rest—about 385,000—are left out.[58] If these individuals are added to the picture, there would be 3.3 million Chinese living in the United States at the turn of the twenty-first century. The half million undocumented Chinese, though not as numerous as those from Mexico, form 18 percent of the entire Chinese American population, a proportion that is far too large to remain overlooked.

One noticeable demographic characteristic of contemporary Chinese America is the renewed dominance of the immigrant population. The 1940 census indicates that the number of U.S.-born Chinese had surpassed that of Chinese immigrants in the United States. Although the group of U.S.-born Chinese continued to grow after 1965, the immigrant population began growing far more rapidly. This is most apparent during the last two decades of the twentieth century. The 1980 census recorded only 36.7 percent of the Chinese population in the United States as U.S.-born; a decade later that percentage was lowered to 30.7. By the 2000 count, only 29.1 percent of Chinese Americans were born in the United States (see table 1.1). If the number of undocumented immigrants left out of the census were included, the fact that the new Chinese America is an immigrant community would become even more apparent.[59]

Going beyond numbers, making the hidden population visible is crucial to our understanding of social relations within the ethnic community. The study of undocumented Chinese is not new, but scholarly maneuvers to focus on the smuggled and link the undocumented with criminal activities have worked to separate these individuals from the larger Chinese American population, which has enjoyed a model-minority image in American society. It is important to see that undocumented immigrants are a diverse and complex group. The daily struggles of these people to find work and shelter, to remain hidden from government agencies, to pay off enormous debts and send money to families overseas, and to try to gain legal status are intertwined with other factors in the development of the community. The fact that the undocumented Chinese continue to depend on ethnic networks for survival allows the creation of a new ethnic economy, new social classes, new social hierarchies, and new social relations.

The combination of a high percentage of immigrants and the presence of a large number of undocumented immigrants requires reevaluation of the criteria and concepts that have been commonly adopted by ethnic studies scholars. The struggle for the rights and privileges to racial equality and social justice promised to citizens by the U.S. Constitution is only one aspect of Chinese American history. As George Lipsitz points out, strengthening "the distinctions between citizens and aliens" would provide "legitimation for nationalist and nativist policies that impose enormous suffering on humans precisely because they are not U.S. citizens."[60] Overemphasizing the distinction between documented and undocumented immigrants, and marginalizing the latter because they are "illegals" risks the same tendency against which Lipsitz cautions.

The recognition of demographic changes in post-1965 Chinese America obliges researchers to examine the different forces that have come into play. An acknowledgment of internal diversity, contradictions, and conflicts is not a denial of common ground. Rather, it can illuminate the strength of ethnicity in bonding people together. Throughout their history, diverse and sometimes opposing Chinese American groups have used ethnic ties as a means to further their own ends. Their networks have allowed individuals to find work, achieve wealth, and establish ethnic solidarity and pride. The relationship between the presence of a large number of undocumented immigrants and the expansion of the ethnic economy, and whether every person has had an equal opportunity to benefit from the enclave, are issues that we must explore next.

CHAPTER 2

Drawing Lines
of Class Distinction

As she reflected on her ten-month tryout as a member of a Chinese Presbyterian church in Houston in late 1994 and early 1995, Min reminisced about a rather uncomfortable experience that led to her departure. She was thirty-five then and recently divorced. After living in Atlanta, Georgia, for five years, she wanted to leave the past behind and start anew. Working at a furniture store six days a week, she volunteered her time at the church, helped organize a big Thanksgiving party, and spent countless hours on Christmas decorations. She was eager to make friends. Before Easter, however, she stopped. "I just felt that I couldn't fit in," she recalled. "People were friendly, but I somehow had the feeling that they also tried to ignore me. If I had a good job then, or if I was young and pretty, things might have turned out to be different. Of course there were people I could be friends with, but these were people in not-so-good situations."[1]

That Min believed that she was alienated by some church members because she possessed neither wealth nor youth, and that she was not interested in getting close to the members who were probably less fortunate than herself, suggest the importance of class status in social identifications of Chinese Americans. The ethnic community today is diverse and complex. While most immigrants of the late nineteenth and early twentieth centuries originated from rural areas of Guangdong province in China, those who arrived after 1965 came from all walks of life from mainland China, Hong Kong, Taiwan, Southeast Asia, and many other parts of the world. Outsiders visiting a Chinese-language school or a church gathering might be impressed by the homogeneous appearance of the ethnic group. These individuals' diverse backgrounds, complicated

d War II and Cold War–era geopolitical conditions
ds, as well as the mobility that many individuals are
in the United States, have created clear distinctions
rdly be a Chinese American without belonging to a
s of the ethnic group.

STUDYING CLASS

Class has been largely absent in the study of Chinese America. To
some scholars, the Chinese, regardless of their history in the United States
as a largely oppressed group prior to World War II, have emerged since
the 1960s as a model minority. Within a relatively short period of time,
many Chinese have already reenacted the success story of earlier American immigrant groups through their hard-work ethic, entrepreneurial
skills, and higher education. Individual successes, well circulated by the
media, have helped fashion an image of Chinese Americans as basically
a "middle-class" group. When researchers cite census data suggesting that
Chinese Americans' level of economic and educational achievements
is higher than the national average (these statistics usually do not take
undocumented immigrants into consideration), their scholarship further
enhances the model-minority image of a middle-class Chinese population. Few actually deny the importance of class analysis; next to race
and gender, class is probably one of the most commonly used terms by
Asian American studies scholars. More often than not, however, analysis
of class in the study of Chinese America is mixed with (if not replaced
by) discussions of race and ethnicity. Except for studies by Peter Kwong,
Renqiu Yu, and a handful of others, very few works frame Chinese
American experience within a class analysis.[2]

Approaching Chinese American history using a class analysis rather
than race and gender is complicated for various reasons. In the McCarthy
era, the classic, radical theory of class defined in the Marxist framework,
which emphasizes class struggle and working-class revolution, was often
linked with communism and deemed anti-America or un-American. At
a time when China was identified as an archenemy of the United States,
Chinese Americans were pressed to sever their ties with their ancestral
land and distance themselves from any notion that might be associated
with communist ideology. Meanwhile, describing ethnic minorities'
struggle for social justice in terms of race and gender is relatively safe

in the post-civil rights era. Class analysis is also theoretically challenging because class has different meanings for different people. Although there is a huge body of revisionist literature on class theory by scholars in various academic disciplines, no conclusion has been drawn about whether class is based on material possessions alone or is seen mainly as a product of culture. Moreover, assessing class status is not an easy task. Although it is possible to measure an individual's education, income, occupation, and property value, measuring one's level of authority and social prestige is a different matter.[3] The relationship between class and race is also difficult to define. And when racial equality is the central concern of ethnic studies scholars, would an emphasis on class division, which inevitably discloses some degree of exploitation and conflict *within* the group, somehow work to erode ethnic solidarity?

The reluctance of scholars to reveal class differences among Chinese Americans also has much to do with the improved socioeconomic status of Chinese Americans. Most Chinese Americans of the pre-World War II generation, individuals who were born into immigrant families of modest means and grew up during the exclusion era, can no longer be described as working class. Social mobility is by no means limited to the second or third generations of Chinese Americans, as a good portion of post-1965 immigrants, especially those who came with financial or human capital, have moved up the socioeconomic ladder. Chinese Americans are visible everywhere and in every field. With seven Nobel laureates, they are well recognized in science. Internationally renowned Chinese Americans are also found in architecture, the arts, music, sports, business, and many other fields. Although only relatively few have achieved a high level of success, their stories helped change the image of Chinese Americans from a lowly class of worthless, excludable, unassimilable subhumans to an American middle class, featuring affluent suburban dwellers and high achievers in elite schools and colleges. To scholars who strive to demonstrate that people of Chinese ancestry *are* Americans, it is more important to celebrate than to question the new social position Chinese Americans occupy in the post-civil rights era.

It would be naive, however, to think of Chinese America as one homogenous middle-class group. Chapter 1 challenges the assumption by revealing the existence of a large number of undocumented immigrants who struggle below the poverty line. This chapter moves beyond that concern and examines the ways ordinary Chinese Americans draw lines of class distinction among themselves. More specifically, it will explore the ways that Chinese Americans view their upward mobility and how they judge one another accordingly. It will illuminate how class matters in Chinese American experiences and how wealth, education, social prestige, native origins, and legal status are weighed in defining an individual's social status.[4]

Class has always been important to Chinese Americans. During the time period when Chinese laborers were barred by exclusion laws (1882–1943), merchants enjoyed the privilege of free entry, which gave them an edge, in addition to their economic advantage, over the laboring class. The merchants also used their own class status to challenge anti-Chinese ideologies in America.[5] Controlling leadership positions in major community organizations, the merchants oversaw the day-to-day lives of their fellow immigrants. When the community was divided over China politics in the late 1940s, many viewed their struggles along class lines.[6]

Although wealth and prestige were important, class distinctions were obscured in the early Chinese American community for several reasons. Overwhelming racial antagonism from the larger society before World War II called for ethnic solidarity, which worked to a great extent to suppress class differences. A segmented ethnic economy built upon segregation limited not only employment opportunities for the laborers but also possible business expansion for able entrepreneurs. Although business owners such as shopkeepers and labor contractors should not be categorized in the same class as laborers, their incomes and lifestyles were not significantly different from those of shop clerks, factory hands, and restaurant workers.

As a teenager in the 1930s, Jade Snow Wang, author of *Fifth Chinese Daughter*, sewed in her family-owned garment factory, alongside her mother, siblings, and hired workers.[7] Elizabeth Lew, who started to work in a garment shop when she was ten, remembered her childhood as a time when "everyone worked." When she and other workers sewed, the factory owner's children "ran button-hole machines" and "fold[ed] every-thing."[8] Moreover, as a common practice of the old days, many Chinese actually worked at places in which they also owned shares—making themselves both partners and laborers in these business establishments.

Under these circumstances, class lines between bosses and workers were difficult to draw, and the employers often shared the same interests as their employees. One of the most powerful anti-establishment organizations of the time, the Chinese Hand Laundry Alliance of New York, for example, was a union of both laundry owners and their workers.[9] Class boundaries were further blurred by native-place affiliations and kinship ties, toning down potential conflicts between the bosses and workers. The majority of the early Chinese immigrants originated from a few regions in two southern China provinces and shared rural roots and similar cultural and socioeconomic backgrounds. In confronting a hostile social environment in confined communities, as Sucheng Chan points out, it was crucial for the immigrants to "get along with each other in close quarters."[10] These situations led the relatively well-to-do Chinese—merchants, store, and factory owners—and the working poor to form what several scholars described as reciprocal relations.[11]

If there was a class in a distinctly higher position, it was not in contact with the rest of the Chinese American community. People who lived in racially segregated Chinatowns in those days were fully aware of an elite class of students beyond their neighborhood's boundaries. Since the late Qing years, the Chinese government had been sending students in an effort to import Western education to cope with China's problems in adapting to a changing international environment. Their numbers increased significantly after the turn of the twentieth century, as the U.S. government used part of its share of the Boxer Protocol indemnity to fund their studies.[12] By then a small number of wealthy Chinese families were also able to finance their own children's education overseas. A total of 3,797 Chinese students were in the United States in May 1949; many were enrolled in prestigious colleges on the East Coast.[13] Coming mostly from prominent families with considerable wealth, prestige, power, or intellectual heritage, few of these students had experienced economic hardship in China. Nor did they care for making a living in the United States as laundrymen or even small merchants. Their mission was to introduce Western technology to their homeland; they wanted to return to become the leaders of modern China. One survey revealed that 56.2 percent of the highest-ranking officials in the Chinese government, academic institutions, and the military by 1939 were educated in the United States.[14]

As a privileged group of Chinese who were exempted from the exclusion laws, the students did not see themselves as part of the Chinese American community. Living in university dormitories or with American families, in their eyes people in Chinatowns were "laboring hands (*laogong*)"—a low class that they knew very little about. And to the immigrants, this class of elite students served as a reminder of their own humble status. Ji Chaozhu, who later became a diplomat, recalled a childhood incident that took place on his first day of school in New York, shortly after he followed his father to the United States. Because of his family connections, Ji and his sister received a warm reception in school, and they were served rice for lunch. This special treatment, however, disturbed the then ten-year-old Ji so much that he threw a tantrum. "We educated northerners do not like rice, only the uneducated Cantonese eat rice! We educated northerners would only eat things like noodles and bread," he cried out, until the rice on his plate was replaced with potatoes.[15] Like most people from northern China, Ji, a native of Shanxi province, probably indeed preferred wheat products to rice, but what he said that day in front of his American teachers and classmates would make little sense if he had said it in China. There were indeed social prejudices among the Chinese due to regional differences, but the argument he made regarding the northerners' superiority in education is worth noting. Southern China, especially the Yangzi River delta and Pearl River delta (where Canton was located) were by no means the country's poorest regions. In contrast to cold and harsh weather conditions in most northern provinces, the mild climate and plentiful rainfall in most southern regions allow two crops to be grown each year. As a result, the population density in China's southern regions is much higher than that of the north, and there is no evidence to suggest that the northerners were better educated than the southerners. But Ji's point was well made (well taken by his audience, too), for the young boy was not comparing himself to people from southern China. Rather, he referred to the only southern Chinese his teachers and classmates had known, the "Cantonese" immigrants, who were seen as uneducated. Even at the tender age of ten, Ji understood how Chinese immigrants were perceived by the Americans, and apparently he was afraid of being seen as a member of that group.

Celebrated as a source of ethnic pride, the elite class of Chinese students has not been associated with Chinatown Chinese. Studies on the early Chinese American communities often mention little about these students because their experiences were distinctively different from those of the immigrant laborers; they did not belong to community organizations and were largely absent from community activities. Studies focused on students often used "the educated elite" to emphasize their uniqueness in class terms.[16] Indeed, these students and the immigrants had their own separate paths. The two groups neither shared common ground nor did they conflict with one another.[17]

The end of exclusion changed the way in which Chinese Americans connected to one another. Desegregation undermined the governing power of community organizations, thereby changing the ways individuals related to their community. Most post–World War II immigrants originated from regions other than Guangdong; coming from many different regions in China, Taiwan, Hong Kong, and the greater Chinese diaspora, they did not find traditional community organizations appealing. When reduced racial tensions made the mainstream job market more accessible, Chinese individuals no longer depended on their ethnic communities for survival. Demographic changes also produced more and different economic opportunities. After 1965, Chinese American entrepreneurs found new ways to launch business ventures utilizing a steady supply of immigrant labor and a greatly enlarged ethnic-based consumer market (see chapter 3). The rapid growth of ethnic entrepreneurship, services, and the market linked Chinese Americans together in ways that were quite different from those of the past. As economic growth both within the community and beyond facilitated upward mobility, it also gave material bases more weight in people's social lives. If, during the exclusion period, Chinese immigrants' success in the United States largely depended on the ability of their community to combat discriminatory laws and practices, then in the post–civil rights era, one's socioeconomic resources become crucial to his or her chances. Perhaps because there is a clear understanding that not everyone in this world is given the same opportunities and rewards, Chinese Americans have become quite class conscious.

Defining Class

Like people of other ethnic backgrounds, Chinese Americans understand class as some combination of a variety of economic, social, and cultural factors. While material possessions and income, education and occupation, and authority and prestige are all acknowledged as important dimensions of class, as an immigrant group, Chinese Americans also take into serious consideration historical circumstances that brought them to the United States and the means by which individuals crossed the borders, as well as the geopolitical and socioeconomic development of the regions that shaped their backgrounds.

That theirs is an immigrant-majority community makes defining class a rather complex matter for the Chinese. Initially, an individual's class comes from the standing of the family into which the person is born. In less-developed agrarian societies where mobility is limited, people's family roots are public knowledge. Immigration uproots people from different places and regroups them in new localities. This process allows some to hide their past, while creating anxieties about others at the same time, as the new immigrants suddenly find they are living among strangers. Disclosing information regarding wealth or prestige that their families once enjoyed in their native land becomes important to some, if they believe such information will help them gain social recognition in new settings. Others may see this as an opportunity to boost their social status, as no one knows their background anyway. The problem, as librarian Tammy Tang sees it, is the fact that "some [Chinese] people have no respect for the privacy of others and they ask way too many questions."[18] Apparently, information about one's past is important, whether volunteered or obtained through interrogation, because without it one's social status cannot be easily determined. While "my father is an American-educated scholar" means the person's family is Westernized and probably wealthy, "I am the offspring of highly ranked government officials (*gaogan zidi*)" implies power and prestige that the person's family enjoyed back in China. More often, the reference is to material possessions: "My house in Taiwan has six bedrooms with six baths," or, "I don't have to work, I can call my father-in-law if money is ever an issue." Genealogists can trace their family roots back for hundreds or even thousands of years to an emperor or some heroic figure, and writers can also find ways to impress their readers with the high-class status of their families.[19]

Although class status is inheritable, having more of what everyone values in one's ancestral land does not necessarily mean that high social status in the adopted country is forever guaranteed. It is relatively easy for immigrants to bring material resources with them, but turning family authority or prestige into practical use in a new environment is a different matter. Asked whether he gave any special privilege to the son of a notable intellectual in China, restaurateur Sammy Luo thought about it for a few seconds and offered the following remarks, "Well, he should be in school with books. But his father cannot take care of him in America. If the job is too hard, why bother to come?"[20]

To immigrants who are yet to be successful, comparing their current situation with that of their families can produce a sense of shame. A man in his early fifties said that he usually referred to his parents as petty office clerks (*xiao zhiyuan*) instead of government officials, and that he had never told his parents that he made a living in the United States painting other people's houses. "Not that I have something to hide," he said, "I just don't want to be compared with them. I am doing what I choose to do; I don't want people to feel sorry for me."[21]

For the same reason, those who have risen above their origins often feel especially good about themselves. In that case, revealing their humble past can work to demonstrate how much they have accomplished. Most immigrants were children in families with modest means in their country of origin; they came to the United States for better economic opportunities, and most of them started as menial laborers. Once they have climbed up the socioeconomic ladder, however, their humble past is no longer a source of embarrassment but, rather, a source of pride. One well-to-do businessman was quite satisfied when he compared his achievement with that of a fellow church member: "John went to one of the most prestigious high schools in Taiwan. Not far away from there was my family's food cart. Those kids sure looked different from my brother and me. To me, it was like heaven and earth. When my first son was born, I swore to my wife I would do anything possible to send him to a good school. Both my kids are attending the most expensive private schools here. I doubt John's job pays him enough to send his kids to that school [laughter]!"[22]

Schools, neighborhoods, and the price tags of one's material possessions are all markers of a person's class profile. Jumei Cheng, a forty-nine-year-old woman who has been in the United States for twenty-five years, said that it was "impolite" to make inquiries about other people's income or bank savings. She acknowledged, however, that she knew who lived well and who did not by observing people's spending habits: "All you have to pay attention to is their financial strength (*caili*). I don't know exactly how much money some of my friends are making, but I do know who can afford what."[23] Commenting on one of his old friends, a middle-aged man said, "He is rich (*fa le*). The wage-earning group (*gongxin zu*) would not be able to afford anything in that neighborhood!"[24] Xiyao Peng, a sharp dresser with a high-pitched voice, seemed to have expensive taste. But the ladies from her singing group in Los Angeles did not think highly of her financial situation. "Who knows what's going on with them [Peng and her husband]," one woman remarked, "If they have the money, why are they still renting [in other words, why couldn't they afford to buy a house]?"[25]

The importance of class status compels people to find ways to showcase their wealth. "Do you see the cars parked in our church lot? Our people are very much into brand name cars, even though some have to stretch," said one woman from Hong Kong.[26] George Wu, a restaurant owner, knew the value of driving fancy cars:

> When I bought the restaurant fourteen years ago, my brother told me to lease a Mercedes. I was reluctant. Those days were nerve wrecking. We borrowed too much money. Business was slow. We could hardly pay the bills. My wife had to come to work shortly after our daughter was born; we couldn't afford an extra hand. But my brother said I had to keep the Mercedes no matter what. He said I had to show people that we were financially strong. If I couldn't afford a Mercedes, he said the devils who loaned us the money (*taozhaigui*) would come to knock on our door. Now, if I suddenly drive around in a cheaper car, people would wonder what happened. They would think that I had gambled away my money.[27]

As more and more people own brand-name cars and other luxury items, standing out in a crowd becomes difficult. A woman who described herself as "very rich" said that people's possessions and affordability needed scrutiny. Her Lexus, she said, was very high end, and her taste differed from that of others because she had more money to spend:

"When I went to shop for a car, I told the dealer to show me the very best. You won't want to drive a cheap Lexus if you tried mine—there is no comparison! I have very high standards. Not many people could afford my taste."[28]

Social pressure plays an important role in the development of expensive taste, compelling individuals to put their socioeconomic selves eagerly on public display. Jerry Yi, an engineering professor, said that he and his wife did not share the same taste because they belonged to different social circles. "I don't drive a brand-name car, but my wife's friends all drive fancy cars. She cares about saving face, so she has to have one. No one cares what car I drive."[29] Bob Sun, a medical device salesman, said that the BMW he drove is his "cover" (*baozhuang*). "In my early years here I paid five hundred dollars for a salvaged car. People threw mean looks at me all the time. This is America; no one respects you if you are poor. In my BMW no one looks at me like that anymore."[30]

Material possessions play an increasingly important role in social circles. Wendy, who identified her family as rich, said that knowledge about one another's socioeconomic status would make it easy for people to socialize. "It is natural for people to want to hang out with those in similar or higher circumstances. You wouldn't want to mingle with people who are lower because you don't want to be seen as one of them. Everyone would like to move up, not down like water."[31] Clearly, lines of class differences are consciously drawn by individuals through group affiliation.

Julia Tai, a southern California realtor who has a Master's degree in English, said that the fact that her clients (almost all Chinese) were status conscious helped her business a great deal. Accordingly, the Chinese are more willing to stretch financially than average American consumers when it comes to property purchase. "In my trade, knowing what your clients are looking for is the key. You buy a house to live in and to show to others. One time a couple checked out a house that was over what they had budgeted, but when I told them the next door neighbor was rather well known, the wife became very interested. That played a big part in their decision to making the purchase." In early 2004, Julia sold a house that needed a lot of work. "The buyers had two little kids and did not want to consider fixer-uppers. I pointed out, however, that it was an almost all-white neighborhood. They eventually came back and made an offer." Asked whether her clients preferred white neighbors over Chinese, her response was affirmative.[32]

To some extent, class and race are closely connected, and an all-white neighborhood basically means a middle-class neighborhood. While some homeowners did not say that race was a concern, they did acknowledge class as a factor. "Being a homeowner exemplifies middle-class status, but you really aren't unless you live in a middle-class neighborhood," said one businessman bluntly.[33] A man who identified himself as an employee of Los Angles County asserted that neither race nor class were issues for him. What he and his wife strived for at the time was simply a "safe" place. "As long as it is a good neighborhood, we don't care whether our neighbors are white, black, or Chinese. Diversity is a good thing; it is good for our children." He did add, however, a "good" and "safe" neighborhood was more likely to be a middle-class neighborhood.[34]

Regarding Chinese neighbors, the views are mixed. One woman said she liked the fact she had Chinese neighbors because it was "easy to find people to watch the house" when they were away.[35] The presence of other Chinese, said another woman, made the living environment more "relaxed."[36] Meimei Ling, a resident of Arcadia, California, considered Chinese neighbors easy to deal with: "My son was a real headache in his younger years. The Chinese [neighbors] were sympathetic to us, but we were scared when he bullied non-Chinese (*yangren*) kids."[37] Henry Kang, a research scientist in Oakland, California, felt that having Chinatown within walking distance was especially good for his parents, who were living with him and his wife. "They like to get groceries and the Chinese newspaper when we are at work. They also enjoy spending time with their friends. Otherwise they would be like caged birds." Henry's friend Danny, however, had a different take on this. He said that having too many Chinese in the same neighborhood would "prevent his children from becoming Americanized," and he seemed to be quite pleased that most of his daughters' friends were non-Chinese.[38] A woman who immigrated to the United States in the early 1980s said that she didn't want to have anything to do with the Chinese couple on the block because they didn't have any class: "They grow vegetables in the front yard and air-dry their clothes. It's disgraceful (*diuren*)!"[39]

Those who avoided Chinese neighbors also highlighted the issue of privacy. Yan Zhou, who owned a home in the San Francisco Bay area, said that the Chinese were nosey. "We did not specifically look for a white neighborhood, but too many Chinese together is no good; we wouldn't want to be constantly compared, judged, and gossiped about."[40] Weiwei Chan, who has a teenage son, said that it was the competitive nature of the Chinese that made her try to avoid them. "You are right that they [Chinese] often live in areas with good schools, but honestly, I hate to see my kid compared to them. We would rather be left alone."[41]

Wendy Wang, a college student, said that her mother could always tell the "haves" from the "have-nots" by looking at their cars or other belongings. Her friend Stephanie Poon said that her mother was like that too, and that she had teased her mother after she got her driver's license. "I said, mom, please buy me a BMW, I want to be seen as rich. And my brother seconded immediately, 'Come on, Mom, I don't want other people to think that my sister is from a poor family.'"[42]

Although high-end cars and trophy properties are good indications of realized American dreams, these luxuries can also work to distance those who cannot afford them. Le Ye, who owns a 6,000 square-foot mansion (*haozhai*) on a green hill in southern California, was especially pleased when people nicknamed his residence the "White House." In a letter to a Chinese-language newspaper, he says that the house gives him a sense of "satisfaction and accomplishment" and makes him feel "superior (*gao ren yi deng*)" and "proud." However, he does realize that this sense of success comes with a price, as several old friends don't want to come over. "After seeing our house, those with an inferiority complex feel they cannot rise up to be our equals (*gaopang bu shang*) and refuse to have anything to do with us."[43]

Alienation was what Limin Yao felt from other people in the community. As a hotel clerk in Queens, New York, she is frequently reminded of her low social status. "I send hotel guests regularly to travel agencies and restaurants. But in the eyes of many people here, I am just a chore runner (*dagongde*). They all say that my boss is mean and stingy. In public, however, she is always warmly greeted and I am the one who's ignored."[44] Beautician Anna still has bitter feelings about some of her church members. Once she overheard some ladies at the church talking about trips to Europe. "When I walked over and asked a question," she reflected, "they stopped talking all of a sudden, and one of them gave me this stare. It made me feel like a fool."[45] Tony Chang, an engineer, said that he basically went into hiding after being laid off. "I turned down many dinner invitations. I can see myself having a good time there if I am doing well, but I have nothing to say about myself. I would rather be left alone."[46]

Ran He, who helps out at a Chinese-language school on the weekends, thinks that the Chinese in America are rather "vulgar (*suqi*)"—worse than those in China. "People with good manners (*xiuyang*) in China would not brag about money; you simply do not have the word 'money' on your lips all the time. Look at the [Chinese] people here, all they care about is how much money they could make!" Sharon Li, who has a good career in the real-estate business, is seen by her friends as unusual because she is quiet and modest. Apparently a very considerate person, she remarked, "My luck is good. I have a good business due to the trust I receive from the Chinese clients around here. Not everyone is as fortunate. It would be too much for me to show my wealth because it would make others uncomfortable."[47]

Along with money come social prestige and power, which are not always measurable. Richard Ho, who never attended high school while in Taiwan, was proud of the amount of money he has been able to make in the United States. "My restaurant generates a good income; I bet not many with Ph.D. degrees (*boshi*) can compete with me." He, however, does not want his sons to follow in his footsteps. "My children should go to college and work with their brains. I make money serving other people (*ciho ren*). That's hard. My children should be served by others."[48]

As was the case in their ancestral lands, the Chinese in the United States are quick to recognize education as the key to upward mobility. Doctors, lawyers, professors, and other members of the professional class are highly respected, and children are often pushed to join them. Community organizations and business associations often provide scholarships to honor talented students, which is also a way to recognize good parenting. Chinese parents of high achievers automatically become experts on child-drearing, and they are invited to speak at community-hosted conferences on children's education. An immigrant couple from Fujian province in China received high honors from his regional community organization because they had sent all three of their sons to Harvard.[49] The community provides support and encourages families in their efforts to educate their children, but it also generates tensions when parents pit their children in fierce competition against one another. "When I did not make the debate team in high school," recalled Patricia Li, then a freshman in college, "my mom thought it was unfair because this Chinese friend of mine got in, and she thought I was better. Our families were always in some kind of competition, which made us very uncomfortable. When she [the friend] got higher SAT scores, her mom told everyone that she beat me; my mom was really upset."[50] Jenny Zhuang, a nurse, thinks that Chinese focus too much on their children's accomplishments: "All you hear is so-and-so's kid did this and so-and-so's kid did that, making us feel like we are bad parents because we are too busy to supervise our daughter's extracurricular activities. Why should we worry about whether she will be able to get into a good college now? She is only twelve!"[51] Another mother said that she was so nervous before her son was admitted to college that she did not want to talk to any of her friends. "I did not want to hear where the other kids were getting into, but in those days, that was the topic everyone was interested in. If Bob [her son] was rejected by all the UCs [Universities of California], I would not have the courage to face others."[52]

The concern, apparently, is not getting into college, as higher education is available for just about everyone in the United States. Yuting Lei, a businessman who came to the United States in 1994, said that he felt very relieved. "It's too hard to get into college in China, and we were very concerned about our son's future. Otherwise, why would we go through all the trouble to come here?"[53] But many parents set high goals for their children and work hard to achieve them. One devoted parent said that growing up in Taiwan, his parents were not involved in his school activities because there college admission is determined by the scores of a single entrance exam. "But high grades and good test scores are not enough here," he said, "and the emphasis on extracurricular activities requires parents' participation. My parents did not care for my playing basketball in high school. They would rather see me carrying books all the time. It is hard for me to explain to them why I have to spend so much time at my son's tennis matches. Look at the kids who excel in music and sports, every one of them has devoted parents behind them.

I don't want my son to be left behind."[54] Amy Yuan, who fulfilled her dream by sending her son to Columbia University to study business, said that she had been thinking about her son's college applications since his freshman year in high school. "We can save a lot of money if he goes to a public university; many of them are not bad. We just don't want him to end up in a college where everyone else also goes."[55] In other words, when a college education is available to all, it is a privilege to none. To be seen as superior, one has to be admitted to institutions that relatively few people can actually get into.

Degrees associated with elite institutions are highly valued by many who still have vivid memories of their own college experience. Those who failed to reach their goals have lived with the consequences. One woman, who was very proud of her husband's accomplishment, referred to his alma mater, *Taida* (National University of Taiwan) as "Taiwan's Harvard." To Alicia Hsu, who also came from Taiwan, the significance of her son's college could not be overemphasized: "My husband is from an academic family. When he failed to get into Taida, his parents felt they lost face. When my son received his college admission, I informed my mother-in-law: 'Your grandson is admitted to Princeton University. This is the highest-ranked university in America—the very best in the whole world!'"[56] Diana Wang, who came from China in the late 1980s, was especially pleased that her daughter went to Yale University, something that the children of many of her wealthier friends could not accomplish. "We would pay for her to go even if we had to sell our house," she said. "Some people say you can do anything with money. Could they purchase a ticket to get into Yale?"[57]

The privilege associated with elite colleges is not quite the same as that which comes with wealth. Coming from an ancient tradition where the Confucian doctrine of "a good scholar makes a good official" was common practice, where the top stratum of the social structure was made up of scholars who had distinguished themselves after a series of imperial examinations, it is easy for Chinese Americans to link educational success to the accumulation of wealth and power in the United States. Most new immigrants are struggling to make ends meet and do not see big changes in their lives. But their children's success in getting into prestigious colleges is real, and they want it to be recognized. When parents of high achievers demand recognition from the ethnic community, however, they inevitably put others down. In a recently published novel, historian Yu Renqiu tells a story of an immigrant who throws a big party and uses the occasion to brag about his earned success—his son has graduated from Harvard and his daughter has been admitted there. Yu's nuanced details, with the exasperating host on the one side and his guests (many attended the party reluctantly) on the other, capture the tensions among the Chinese when some try to renegotiate their social status using their children's academic achievements.[58]

Efforts to put their wealth on public display, to compare one's success with another's, and to demand social recognition of their newly achieved mobility, reflect both the desire for higher class status and the pressure to get ahead. Since the California gold rush, generations of Chinese immigrants have come to the United States to pursue their "gold mountain" dreams. Who gets to realize such a dream is subject to interpretation, and mobility is understood from a multidimensional comparative perspective. Cindy Jeu, who came from Hong Kong, thought comparison has its purpose: "America is a paradise for risk takers; one can move up overnight. Our people do like to compare everything back and forth, but how would you know who is successful and who is not without the comparison?" Available opportunities as well as success stories encourage individuals to try hard and take risks. At the same time, however, no one is immune to failure. Constant comparison with one another creates more uncertainty, anxiety, insecurity, and stress.

CLASS AND REGIONAL VARIATIONS

To some extent, the effort to draw class boundaries is a result of increased interactions among Chinese of various socioeconomic backgrounds after World War II. The early Chinese immigrants came from Guangdong province, China, and were mostly of humble rural origins. Before the war, they concentrated in highly isolated ethnic ghettos in San Francisco, Oakland, Los Angeles, New York, Chicago, and Honolulu, with little chance for social mobility outside their community. The participation of Chinese Americans in the war effort signified the beginning of desegregation. When the war ended, Chinese American war veterans and former defense industrial workers ventured out and moved up.

In workplaces, children of the early immigrants met people of their own ethnicity from a different stratum of the Chinese social structure;

many of the latter were Western-trained students who came to the United States in the late 1940s and early 1950s, during and after the Chinese civil war. The victory of the Communist revolution created a great deal of uncertainty; many students in the United States decided not to return. In the two decades following the founding of the People's Republic of China in 1949, the United States also admitted a few thousand refugees from China; among them were top government officials and military officers, bankers, business owners, and intellectuals. An increasing number of young students from Hong Kong and Taiwan also began to arrive. All these changes facilitated interactions among Chinese of different socioeconomic backgrounds and made some people anxious about the blurring of class distinctions.

George Lew, an American-born Chinese who grew up in Oakland, California, and went to college at the University of California, Berkeley, under the G.I. Bill, remembers this time of change. "It was a very interesting time," he said. "Suddenly, I found myself talking to Chinese people in English. You see, I had to speak *English* to *Chinese* people. They had a strong accent, but they didn't understand a word of Cantonese! [laugh]"[59] Andrew Wong, who worked in a company in San Francisco, was called by his boss to meet a newly hired engineer. "I showed Dan around," he recalled. "I grew up here, so naturally I became the host. He slept on our living room sofa for a few nights before moving into his own apartment. That's before we bought this house. He left in the late 1970s to start his own company, a smart guy. He must have been twenty-seven or twenty-eight then, in the early 1960s. I ran into him last year and was glad that he remembered those days—sleeping on the sofa."[60] Maggie Gee, a retired research scientist at Lawrence-Livermore National Laboratory in California, became friends with some scholars who came to work at the lab, most of them from Taiwan and Hong Kong: "I watched these kids grow. Some of them are now quite Americanized."[61]

To the highly educated and mostly non-Cantonese new immigrants, differentiating themselves from earlier immigrants, and the class connotations associated with them, is of great importance. They do not like to be seen as the same as earlier immigrants. Asked whether class was an issue among the Chinese she got to know from work, Caroline Jin, a medical research scientist born in San Francisco, at first said she did not think so. She saw everyone as her equals because they were all educated in the United States, and they were doing the same job. But she took it back moments later, after she had a chance to reflect; she commented, "It's interesting that you brought this up. Actually, as I think about it, class was a point made from time to time. Not directly, but implied. Do you remember Kenneth? I don't mean to criticize; I like him a lot. But he was quite status conscious. I don't remember exactly how he put it, but there's this sense that people from Taiwan were the best—they were the upper class. My grandfather came here to make a better living. His grandfather, being well-off, wouldn't do that, I guess."[62]

To distinguish themselves from the laborers, some of the newer immigrants stayed away from traditional community activities. Kathy Yan, who came from Taiwan with her husband in 1967, recalled a "weird" time when every Chinese was seen as associated with Chinatown. "One of my American friends got into the habit of passing on information about Chinatown events to us. I eventually told her that we didn't like Chinatown at all—I hated the way it smelled, and I didn't even care for the grocery there since my son wouldn't eat Chinese food. She was very surprised. She thought all Chinese are the same—that's frustrating!"[63] There were signs of clashes in Chinatown, as well. Growing up in San Francisco, Mary Lew recalled seeing a new restaurant started by a new immigrant on the same block where her uncle worked in the 1960s: "People were saying that the food there was overpriced. The owner said, 'Too expensive? Find a Cantonese restaurant then. Mine is not here for the poor people.'"[64]

But class is not immutable. A family's past in the old country may not determine a person's success in the United States. Once uprooted, an individual often has to start anew in his or her adopted country. If backgrounds should be taken into consideration, then some believe those associated with American citizenship, a higher level of assimilation, or the seniority of one's family in the United States should carry more weight. The value of citizenship has been perpetuated by government legislation. During the exclusion era, only American-born Chinese were allowed to participate in American politics, and their birthright has played a big part in the articulation of ethnic identity by second-generation Chinese Americans. As part of the struggle to gain recognition and acceptance from mainstream American society, scholars also maneuvered to draw lines between immigrants and their American-born children. Equipped with citizenship status, a good command of English, a higher level of cultural assimilation, and family wealth accumulated in the United States over a relatively long period of time, the senior members of the ethnic community are indeed in a better position to make the best of what America has to offer. The later arrivals, in contrast, do have more obstacles to overcome. Unless a person comes with sufficient financial resources or marketable skills, social status back in the native land probably will not have a big impact on his or her accomplishments in the United States.

The value of a made-in-USA tag was quite clear to Wen Li, a naturalized citizen who came to the United States in 1991. Wen said that she was used to receiving questions from strangers about her immigration background (when did she come, how did she come, did she gain citizenship through marriage, etc.), questions her U.S.-born husband did not have to face. "Once people heard that he was born here, you can see a kind of approval on their faces, and no more interrogation. They would consult him on legal issues, financial issues, or politics as if he were an expert on everything."[65]

After the United States established diplomatic relations with the People's Republic of China in 1979, new waves of immigrants from the Chinese mainland began to arrive, adding more complexity and anxiety vis-à-vis class status. The opening of China allowed reunions for members of thousands of Chinese American families that had been separated for three decades and introduced new Chinese faces on university campuses. In many ways the newcomers from the PRC are very similar to their counterparts from Taiwan and Hong Kong. Most of them speak Mandarin instead of Cantonese, and they come from all walks of life. A large number of students and scholars from the mainland are graduates of China's top universities.

In the eyes of those from everywhere else, the newcomers from the PRC, known as the mainlanders (daluren), are not only different but also inferior. As their fellow ethnic Chinese in Taiwan, Hong Kong, and the United States enjoyed the fruits of capitalist economic development for several decades after 1949, the largely isolated mainlanders devoted most of their energy to one political movement after another called by the Communist party. To the new immigrants, the United States resembles little of the world that they had left behind. Their proletarian outlook, rather than political ideology or family backgrounds, subjected them to prejudice, alienation, and resentment once they set foot on American soil. (Before the late 1990s, the vast majority of immigrants from China came with very few financial resources.) "I can spot a mainlander on the street by a single glance, their mannerism is very awkward," said one woman.[66] A businessman said that the mainlanders in his garment shop and restaurant were lazy because they were products of the socialist system: "People who are used to getting their rice from the big pot (*daguo fan*) cannot do the hard work."[67] A restaurant owner from Taiwan said that she never let her husband's nephew, who was from China, near the cash register because she was afraid that he might steal: "Precautions are necessary (*fang ren zhi xin bu ke wu*). I don't mean to say that he is a bad person, but who knows what poverty-stricken people might do?"[68]

Jerry Tong, now a software engineer, came to the United States in 1981 with the assistance of his uncle. Jerry's grandfather, an entrepreneur from Shanghai, took the family to Taiwan before the Communist takeover in 1949, leaving Jerry's father behind. "My father did not leave because he was in love. When my grandparents were busy packing, he hid in his college dorm and refused to go home. Thirty years later, when word suddenly came from my grandparents, father burst into tears. He had never mentioned anything about his family to me until then." Jerry's uncle, who had settled in New Jersey, was the first to go back to visit, and he helped Jerry, then a college student, apply for college in the United States. Jerry would stay with his uncle for two years while finishing college, but was on his own the two months after he arrived. "My uncle promised to take care of me, but in his house days wore on like years. It's torture, mentally. My parents could not afford to cover my expenditure here; what else could I do? I moved in with some restaurant workers and someone tossed me two blankets. Oh, let's not talk about this anymore."[69]

Some reunited families were torn apart due to such prejudice. Annie Feng, now an accountant in Simi Valley, California, came to the United States to be with her family. Born in 1949 in Shanghai, Annie was left to care for her grandparents when her parents went to Taiwan. Thirty years later, when her parents sent for her to come to the United States, she was the envy of many of her peers in China. But she soon sensed that she was a shame to her family because she was from the mainland. The adjustment she tried to make was never enough. Tensions mounted when she refused to go out with guys her mother introduced her to:

She [mother] introduced me to a few men, quite a few. This one was the father of two kids—I don't remember what happened to his previous wife. I was told he was an honest person, with a good job and a house. He was on the shorter side and plump. When we met, he looked me up and down, critically, as if I was a commodity in a store. That turned me off. He ordered food, but I barely touched it. I said I had a headache—which was true—and he had to drive me home. My mother and sister were furious. I was thirty-two and eager to get married, but no one ever asked what kind of person I would like to live with. Since then, my mother and sister—my father was not like that—have not shown me a smiling face. When Luke and I were seeing each other, I overheard my mother saying something to the effect that she could not afford to deal with another pauper (*qiongguangdan*). Imagine: I was a pauper to my own mother![70]

Wilson Wang, who was stationed in Los Angeles for a Chinese export company in the late 1980s, had mixed feelings about dealings with coethnic entrepreneurs. Common language and cultural background made it easy for him to establish business ties with other Chinese, but the fact that he represented a mainland company made things rather complicated:

Once I delivered two containers full of dry chili pepper to a whole-saler. The owner, who was from Taiwan, told me to find a pest inspector and leave the goods in his parking lot. When I returned with the inspector, the containers were gone—they were found a few days later near the freeway, empty. My first inclination was to report it to the police, but he was very much against it. He said he would give me some money and I should just tell my company that the goods were stolen. He said that this would be a small loss to a government-run company, and that since I had job security there was nothing for me to worry about. It's hard to believe. We had businesses with several Mexican-American wholesalers; no one treated us like that.[71]

In institutions of higher learning that reward academic merit and hard work, it is relatively easy for mainlanders to ignore bias against them. Min Jiang, a division manager of a pharmaceutical company, said that she never let stereotypes bother her. "I got along fine with other Chinese students. Of course there were unfriendly things said about us in general. We dressed differently and did not know much about American social etiquette. Most important was the fact that we did not have the money to buy fancy things. But so what? Honestly I didn't care what they had to say. What matters in school are merit and ability. So if you have them, who cares how much money you have?"[72] Hua Xie, a research scientist, said that sometimes people would say that she did not look like a mainlander, "I suppose that's a compliment, but it's annoying. It assumes that people from China are inferior."[73] Weiping Wu, a college professor, said that when some students from China were found to have problems, their origins would be seen as the causes. And some people used that as an excuse for not admitting mainland students.[74] Another professor recalled an incident when he first entered the job market in the early 1990s. When he called to inquire about his status in the application process for a faculty position, the search committee chair, who was also a Chinese immigrant, told him he had no chance: "Do you know what he said to me? He said that 'the job market has been flooded by you mainlanders.'"[75]

While memories of the cold receptions from others are still fresh to some immigrants from China, others said that they can now understand why. A few even admitted that they had changed as well. "Only after I came to America did I learn how important it is to have money," said Rick Li, who immigrated in 1989. "I should not expect people to respect me when my pockets are empty. I tell every newcomer the same thing: work hard and earn a lot of money. Everything comes your way when you have money. I don't think rich people and poor people behave the same way. That's just a fact."[76] It took only five years for Diana Yang, a graduate student, to develop a very critical eye toward people in her homeland, and the latecomers: "You can say that I have changed; it is inevitable. Obviously what I think and do is very difficult for people in China to understand."[77] The impact of the American experience upon the value system of individual immigrants is revealed in a television series, *Beijing ren zai niuyue* (Beijingers in New York). The main character, Wang

Qiming, a cellist from Beijing, is outraged when he and his wife first arrive in New York because their relatives, after dropping the couple off in a cold basement apartment, refuse to offer additional help. Years later, when an old friend arrives in New York from Beijing, it is Wang, well on his way to become a middle-class American, who emulates what had happened to him.[78]

Similar to the experiences of the Okies in California in James Gregory's study, prejudice against mainland Chinese is not directed at all Chinese from the PRC. Students and scholars have encountered relatively less resentment, and those who came with sufficient money have no problem getting accepted. Internationally renowned athletes, movie stars, artists, and scholars, as well as successful businessmen from the mainland, are often quickly embraced by Chinese Americans as their own people. The stereotype was not a matter of regional prejudice. "Class," as Gregory puts it, "is the essential dividing line."[79]

THE UNDERCLASS

Sitting outside a Starbucks on a fine spring afternoon in Queens, New York, Lisa helped a two-year-old girl clean up after a snack of milk and cookies. Next to her chair was a light-colored stroller, where the girl's five-month-old sister was asleep under a white flannel blanket dotted with pink roses. For fourteen years since she first left Haining in Zhejiang province, Lisa has worked for more than a dozen Chinese American families. She was able to get legal status with the assistance of one of her former employers, but her situation did not improve much after that.

The young girls' parents were both at work. Their father, a lawyer, traveled often, and their mother, a free-lance architect, worked in her home office. For ten hours a day, Lisa took care of the girls and cooked meals. Occasionally she would be asked to stay for extra hours in the evenings or over the weekend with additional pay. Dinner with her own son after work was usually simple; only on weekends would she cook something special. When the subject shifted to her son, Lisa's face lighted up. It turned out that he had been accepted by a state university, and financial aid from the government would cover tuition and fees, plus room and board. At forty-four, Lisa had developed lower-back pain from lifting and carrying children over the years. She could not envision herself doing anything else, however, due to her lack of marketable skills. "My life is going to be the way it has been; I do not expect much for myself," she said. "He [the son] has a shot. I know he will do better, that's enough."[80]

In California, Yamei (see chapter 1) still worked in a restaurant after seven years in the United States. Her son, Lulu, was finishing his junior year in high school, his third year of American education after his mother got him out of China through political asylum. He was quite relaxed. While his old classmates back in Shanghai must work hard to prepare for their college entrance exams, the door of community colleges would be open for him. Through Yamei's connections, Lulu got a job in a restaurant, working twenty hours a week. In the small one-bedroom apartment that he shared with his mother and her boyfriend (Yamei divorced her husband shortly after he came to the United States) was a large-screen television in the living room, facing a couch right next to Lulu's bed. Lulu and his mother split the cost for the television. He had a second job lined up for the summer, in another Chinese restaurant. The next goal was to buy a used car. After that, he said he would take a trip to China. Yamei was proud of her son: Lulu had matured since coming to America. She also understood the price they had to pay; he was not spending time on his school work, he had not touched his flute since coming to America, and he had absolutely no time for sports, although through their apartment window they could watch boys his age playing basketball downstairs. "I asked him to work fewer hours, but he wouldn't listen. I have no way out, but I don't want him to spend the rest of his life working in restaurants." There was not much more that Yamei could do to change the situation, however. She could not afford music lessons or summer camps for her son. The real irony is that if her son could contribute more to the family budget, she could see the possibility of purchasing a restaurant herself.[81]

Starting out as undocumented immigrants, many Chinese like Lisa and Yamei come to a new country with no money, no knowledge of English, no marketable skills, and no work permit. Through personal contacts or ethnic networks they find work in restaurants, garment shops, or private homes. These contacts and networks allow the undocumented to survive, but in doing so they also funnel the workers into dead-end occupations. Both Lisa and Yamei eventually adjusted their legal status;

but only after they were freed from their illegal status did they realize how difficult it is to move up. They are trapped. They have no property and no money to purchase property. They have no skills to find better jobs and no time to train for career advancement. Their past experiences have made them a permanently disadvantaged group within their own ethnic community: the Chinese American underclass.

Scholars and political commentators have long attempted to divide poor people into different categories. In recent decades, studies on the underclass have focused largely on contemporary inner-city crises associated with drugs, crime, teenage pregnancy, unemployment, and welfare dependence. Some scholars examine the moral character of certain urban groups as well as the relationship between the behaviors of individuals and the poverty that they endure.[82] Their critics argue that the approach itself, which divides the urban poor into deserving and undeserving individuals, has "reinforced images of social pathology," imposed stereotypes, and put the blame on the victims.[83] The heated debate, joined by both liberal and conservative researchers and political commentators, has generated a large body of scholarly work, which has impacted the formulation of government policies on poverty. Unable to come up with acceptable ideological arguments and theoretical solutions, some advocates of underclass research have suggested that the term should be simply abandoned.[84]

My use of the term "underclass" in this study is not an attempt to solve the unsolved theoretic or political issues (although studies on the underclass have never taken Asian American experiences into consideration), as I have no intention of reviving a historical debate. I am using the term for practical purposes. In regard to social mobility, opportunities for the "have-nots" are not equal; among Chinese immigrants, there is a permanently entrapped group that cannot be easily classified with other poor immigrants as working class or lower class. Although discussions of the undocumented Chinese may at times appear similar to those in Douglas Glasgow's *Black Underclass*, because as a group they are also "collectively different" from and "left behind" by the others, no effort will be made to draw parallels between the two.[85] Nor do I link the enduring hardships of this group of Chinese with inner-city problems or social pathology.

What differentiates the undocumented from the general working-class or lower-class Chinese is their legal (or illegal) status. It is not unusual for a person to start poor in the United States; relatively few new immigrants come rich. This group of individuals shares a unique social status not because its members are poor, but because they are excluded from the system that provides ordinary Americans, immigrants included, basic rights, privileges, and protections. Since these individuals have no legal rights to remain in the United States, sociologist David M. Heer sees them as members of a "legal underclass."[86]

The undocumented Chinese come from all walks of life; most of them originated from different regions of China, but some are from Taiwan, Hong Kong, Southeast Asia, and many other parts of the world. Among them are former peasants, factory workers, office clerks, students, and professionals of different kinds, including individuals who could have distinguished careers in their native places. But the lack of legal status, which is required for formal employment in the United States, means that these individuals have no access to the formal job market. They are referred to as "blacks" (*heiren*) in the community because they are hidden in the dark, and they are a vulnerable target for economic exploitation and other forms of abuse. An old couple from China in the United States to visit their daughter, for example, answered a call to take care of two young children for a Chinese American family. Although the going monthly rate for such a job would be $1,200, they accepted $800 instead, fully aware that they did not have work permits and their visas would soon expire. The employer seemed to enjoy their service, but said that she would like to pay them all at once at the end of the year. Eight months passed before they finally asked for their paycheck. By then, however, the employer requested to see their work permits. When the couple's daughter protested, the employer ignored her and threatened to call the police. Unfortunately, aside from the community newspaper, there was no formal channel for the couple to file a grievance. Fearing their expired visas would have a negative impact on their daughter, who was a student, the couple had to swallow their plight.[87]

Huiling Zhao, who came from Malaysia in 1985, said that she was paid $700 a month when she started to work in a Chinese restaurant in Manhattan, New York—$100 less than what the other employees received. Moreover, throughout the years when she did not possess legal status, she was frequently bullied but had to submit to humiliation.[88] When it was revealed that two New York immigration firms swindled more than four million dollars from about 150 Chinese immigrant clients, most of the victims, almost all of them undocumented, did not come forward to talk to reporters or help with the police investigation; many tried to hide instead.[89]

Legal status can complicate domestic disputes as well. Writing to a Chinese-language newspaper, Ms. T says that her ex-husband has not paid his share of child support. She came as a spouse in 1993. For eight years when her ex-husband was a graduate student, she supported the family by working long hours in a Chinese restaurant. They divorced in 2001, shortly after their son was born and right before he received his Ph.D. in electrical engineering. He later landed a job and gained legal status, but she was left out. The child support and alimony she has received since then was calculated based on a $20,000 annual income, $50,000 lower than his actual earnings. In a telephone conversation with a Chinese-language newspaper reporter, the unapologetic ex-husband, a senior manager of a company, maintains that T should be thankful because he has not "reported her [illegal] status" to immigration authorities. And, he adds, should publicizing his personal issues cause him to lose his job, he will have no money left to pay her at all.[90] According to many reports that have appeared in community newspapers, undocumented immigrants are often targets of swindles by lawyers, doctors, accountants, and employment agencies.[91] Although from time to time the victims will receive sympathy from community newspapers, they rarely seek formal protection from law enforcement agencies.

Socially, the undocumented are isolated and excluded. According to a March 6, 2007, *Shijie ribao* report, the Chinese in America can be divided into two categories, and only one of them is "clean." The reports reveal a new and "strange" phenomenon in the Chinese American community (*huaren shequ*): the emergence of *xiaobailian* (handsome young men) as companions of wealthy women. In an age of globalization, a transnational lifestyle is common for businessmen. Some of these men have cultivated extramarital affairs with women on the other side of the Pacific, making their middle-aged wives, the mothers of their children, deeply depressed. But now, say the reports, the married women are fighting back. Erika, financially independent and physically attractive, is one woman who has turned the corner. Although her husband has an *ernai* (a female companion outside of marriage) in China and spends little time at home, Erika does not let herself get upset. She takes dancing lessons to stay in shape—no one can tell from her appearance that she is in her fifties. She is not lonely either. In the absence of her husband, Erika enjoys romantic companionship from a handsome young man—a world-class dancer from China.

In the eyes of her peers, Erika handles her love affair "wisely" because the man she sees is "clean," meaning he has a green card. The young dancer is shy of money, of which Erika has plenty. She bought him a house and pays him to stay at home. However, the situation can be complicated if the person is not clean—without legal status. For example, another rich woman reportedly has defeated many competitors to win the love of a super handsome xiaobailian only to learn that he is undocumented. In this case, the guy needs more than money; he wants to marry a citizen to gain legal status. This, however, is more than the woman can afford, as her current marriage is the source of her wealth.[92]

Money, talent (which can be transferred into wealth), age, appearance, and legal status are some of the most important elements that intertwine in the highly commercialized world of intimate relations. Age might be an obstacle for these women, who are also married, but their wealth can work to tip the balance. The bargaining chips of the xiaobailian, on the other hand, are what these ladies do not have: youthfulness, presentable looks, and dancing skills. Relationships that cross class lines and age gaps are not necessarily insurmountable; they can be mutually beneficial for both parties. But legal boundaries are more difficult to cross. The undocumented are seen not simply as impoverished but rather as members of an alien social group rejected by American society. These are the untouchables. For wealthy women, associating with these people means to enter into unfamiliar and dangerous territory. Although undocumented immigrants might be able to upgrade their social status through intimate relations, their vulnerability is obvious. According to one of the reports on xiaobailian, two rich women in Los Angeles got into a fight over an actor from China. When one of the women lost the battle, she angrily reported the man's legal status to immigration authorities. "The poor guy," writes the news reporter, "is forced to leave the country without getting a green card."[93]

Jennifer Hsu, a twenty-six-year-old waitress in Pasadena, California, understands well the social implications of being undocumented. When she came from Taiwan in 1998 with a student visa, Jennifer was introduced to restaurant work by her roommate. She visited her parents in 2002, but could not get her visa renewed because she had not been enrolled in a U.S. school for some time. She did manage to return, this time as the fiancée of a U.S. citizen, though that was just a role she played to get back into the country. She continued to work and did not seem to be bothered by her legal status. "If caught, I will just go home to Taiwan," she said. She has a meticulously maintained bright red Volkswagen Beetle, and is apparently enjoying the freedom away from her parents. She can be taken as any independent young Chinese American woman or student. When the topic of her legal status came up during our interview, a male co-worker of hers joked that all she had to do was to marry a rich guy, a citizen. Jennifer gave her co-worker a sharp look and took a long pause. Then she threw her cellular phone into her Coach purse and let out her frustration: "It is easy for people to say that. Once the guys knew that I had an expired visa, they would try to take advantage of me. I have met too many guys like that. People see me as a happy-go-lucky person. Who has seen me cry? Every time I talk to my mom on the phone, I cry for hours. Where can I go to find the right person [to marry]? If I stay here, I am afraid that I will be by myself for the rest of my life."[94] Then would she consider a relationship with someone in the same situation? To that Jennifer's answer was a firm "No." "Not that I look down on them [the undocumented], but I can't double the burden. My whole life would be over if I make a stupid move like that."[95]

For the undocumented, marriage is one of the few options to legality, and it is commonly believed that this path is easier for women to take. Liye Chang, a hairdresser, had a short-lived second marriage three years after she and her young son came to the United States in 1990 from Hong Kong. She said that from the very beginning she was fully aware that this relationship would not last. "You can say that everything about him was the opposite of me," she remarked. "He was a spoiled playboy—did whatever occurred to him, and had several run-ins with the police; I worked hard and was frugal. My English was bad, and he could hardly understand a word of Chinese." She acknowledged, however, that she was eager to get married; her mind was made up the first time when she was invited to his parents' house. "I had no legal status and no money. Marrying into that family would give me everything I wanted so desperately." Narrowing her eyes in search of memories, Liye's face began to glow as she described the wedding reception: "My friends were stunned when they saw with their own eyes the swimming pool and tennis court at his folks.' I was the 'Cinderella,' and some must have wondered how the 'prince riding a white horse' came my way!" That marriage allowed Liye to gain legal status, though the subsequent three years were full of trauma and misfortune.[96]

To secure their legal status through marriage, undocumented immigrant women often have to tolerate abuse. Ping Lu, who received her permanent residence in 2005 before filing for a divorce, described her three years of marriage as "endless torture" from her ex-husband's family—"a houseful of monsters." Ping's in-laws became possessive once she started to take classes at a community college, and she was not allowed to go out to meet friends. Once Ping returned at about 9:00 pm from a classmate's birthday party, only to find one of her sisters-in-law sitting on the doorstep of their apartment (Ping shared a three-bedroom apartment with her husband's family). "She pointed and shouted at me with obscenities for a long time, while my ex-husband watched and listened," she recalled. "They [her ex-husband's sisters and mother] said that it was bad luck for the family to take me in as an in-law. They said repeatedly that he could have entered a fake marriage and easily made $30,000, and that instead they had to feed me so that I could get my green card and leave him with nothing. I would have run away from them long ago, but I couldn't because I needed legal status to become independent."[97]

The presence of a large number of undocumented immigrants places real monetary value on U.S. citizenship for both men and women. Katherine Fan, whose family came from Vietnam, said that her sister bought a house for the family in Oakland, California, with financial assistance from Denny, a clean-cut young Chinese man. Katherine was ten or eleven when the purchase was made. Denny would come to visit every once in a while, and he would hand her sister checks. She thought he was her sister's boy friend, but her sister, who had a child out of wedlock, never acknowledged that. The memory of Denny was fresh in her mind: "Once he came to tell my sister that he would need a few more days to deliver the money. My sister was furious; she let out a loud scream and threw a cup of coffee at him. I didn't understand what was going on and felt very sorry for Denny. My sister was so mean and crazy, but he did not talk back or move a muscle. He just stood there, and I could see one of his arms was soaked with coffee." Long after he stopped coming, Katherine's family ran into Denny in a shopping mall and everyone asked how he was doing. Only then did Katherine learn from her parents that he and her sister had a legal, but fake, marriage. The deal was mutually beneficial: Denny needed legal status; her sister needed help paying the mortgage.[98]

Still, Feng Yang, who turned thirty-five in 2004, believed that the need for a green card was not important enough to violate the sacred union of two human beings. Feng came from China with a temporary visa in 1992 and went to work in a relative's restaurant in Queens, New York. In 2002, he met May, a naturalized citizen from Malaysia, at a church gathering. The two spent some time together, but when May expressed her desire to get married, Feng backed off. The fact that all of his friends thought that he would have more to gain from the marriage made him hesitant: "She was serious, and that bothered me," he reflected. "Marriage should be a solemn matter; the problem was that we couldn't begin on the same mark (*qipao xian*). Maybe it would be different if I were a woman. Maybe. But I found it hard to face her and had to end the relationship." While some of his friends laughed at him, Feng did not think he could marry anyone for the purpose of getting legal status. "People would ask what my next plan is. Honestly I have got no plan at all. I will just plan things one day at a time."[99]

Even for those who overcome adversity and find true love, getting acceptance from their families and relatives can be a difficult matter. Tommy Huang, who came from China with a temporary work visa in 1992, was on his own after his work contract expired. In San Francisco and then Los Angeles, he bused tables and waited on customers before being promoted to a managerial position. Tall, slender, and with a radiant smile, he was popular at work and in his church. Sharing a house provided by his boss with eight co-workers, he and his fiancée,

Shuhui, were saving every penny for a property of their own. It took a lot of courage for the two to stick together, as Shuhui's parents were furious when they learned that Tommy did not have legal status. "They [the fiancée's parents] didn't want to see me; we never met. They had no desire to know what kind of person I am and just ordered her to end the relationship. When she disobeyed, her parents cut her off completely." Shuhui would have gained legal status with her family, which was from Hong Kong, but her parents were so mad at her rebellious behavior that they removed her name from their application. Still, Tommy said he could understand her parents' harshness, "If my own daughter wants to marry an undocumented alien, perhaps I will be angry too."[100]

Social isolation can be initiated by the undocumented immigrants themselves, out of a reluctance to reveal their legal identities to the public. Xinnian Guo, a man in his forties from northern China, said that he decided to be a day laborer instead of a restaurant worker because he did not want to get to know anyone. "Occasionally I would run into someone with a familiar face in Manhattan and we would nod to each other. I don't like to talk to people. There is nothing to say and I don't have any questions for others. The rich ones are nothing but living reminders of my failure."[101] In two separate accounts to the *Shijie ribao*, one woman from Taiwan, Zhen Ling, describes her years in Texas as an undocumented immigrant as "pain beyond words." Most unbearable is the fact that some Chinese people seem to take great pleasure in talking about other people's illegal status. When people make loud inquiries in public about her status or ridicule her for getting a "good deal" because she does not have to pay taxes, she writes, "my heart bleeds." Concealing her legal identity is especially difficult for her teenage daughter. When classmates her age began to drive, the daughter had to make up reasons for why she could not get a driver's license. When Zhen Ling and her daughter finally gained legal status, the youngster was so excited that she had the green card laminated and attached it to a necklace. Since then, Zhen Ling writes, "my daughter's life has changed from night to day; there is no reason for her to hide anymore."[102] Alice Fu, who came from Wuhan, China, as the wife of student, worked as a domestic care provider after her husband died of cancer. A trained nurse back in China, she had no problem finding work. Her most recent employer lived in Las Vegas. The lady was partially paralyzed but with "a sympathetic heart."

She asked Alice to call her "cousin" and advised her not to mention her undocumented status to anyone. "She is such a considerate person," Alice said. "She makes my life a lot easier. Because people believe that I am her relative, they are less curious about my identity."[103]

To Yinyin, who manages a matchmaking service in New York, the lowness of the undocumented immigrants is quantifiable. Beginning with a preliminary evaluation, she calculates each client's worth, using a formula based on information regarding the person's occupation, education, income, personal assets, age, legal status, and marriage history. She gives a college graduate five points, while a citizen of the United States receives ten. A client on a short-term visa or without legal status, on the other hand, is subject to a ten-point deduction. The biggest reward of her job, said Yinyin, was to find marriage partners for undocumented Chinese women. "I had quite a number of young, pretty, well-educated, and capable girls. I helped them find what they needed most in America—legal status. They did not feel secure without status, and I understand that well," she remarked. As she recalled, most of the "girls" were easy to work with because they "understood their own situation" and were not "picky." And several of her former male clients tipped her well because they got "really good deals." One of Yinyin's clients, a fifty-five-year-old, divorced father of three children, was matched to a woman about half of his age. Before the two tied the knot, Yinyin said, the man made his bride-to-be agree on terms set by his family. Although this was the woman's first marriage, she agreed not to have any children of her own. According to Yinyin, the marriage worked out very well.[104]

Without legal status, undocumented immigrants are basically seen as outsiders by people in their own ethnic community. One recently naturalized citizen thought it was "natural" not to include them because they were not "Americans." To him, legal status differentiates a *Chinese* from a *Chinese American*: "I didn't think of myself as an American until I applied for permanent status. Why would anyone want to stay here forever if they did not have the right to stay?" Xiao Chen, who was waiting to hear the results of his asylum appeal, acknowledged that he did not consider himself American even though going back was not an option. "I wish there was no appeal process; the pain would just end if there was no more hope." Because his wife in China was counting on him to bring his daughter over, he had to do anything possible to stay, even if that meant being an outsider for the rest of his life. One restaurateur who had employed a few dozen undocumented workers between 1983 and 2000 said that more than half of these workers had eventually adjusted their legal status. Although a number of them were still undocumented, only two of them returned to China.[105] One construction worker said that he would have returned if he had saved enough money: "Some of my friends in China have become rich; I missed out on the opportunity. I cannot go backwards; I cannot return empty handed."[106]

Over the decades many undocumented Chinese have gained legal status and become American citizens, and probably many more will eventually join them. However, the avenues that are open for them to adjust their status are few, and the price they have to pay to go through the process is high. Moreover, their low-income occupations and inferior social status often continue after they receive green cards. Although their ethnic community provides them the only means available to survive in the United States, the same networks that utilize their labor also work effectively to isolate them socially and prevent them from entering the mainstream job market. They have a long way to go before they can catch up because they trail so far behind the others. To many undocumented immigrants, to see their children rising from obscurity is their only hope, and it is this hope that leads them to view their move to the United States with a sense of optimism.

Changing patterns of immigration after 1965, accompanied by new social and economic developments in the United States, have caused class to play an increasingly important role in Chinese America. This is understandable because class matters in everyday life. More often than not, success is still directly linked to social status. The next chapter will examine the relationship between class and the development of an ethnic economy and show how the ethnic community itself has worked to perpetuate class divisions.

Chapter 3

"Serve the People"

The Ethnic Economy

World War II triggered the greatest social changes the Chinese American community had ever seen. Back home in San Francisco after three years of naval service that took him to several European cities, Jimmy Leong was restless. "My father expected me to help out in the garment shop, but my mother knew that my heart was not [in it]. Imagine: I had spent the first twenty years of my life, right up until the start of the war, living in Chinatown. I missed home badly while I was away. Now I was back again, but I couldn't stand it any more." With the G.I. Bill, Leong began studying engineering at the University of California in Berkeley. He and his wife, a onetime Rosie the Riveter, raised two children in Berkeley, then moved to Castro Valley in 1960.[1]

Like the Leongs, many young Chinese men and women who left Chinatowns after World War II never looked back. Fanning out seemed to be inevitable once the postwar economic boom provided greater employment opportunities for ethnic minorities, and racial restrictions on real estate purchases eased. After many decades of legal exclusion and social and economic segregation, the postwar generation of Chinese Americans was poised to enjoy the opportunities that American society had to offer. The historical mission of Chinatown seemed to have been accomplished. At a time when the ethnic economy had loosened its hold on the young and able-bodied members of the community, few would see the need for future development. Over the next twenty years, hardly any renovation or construction projects were undertaken in the largest Chinatowns of the nation, San Francisco and New York.

The ethnic economy did not die out, however. The postwar years witnessed a historical transformation of the Chinese American community and its ethnic economy, paving the ways for rapid changes in the decades to follow. After 1965, a new wave of Chinese immigrants began flooding in, and in the 1980s and 1990s, historic urban Chinatowns were revitalized and many new suburban ones emerged, reconfiguring the shape of the ethnic economy. Instead of filling a few local traditional ethnic entrepreneurial niches, hundreds of business ventures reach a far larger and far more diverse ethnic population all over the United States. According to a 2002 survey released by the U.S. Census Bureau, of the 1.1 million Asian-owned businesses, 290,197 were owned by the Chinese.[2] This development reflects many of the changes within Chinese America.

Scholars emphasize business ownership and coethnic employment when defining the ethnic economy. After a thorough examination of an enormous body of literature, Ivan Light and Steven Gold identify the three key aspects of the ethnic economy as: the ethnic ownership economy, consisting of business owners and their coethnic employees as well as unpaid family members; the ethnic enclave economy, "an ethnic ownership economy that is clustered around a territorial core"; and the ethnic-controlled economy, consisting of businesses in the general labor market in which "coethnic employees exert appreciable and persistent economic power."[3] The demand side is absent not because of any accident of omission, but because several multiethnic-group and multilocality studies fail to show significant correlations between local demands and the rate of minority self-employment.[4] Thus, Light and Gold conclude that ethnic minorities "had a much greater propensity to form strong niches in a few low-income retail or service specialties," and that immigrants of the same ethnicity were more likely to cluster "in the same occupations."[5]

In this chapter and throughout this book, however, the term "ethnic economy" is used in a rather broad sense to describe a unique ethnic experience. Unlike most other ethnic economies, the large and diversified Chinese American economy encompasses far more than a few niches.[6] Although the Chinese have formed clusters in both historical and contemporary settings, where ethnic enterprises are most visible, their economy has expanded far beyond the boundaries of Chinatowns and ethnic commercial districts. Most important, it is impossible to get a good picture of this economy without taking into consideration its enormous ethnic market. Of concern is not so much a balanced approach to both supply and demand issues, but rather the relationship between business establishments and their clients, and the strength of ethnicity itself in bringing together large contingents of people from near and far as business owners, employees, clients, and consumers. When demand is studied, the agency of entrepreneurs requires special attention, for demand cannot be understood as simply opportunities up for grabs but, like crops for farmers, it results from long-term cultivation. A generation ago, some economically disadvantaged immigrant groups from underdeveloped nations cultivated their own ethnic economies within the larger society mainly to escape discrimination.[7] Will ethnicity lose its ability to unify large and highly diverse populations into collective activities as circumstances change in the United States and abroad in an age of globalization? This question is important to the study not only of ethnic economies but also of ethnic communities, as the two are closely related.

Although it is common for researchers to use national origins to define ethnic economy and ethnic entrepreneurship, it is practically impossible to assess economic activities of Chinese Americans in this way. Chinese immigrants in the United States have come from diverse roots. Although subethnic organizations may be formed along the lines of native places or national origins, and although some subgroups may concentrate on certain business endeavors, as a whole the ethnic economy does not operate along these lines. Generational lines are not easy to draw, either, as immigration, marriage, adoption, international exchange, and transnational employment opportunities have affected family structures and the cultural-economic behavior of individuals in very complex ways. Many Chinese American families include immigrant parents and American-born children, and it is not unusual for second- or third-generation Chinese Americans to marry new immigrants. It is true that new immigrants are more likely to be self-employed, and the cost of labor is a major concern for initiating ethnic enterprises, but that does not prevent American-born Chinese from being self-employed or working in ethnic firms.[8] There is considerable evidence that the Chinese ethnic economy is strong enough to attract investors, entrepreneurs, professionals, and laborers of different backgrounds. For that reason, in order to understand the Chinese American community, it is necessary to examine all participants in the ethnic economy.[9]

Because the ethnic economy is examined in relation to the development of the community, whether a business is included in this study is determined by three factors: ownership, labor, and market. A business employing mostly Chinese workers is considered an ethnic establishment, whether or not the owner was born in the United States. A law office led by an attorney of Irish American heritage may also be included if most of its employees are Chinese and it caters primarily to Chinese clients. Companies that are owned by ethnic Chinese but do not operate with a distinctive Chinese labor force or cater mainly to Chinese customers, such as Yahoo Inc. (co-founder Jerry Yang is an immigrant from Taiwan), will receive less attention.

HISTORICAL TRANSFORMATION

The transformation of the ethnic economy began immediately after World War II. Until then the Chinese had been highly concentrated in three types of businesses: laundries, restaurants, and small groceries and dry-goods stores. After the war, there were noticeable signs of change, causing some concern but at the same time offering new hope. The decline of the laundry business, largely a byproduct of postwar social and economic developments in American society, came first. Although the high marriage and birth rates of the 1950s and 1960s meant more laundry had to be done, the advent of automatic washing machines and dryers, along with the appearance of new fabrics that required no ironing, made it feasible for women to wash their family members' clothes themselves and significantly reduced the need for hand laundry services. Staying competitive was a challenge for the old Chinese laundrymen because they lacked the capital to upgrade or replace their equipment. In 1949 there were 10,232 Chinese laundries in the United States. A decade later more than 30,000 individuals—about a third of the working Chinese population—were still in the trade. By the end of 1960s, however, about half of the laundries had gone out business.[10] To many observers, the downsizing of this business, a trade that Chinese had dominated for almost a century, indicated that the traditional ethnic economy had lost its appeal for the younger generation of community members. Indeed, few educated and able-bodied Chinese Americans were willing to toil long hours alongside their parents in this occupation. A different lifestyle, the one that was enjoyed by middle-class Americans outside Chinatowns, seemed far more desirable.

Developments in the restaurant and grocery/dry-goods businesses, on the other hand, pointed in a different direction: they showed enough vigor for future growth. There were 4,304 Chinese restaurants in the U.S. mainland in 1949. Ten years later, 750 could be found in New York City alone. By the end of the 1960s, the number of Chinese restaurants in the United States had reached ten thousand.[11] Grocery and dry-goods stores were hit hard after the United States prohibited the importation of products from China during the Cold War, but entrepreneurs soon turned to Hong Kong for supplies; some opened new shops outside Chinatowns. In the 1950s and 1960s, Chinese store-owners organized several alliances to secure ethnic business power and fight against discrimination. They also circulated their own journal, the *Chinese Grocers Magazine*, to business owners on the West Coast, in the South, and in Honolulu.[12]

The postwar years witnessed changes in the ways that individual Chinese related to their community. Under pressure from a hostile host society, the early immigrants had created mutual aid networks based on kinship, native places, and common interests. These networks assisted immigrants in finding jobs and raising business capital, and they were crucial to the development of ethnic businesses. Some occupational specialties were clan-based, because newcomers usually took the types of jobs held by those who had arrived earlier. Atop the kinship and native-place networks were the organizations that functioned as the governing bodies of the community. These organizations controlled the day-to-day lives of the immigrants while providing them with services that would not have been available otherwise.[13] The end of exclusion, however, changed the relationship between individual Chinese and their community establishments. New immigrants arriving after the war often did not see the urgent need to belong to an organization. Political divisions within the community also worked to further weaken the position of the community power structure.[14] By the late twentieth century, many historically important community organizations had been reduced to gathering places for the elderly; their annual meetings were held to mainly discuss property management and rent collection.

These changes meant different things to different people. To the merchants who had once held leadership positions, they meant less control over community members and the ethnic economy. To the entrepreneurs, they meant fewer restrictions from the community power elites. The early ethnic economy was built on the social structure of ghettos, on the mutual dependence between entrepreneurs and their coethnic employees, and between shop owners and their coethnic consumers. Except for the laundry trade, which served non-Chinese customers, the immigrant economy was a model of self-sufficiency and self-reliance, so mainstream economic activities were largely irrelevant. Ethnic resources such as credit, labor, and market were as important to entrepreneurs as jobs, merchandise, and service were to laborers and consumers. There was little room for growth in those days, but the economy was solid, largely because outside competition was not an issue. Their clients' and laborers' increased access to mainstream society after the war deprived the entrepreneurs of a sense of security. But at the same time, there were also new options that allowed business owners to reassess their resources and explore possibilities beyond those that had defined the prewar immigrant economy. With loans directly from banks instead of community-based rotating credit unions, some Chinese were able to initiate new enterprises.

What occurred during the post–World War II years was a gradual process of constructing a new ethnic economy. With restrictions lifted and rules relaxed or abandoned, alternate ventures were investigated and new business relationships formed. Intense competition evolved, compelling Chinese entrepreneurs to find new resources, create new opportunities, build new networks, and cultivate new markets. The combination of fewer restrictions and more possibilities encouraged business adventurers in a variety of areas, laying a solid foundation for rapid economic growth after 1965.

NEW POSSIBILITIES

Economists use the term "demand" to describe economic initiatives. For some sociologists, demand means "market opportunity," a vacant niche that is not necessarily available to all.[15] One big challenge confronting the entrepreneurs in the postwar years was an unstoppable outflow of young and educated residents from the old Chinatowns. Although ethnic resources did not disappear altogether, to assume that the growth of the ethnic economy was determined primarily by abundant opportunities is to underestimate the roles of innovative Chinese American entrepreneurs who have searched, identified, and cultivated various business opportunities. Discovering new territories and expanding traditional specialties were two factors in the restructuring of the community economy.

One phenomenon that emerged after World War II was the development of ethnic professional services. After the decline of the old community power structure, alternative services came into being to handle tasks traditionally performed by old kinship networks. The Chinese Consolidated Benevolent Association (CCBA), for example, had historically filed grievances on behalf of community members. When the association lost its strength and could no longer maintain a legal team on behalf of the entire community, private practices filled the vacuum. After 1965, the demand for legal professionals increased further. Twelve Chinese law firms were in business in New York City in 1958; thirty years later, the number had increased to 186.[16] Other services hitherto handled by traditional community organizations began to be professionalized, leading to the development of ethnic hotels, banks and credit unions, employment agencies, immigration consulting firms, and notary publics.

The changing lifestyles and increasing purchasing power of Chinese Americans also created a variety of opportunities. As more Chinese gained American citizenship in the 1950s, for example, there was a growing interest in property ownership in the United States. Before World War II, Chinese immigrants were classified as aliens ineligible for citizenship, subject to restrictions stipulated in alien land laws and other discriminatory regulations concerning real estate purchases. The difficulties with owning land and homes compelled the early immigrants to invest in their home villages in China; some built elaborate homes there and dreamed of returning to them after they had become rich. After the Communists came to power in 1949, however, the new Chinese government confiscated land and other properties that had been purchased by overseas investors, and many family members of immigrants were identified as landlords—enemies of the revolution. Meanwhile, many racial restrictions were lifted in the United States, allowing Chinese Americans to enter the real estate market. More than one thousand

Chinese bought houses on the outskirts of San Francisco's Chinatown in the 1950s, doubling the size of Chinatown proper in only a few years. Similar changes also took place in New York and other areas.[17] Some Chinese entrepreneurs seized the opportunity to assist their compatriots with their real estate purchases, leading to the development of ethnic real estate agencies and related services.[18] There were four Chinese realtors in New York in 1958 and thirty in 1973.[19] By 2006, 213 real estate agencies were listed in the *Chinese Yellow Pages* of New York, plus 87 in the New Jersey metropolitan area.[20]

That was only part of the story. Often, opportunities are not simply up for grabs; reenergizing an ethnic economy requires imagination, investigation, and innovation. The development of the restaurant business is a good example. Catering mainly to Asian bachelors who lacked cooking facilities before World War II, Chinese restaurants provided affordable meals and free tea, and in after hours the men remained to play mahjong and cards. As families began to fill the social space that was once dominated by male laborers, however, old eateries met the critical eyes of Chinese women, who arrived in the thousands after 1945. Chiu Chun Ma, who came as the bride of a Chinese American war veteran, recalled her first impression of a Chinese restaurant in San Francisco. She said that she almost threw up when she saw a filthy can for fish bones on the table.[21] This may suggest that traditional Chinese restaurants had outlived their usefulness. But they did not disappear; instead, they shifted directions.

Peter Kwong, who has studied New York's Chinatown, finds a significant change in the restaurant business in the postwar years. Focusing on working women who had little time to prepare meals for their families, creative restaurateurs modified their dishes and introduced new services. On their way home from work, female factory workers would see roast ducks and other delicacies displayed in the windows of the restaurants, and a wide variety of take-out dishes made meal preparation simpler.[22] To not only stay in business but do well, one restaurant owner of thirty years said he never stopped doing research. Starting in 1975, he moved from one location to another five times, going from Houston to southern California, changing his specialties from typical Americanized Cantonese cuisine to Sichuan cuisine and then Taiwanese cuisine. When he turned a two-story building in a busy Los Angeles commercial district into a gigantic eatery in 2001, the plan was to combine southeastern Chinese cuisine with Cantonese dim sum.[23] The emergence of upscale restaurants in the suburbs in the 1970s, the proliferation of small take-outs in New York's African American-concentrated neighborhoods in the 1990s, and the introduction of Chinese vegetarian and regional cuisines are all reflections of the innovative efforts of thousands of entrepreneurs who integrated Chinese food into the mainstream American diet. Some restaurants in metropolitan regions with large Chinese populations have even begun to provide customized food services for pregnant women and mothers of newborn babies.

In many cases, opportunities do not exist until discovered. When many Fujianese immigrants entered the restaurant business, others were able to discover opportunities catering to their needs. They furnished supplies for these restaurants, and a few Changle businessmen made fortunes by advertising for their fellow restaurateurs or selling specialized renovation materials (see chapter 4).[24]

In a 1972 study of San Francisco's Chinatown, Victor G. Nee and Brett de Bary Nee point out that most small to medium-sized ethnic businesses probably would not have made it if they had not had an advantage in terms of the cost of labor.[25] A constant supply of immigrant labor indeed gave ethnic entrepreneurs an edge over their non-Chinese competitors. The repeal of Chinese exclusion in 1943 made Chinese admissible and thus subject to general immigration legislation. Under the War Brides Act (1945) and other legislation, thousands of Chinese women joined their husbands in the postwar years.[26] And the 1965 Immigration Act led to a steady influx of Chinese on an unprecedented scale. Abundant immigrant labor turned the community into an employer's market. As several scholars have demonstrated, Chinatown business owners achieved great social mobility utilizing and exploiting low-wage immigrant workers, and they enjoyed great success, particularly in the garment industry.[27]

In sharp contrast, scholars of the enclave theory argue that both business owners and employees benefited from their participation in an ethnic economy. Min Zhou, for example, found that a large number of immigrant women were able to work in the Chinatowns' garment industries while jobs elsewhere were inaccessible due to a language barrier and the women's lack of training. The need to combine wage earning with household responsibilities posed another challenge for these women. The low wages they received was compensated for by flexible working hours and the opportunity to take work home.[28] Because so many women were eager to find work, many ethnic entrepreneurs got started with a relatively small investment. As a result, hundreds of Chinese-operated garment factories mushroomed in the 1980s, especially in Chinatowns in New York, San Francisco, Oakland, and Los Angles.[29]

In addition to garment factories, the rapidly expanding restaurant business became one of the biggest employers of female workers. The demand for domestic service also increased significantly, as more and more educated middle-class Chinese American women have become career professionals. This situation must have had a great impact on the gender composition of Chinese immigration, for since the late 1940s Chinese immigrant women have outnumbered men in most years.

Scholars often link the growth of the ethnic economy to the fact that Chinese America is an immigrant-majority community, and some believe that many post-1965 immigrants have had access to financial resources they brought with them. Lucie Cheng and Philip Q. Yang argue that the new Chinese immigrants, like immigrants from other parts of the world, are "more likely to be entrepreneurs than their native-born counterparts" because of these resources.[30] Many Chinese, in fact, sold their property in their native places and brought the profit as well as all their savings with them. The 1990 Immigration Act, which granted admission and permanent residency to foreign nationals who invested one million dollars or more in a business employing at least ten workers in the United States, has attracted investors from Taiwan, Hong Kong, Macau, and more recently, China. This group of million-dollar investors is small, but many families did come with modest savings, and quite a number of them brought as much as $200,000.[31] For those who came with money and advanced degrees but who could not find good jobs because of limited English-language proficiency or lack of applicable skills, running their own businesses would have been a logical path to take. It is common to find former health professionals operating clinics or herb stores, and some former government officials, teachers, and artists have become shopkeepers. Because ethnic entrepreneurship is no longer regulated by community organizations, and because immigrants who work for themselves often do better than those who are employed by others, relatively few scholars now insist that the ethnic economy works to prevent the assimilation process of immigrants.[32]

But there is a lack of evidence to support the idea that the Chinese have more financial resources than immigrants from other parts of the world. What is clear is the fact that some ethnic groups do not engage heavily in entrepreneurship. Mexican immigrants, for example, have not shown a strong tendency toward business development. Asians have also taken different paths to realize their American dreams. While the Chinese, Koreans, and Vietnamese are most active in developing their own ethnic economies, the South Asians and Filipinos seem more interested in employment opportunities within mainstream society.

Immigrant background is another aspect worth exploring. The Cantonese, who made up the majority of early Chinese immigrants, are known in China for their expertise in trade and business. For centuries before the First Opium War (1839–1842), which resulted in the British forcing China to open additional ports, Canton was the nation's only port for foreign trade. Cantonese merchants have settled in many parts of the world besides the United States, especially in Southeast Asia, and they also played important roles in the economic development of China. Although the post-1965 immigrants are far more diverse, many of them have come from regions with a strong entrepreneurial tradition. Economic growth and expanded trade in both Hong Kong and Taiwan gave birth to a large class of entrepreneurs in the late twentieth century; many of those who emigrated to the United States had previously engaged in trade and business. The ethnic Chinese in Vietnam are another group with a heavy concentration in entrepreneurship. As Nazli Kibria reveals, many women earned income from small-scale trading practices such as "buying wholesale goods and selling them in the market, or selling homemade products in the market" in the war-torn country, before coming to the United States.[33] Market activities have also increased dramatically in mainland China since the 1980s. Those who have come to the United States for educational opportunities and then remained are more likely to search for employment in the mainstream job market. But their fellow immigrants from Fuzhou (in Fujian) and Wenzhou (in Zhejiang)—two of China's most business-active regions—have concentrated their resources in entrepreneurship; they are the dominant force in the ethnic economy in New York.

INFORMAL PRACTICES

The contemporary Chinese American economy is broad and diverse; its appearance is in some ways similar to that of the general economy. The *Chinese Consumer Yellow Pages* for southern California, a business directory of more than 2,000 pages, for example, looks very much like any English telephone book. There are general advertisements for commercial, professional, and production businesses of many varieties. Some are ethnic specific; most others are not. Listed next to traditional herbal medicine and acupuncture specialists are dermatologists, neurologists, plastic surgeons, pediatricians, and general practitioners, and among the different kinds of Chinese food services are sushi bars, steak houses, Mexican grills, Domino's Pizza, McDonalds, and Starbucks. The Chinese sell everything one can possibly imagine, from food, clothes, and household necessities to jewelry, cellular phones, phone cards, carpets, appliances, electronics, cars, and houses. They provide comprehensive services as well, ranging from legal, financial, insurance, medical, and educational advice to construction, remodeling, repairing, domestic care, housecleaning, gardening, wedding planning, and funeral and burial arrangements. Although most Chinese American professionals serve the general population, some have returned to the community for various reasons.[34] Hundreds of doctors, dentists, lawyers, accountants, teachers of special skills, and business managers have opened offices in metropolitan regions with large Chinese populations, and they advertise in Chinese-language yellow pages and newspapers to attract ethnic suburban dwellers. Most of these businesses are run in the same fashion as those in the mainstream economy. Ethnic medical doctors or dentists accept government and private insurance plans, and ethnic banks check credit before issuing loans to individuals.

The difference, scholars interested in segmented labor market theories argue, is that ethnic economies are those that engage in secondary or enclave labor market practices.[35] The secondary labor market is composed largely of small entrepreneurs who can cut business costs by employing unpaid family members and immigrant laborers at low wages, and often make little effort to provide good working conditions. The enclave labor market, on the other hand, has its own structural and cultural components. Min Zhou and Mingang Lin define the enclave economy by emphasizing the geographic extent of concentrated entrepreneurship that relies on ethnic capital and labor, with markets and services initially oriented toward but not limited to ethnic consumers and clients. They find that the shared cultural background of participants in this economy transcends the "commonly accepted norm of reciprocity," which helps build solidarity and trust as well as support and control.[36] In her study of garment workers in New York's Chinatown, Zhou illuminates the ways that the enclave economy helps new immigrant women meet the challenges of both family responsibilities and financial pressure. To her, such an economy has become an effective alternative path to social mobility.[37]

One important component of the Chinese American economy is its informal nature, as a considerable amount of income-generating activities take place outside formal regulations. This situation is by no means unique to the Chinese; rather, it is common in ethnic economies in general. Scholars find that the informal sector of the economy in both the United States and Europe has expanded in recent decades. According to one study, 16 percent of undocumented workers in California received wages in cash—a standard indicator of the informal sector—in 1980, and few legal immigrants were involved in such practices. Twelve years later, however, cash wages were paid and received at a much higher rate, involving 45 percent of undocumented immigrants and 25 percent of legal immigrants.[38] Measuring the size of the informal sector is difficult, but unrecorded income certainly plays an important role in the ethnic economy.

This practice benefits both entrepreneurs and their employees. Off-book transactions allow some small business owners to make ends meet, while cash income compensates underpaid workers. Asked whether he was aware that rejecting payment by credit card would turn away many potential customers, one restaurant owner responded that this was the only way for him to keep his workers: "Mine [restaurant] is a business of little capital (*xiaoben shenyi*). If I have no cash to pay my employees, they will work for someone else."[39] Another restaurant owner said that he did accept credit cards, but his workers expected cash tips: "On days when there is little cash to go around, I have to look at their unhappy faces (*chou lian*)."[40] Xiao Li, a carpet installer, said that he receives about 50 percent of his income in cash. "That's my bonus. I have no retirement fund, no nothing. I feel a moment of satisfaction every time I watch my wife counting the bills."[41]

Behind these practices is a sense of mutual understanding and mutual support strengthened by a shared culture. That defines the relationship between employers and their employees. Judith Yuan, who came in 1980 on a student visa, said that she was lucky in her early years in the United States because people helped her find jobs that would otherwise not have been available to her. Later, when she owned a restaurant, she helped many others. She recollects how she first met Jingjing, now a business woman, some twenty years ago:

> I drove by a bus stop late one afternoon near campus. There she [Jingjing] stood. Our eyes met. I will never forget the look in her eyes—it was the look of a clueless newcomer desperately seeking help. It touched my heart. I turned and offered her a ride. She was delighted to learn that I was also from Shanghai and asked almost immediately if I could help her find a job, any job. I called a former coworker who owned a big restaurant in town. She didn't need extra people, but agreed to let Jingjing try out. She is a very capable person and later even found work for her husband in the same restaurant. I get calls from friends often nowadays since I have my own restaurant. I would try to find things for them to do or introduce them to others.[42]

When providing employment opportunities is seen as a favor, there is little room for negotiation, making immigrant workers vulnerable to exploitation and abuse at the workplace. One restaurant worker described her first employer as stingy (*koumen*) because she was paid only ten dollars a day for twelve hours of work for an entire week. Actually, it is common for workers not to get paid at all during the "tryout" (*shigong*) period. The woman's husband, however, had a different experience. He was told by the owner that there were no openings, but he could go to try out without pay. "As I was about to take off the first night," he recalled, "the owner patted me on my shoulder and stuck a bill into my hand—it was twenty dollars. And he told me to start as a regular the day after."[43]

In the absence of government supervision, hiring and wage rates are regulated and adjusted through informal community practices rather than official rules. Before a new business venture is launched, the owner checks out general practices. "No one is there to set rules (*guiju*)," said one restaurant owner. "But I can't say there are no rules. Some workers are paid below the minimum wage, but they know they can earn good money from tips; they take home more than the minimum wage. I pay the workers a lot more nowadays. I give them a raise when it's hard to find replacements, and I have to raise their pay again if other restaurants are paying more."[44]

Most restaurant workers do not have union protection. Employers know, however, that it does not take long for a newcomer to figure out how well other workers are paid. Mistreated workers can bad-mouth their bosses, and they can also write to ethnic newspapers. The fact that most of these jobs are temporary makes it relatively easy for workers to give them up, and immigrant workers do know how to use their right to quit effectively. On the opening day of the East China Buffet Restaurant on Long Island, owner Zheng Tianming invited a number of guests and local dignitaries to see what the best Chinese restaurant could offer, only to find that the entire kitchen staff did not show up to work because he had refused to meet their demands for higher pay. That collective action caused chaos on an otherwise celebratory day for Zheng and he was quite bitter about it.[45] Most often, however, disputes are settled quietly within the community, for ethnicity plays a central role in bringing employers and employees together.

It is the ethnic bond that has helped to create a comfortable environment for the expansion of the informal sector. Many middle-class Chinese American families, for example, prefer to hire Chinese domestic-care providers, partly because of their low rates, while the workers believe under-the-table payments can be easily arranged if their employers are Chinese. The informal sector is especially important for those who do not have work permits, and a common ethnicity can provide a much-needed sense of security. "We hired our nanny from Monterey Park," said a young mother. "We interviewed four women there, asked a lot of questions, but we didn't ask about working papers. May [the nanny] volunteered some information about herself. I don't know what we would have done if she hadn't wanted to talk about her status. I can understand that, though. She is an honest person; I have nothing to complain about."[46] While it is difficult for undocumented immigrants to bargain with their employers, they do not worry about being exposed to the authorities if their employers are Chinese. In 2000, immigration authorities raided a Chinese restaurant in southern California and filed charges against the owners for hiring illegal aliens. There were more than a dozen workers on the payroll at the time, but the owners were convinced that it was one of the two non-Chinese employees who tipped off government officials.[47]

Informal practices also involve coethnic consumers and clients. One landscaper reasoned why he worked only for Chinese in this way: "My rate is low. I don't start without 50 percent in advance, and I want that in cash. A *laowai* [non-Chinese] would tell me he would not pay me until the work was completed. I don't go by that rule. Once a Chinese customer told me the same. I said 'Fine' and gave him a quote. He looked at me and said, 'That's too much: it's about what the Home Depot would charge.' I gave him another quote and said, 'that's for cash; 50 percent down.' That's it. It's not too hard for Chinese people to get it and I can always reason (*jiang daoli*) with them."[48]

SERVICE NETWORKS

Scholars have long recognized the importance of networks in immigration and in ethnic economies, but few have examined Chinese networks beyond the social fabric of kinship and friendship. The fast pace of this ethnic economic growth has much to do with the development of service networks in recent decades. These networks provide assistance to job and house hunters who do not have personal ties in the United States. Far more efficient than kinship and native place associations, these networks are not only capable of finding jobs and housing in established ethnic destinations but they also work as labor redistribution agencies that can divert new immigrants to locations other than those they might have expected.

This is not to say that kinship and native place networks are no longer at work. Since the 1980s, large groups of New York-bound immigrants have flocked to Flushing, Queens, and Brooklyn each year, following in the footsteps of family members, relatives, and friends. It is not unusual for someone fresh off the boat and speaking not a word of English to find housing and work immediately upon arrival if ties established back in China are utilized.

Nevertheless, traditional networks have their limitations. They work most effectively when jobs and housing are available in established immigrant destinations. They also have little flexibility in terms of social and physical mobility and may hinder economic growth. In times when migratory influx outstrips economic growth, some scholars argue, economic saturation will be reached.[49] Since the networks alone are incapable of creating jobs and housing, unemployment will occur when a shortage of jobs and housing becomes apparent in a particular area, creating fewer incentives for future immigrants. For over a century, Cantonese family and district associations played central roles in providing immigrants with accommodation and employment information. When far larger groups of immigrants from diverse regional backgrounds arrived after 1965, finding available work and shelter for them was beyond the capacity of the few existing family and district associations. When the majority of the Chinese population in the United States was no longer confined to a few established ethnic neighborhoods, the expansion of the ethnic economy posed a new challenge to networks that function best at the local level.

Like those who came earlier, post-1965 Chinese immigrants with no access to the mainstream job market tended to choose established ethnic neighborhoods as their initial destinations, but only a small portion actually settled where they had intended; many were pulled away by better opportunities elsewhere. The fact that the majority of the new Chinese immigrants bypassed inner-city ethnic clusters indicates the effectiveness of the new networks that are capable of placing newcomers with coethnic employers further afield.

Most important in this regard are the Chinese employment services. Exactly when such services came into existence is unclear, but obviously they are a post-1965 phenomenon. In 1970, there were two firms in business in New York's Chinatown, sending workers throughout the East Coast. A decade later Manhattan's Chinatown had about ten employment agencies, while those in Washington, D.C., and Boston, as well as Queens in New York, had their own. Similar developments took place in California, as well. As of 2006, there were 132 Chinese employment offices listed in twelve regions of the United States: the New York region alone had some eighty firms.[50]

The Chinese employment services are unique in two ways. First, they are ethnic-specific, catering mainly to the Chinese American population. Multilingual professionals are able to communicate with immigrants and prospective employers of various regional backgrounds.[51]

The services they provide are largely invisible to outsiders, as most agencies advertise only in Chinese. Second, each agency specializes in only a few trades related to the ethnic economy. A typical agency deals mostly with restaurants, the garment industry, construction, and domestic service employment. These trades provide temporary and seasonal jobs but do not usually offer security or fringe benefits. Because they require minimum training or English proficiency, however, they make it possible for new immigrants to get started. According to one agent, 80 percent of those who come to his office do not have legal status.[52] These laborers would be turned away by mainstream employment agencies. With the assistance of the ethnic employment service, they can find work in trades that tend to involve a considerable degree of informal practice.

Situated mostly in urban immigration destinations, Chinese employment agencies are often one-room offices equipped with no more than a desk, a telephone, and a few chairs, but these firms operate at a highly efficient level. They have listings of existing jobs nearby and far away, and they match these jobs with work seekers in a timely fashion. One woman said that if she had taken the first job offered to her by an agent in Monterey Park, she would have been able to start to work just two days after she arrived in Los Angeles.[53] A service owner in New York described his job as primarily providing psychological consultation to newcomers. Some immigrants had never worked as menial laborers, he said; it is not always easy for them to accept jobs as dishwashers or domestic servants. At the employment services, they would be told that in order to move up to a higher position, one often has to start at the bottom.[54] The main mission of the employment services, as one former agent said, was to "help new immigrants who cannot find work anywhere else to get started."[55]

One service agent said that most of the people she worked with were former clients, especially laborers who had lost their jobs or were trying to find better ones.[56] In that sense, the employment service is actually promoting mobility via the job market. Knowing that there are other jobs out there is as important as finding a job in the first place, because it gives individual workers a sense of power and security. Most immigrant laborers are not protected by government regulations, but they make no commitment to their employers either. Wei Gu, a waiter who took classes during the day at a community college, said that he was not bothered by the job security issues at all because he did not connect his future with the job. As soon as he got his bookkeeping certificate, he would quit restaurant work "for good." Asked what he would do if he was fired first, the young man laughed: "I didn't beg for this job; he [the boss] wanted me to help out. I am doing him a favor. Workers are hard to keep these days; they quit whenever better jobs are available elsewhere. A lady left just the other day. When she didn't show up and didn't bother to call, we knew it was over. The boss needs someone he knows well around, although I told him at the beginning that I couldn't stay here for long."[57] The fact that their jobs are temporary has positive implications for the workers, for few would like to think they could not get anything better.

Recognizing the importance of housing to immigrant workers, employment agencies work closely with employers who are able to provide living accommodations. More than 90 percent of their labor clients are interested in restaurant work and domestic service, mainly because these jobs often come with housing. According to one agent, her Monterey Park office regularly sends workers to Arizona, Colorado, Nevada, Oregon, and Georgia, although most of the jobs were within California. "But unless housing was part of the deal," she said, "the newcomers would not want to leave Los Angeles."[58] Some workers had no shelter at all when they looked for jobs. Alison Liao, a college student, recalled a time when her mother, who ran an employment firm in Los Angeles, brought clients home to sleep on the living room floor.[59] Debby Wang, who works in New York, said that she did not want to open her apartment to accommodate strangers, but sometimes she felt she had to.[60]

"Family motels" (*jiating luguan*) provide an answer to this problem. By the 1980s, it was common for newcomers and immigrant laborers in metropolitan regions to take temporary shelter in such unregistered accommodations in residences or apartments owned by ethnic Chinese. No business signs are visible to the neighbors. A Monterey Park resident said that she could tell the house next door was a family motel: "a lot of people are living there and I can hear the cars late at night."[61] Yamei, who came from Shanghai in 2001, described the family motel where she stayed at when she first arrived in Los Angeles as simply a three-bedroom apartment. The manager and his wife and their young son occupied one room, and six bunk beds were installed in each of the other two rooms. In what was supposed to be the living room were four mattresses behind wood-plank partitions, and Yamei was charged eight dollars per night for one of the mattresses.[62] A couple taking long-term shelter in a another family motel pays ten dollars a day for a private room that is slightly bigger than their double mattress.[63]

Like the ethnic employment services, family motels are indispensable to many newcomers who lack personal contacts in the United States. What they provide is far more than just affordable sleeping accommodations. Yamei, for example, had one friend in America, who was unable to come to the airport to meet her. Instead, she gave Yamei the telephone number of a motel. Yamei called from Shanghai. When she emerged from the customs and immigration hall at Los Angeles International Airport, Ah-Ding, the motel manager, was there holding a sign with Yamei's name on it. The pick-up service was fifty dollars. Every morning until Yamei took a job, Ah-Ding drove her and several others to employment offices and local markets. He later suggested that Yamei seek political asylum and introduced her to a lawyer—a critical move that allowed Yamei to become a legal resident. "I could never thank Ah-Ding enough. I still visit him at the motel when I go to LA. Imagine: I was like a handicapped person without a clue about how things were done here. He pointed me in the right direction." Ah-Ding's services were not free, and he gets a $500 kickback from the lawyer for every client he brings to. But Yamei thought these fees were "very reasonable."[64] Eight to ten dollars a night for sleeping accommodations would have been impossible to find otherwise, and this price often includes cooking oil, rice, and noodles.[65] Efforts to crack down on family motels in southern California have not shown clear results. In addition to immigrant job hunters, some college students find family motels attractive when they travel.

The development of employment services and family motels provide important alternatives to the old ethnic networks. While kinship and other associations based on personal connections continue to assist new immigrants and facilitate the growth of the ethnic economy, services outside these networks reduce the dependency of newcomers on personal connections and make jobs more accessible to everyone. Documented and undocumented immigrants enjoy greater freedom in the ethnic workplace: for the first time they exert a certain amount of control over their own labor. In the age of the Internet, these services can be accessed, compared, and utilized before immigrants land on American soil.[66]

Although the service networks do not create jobs, the extent to which they are able to divert immigrant laborers to different areas has made it easier for entrepreneurs to create jobs, especially in regions outside ethnic clusters. Tim Deng of Santa Maria, California, said that the labor supply was never an issue, even though his restaurant and hotel businesses were three hours away from Los Angeles. "I would call the agent in Los Angeles and tell her what I was looking for. If it was for a chef, I would go there to meet the person and bring him back. A few other times I hired workers over the phone and then picked them up at the bus station here."[67] By sending them to different parts of the United States, employment agencies create links between immigrant laborer and middle-class and upper-class Chinese American employers. And when a family motel manager refers one of his tenants to a lawyer, he connects an immigrant with a coethnic professional service provider.

"SERVE THE PEOPLE":
EXPANDING THE ETHNIC MARKET

Few other groups in the United States are as successful as the Chinese in tying service providers with end users. The largely self-sufficient ethnic economy that developed before World War II was the result of segregation, as isolation worked to strengthen community ties. When circumstances changed and members of the community moved away from the ghettos in pursuit of better opportunities elsewhere, the foundation of the ethnic economy would have been shaken if its consumer market had failed to reach beyond the confines of the ethnic neighborhoods. One solution for some ethnic groups has been to create niches in areas that are largely neglected by the mainstream economy. Korean immigrant entrepreneurs, for example, have entered black and Hispanic urban neighborhoods and opened groceries and other shops catering mainly to these minority groups. The Chinese have searched for niches, too. While many immigrants in the 1980s entered the garment industry, some latecomers, especially those from the Fuzhou and Wenzhou regions, built businesses in inner cities: takeout restaurants, self-service laundries, 99-cent stores, and seafood markets. What sets the Chinese ethnic economy apart, however, is its ability to maintain the tradition

Table 3.1

Table 3.1

Advertised Chinese Businesses in Selected Regions

Regions	Business Categories	Businesses
Boston	167	1,932
California, northern	615	10,004
California, southern	661	21,005
California, southern (San Diego)	387	4,305
Chicago	114	2,035
Houston	290	4,037
Nevada– Las Vegas	155	1,282
New Jersey	201	1,352
New York	386	6,929
Philadelphia	167	1,400
Seattle	164	2,136
Washington D.C.	137	1,422

SOURCE: Chinese Yellow Pages (titles vary), Boston, 2005; Chicago, 2006; California (northern) 2006; California (southern) 2006; California (southern/San Diego), 2005; Houston, 2007; Philadelphia, 2005; Seattle, 2007; Nevada / Las Vegas, 2005; New Jersey, 2006; New York, 2006; Washington D.C., 2007. The Boston edition includes all parts of Boston, Brighton, Charlestown, Dorchester, Hyde Park, Jamaica Plain, Mattapan, Roxbury, West Roxbury, and Suffolk County; the Houston edition includes Houston, Sugar Land, Clearlake, Austin, and San Antonio; the southern California edition includes Los Angeles County, Orange County, and some businesses in nearby counties (Riverside, San Bernadino, Ventura, Santa Barbara, and San Diego counties); the southern California San Diego edition includes the county of San Diego, and some businesses in Orange County and Riverside; the northern California edition includes the North Bay (Belmont, Brisbane, Burlingame, Hillsborough, Foster City, Half Moon Bay, Millbrae, Pacifica, Redwood, San Bruno, San Carlos, San Francisco, San Mateo, San Rafael, South. San Francisco, and Woodside), the South Bay (Alviso, Campbell, Cupertino, Gilroy, Los Altos, Los Gatos, Menlo Park, Milpitas, Morgan Hill, Mountain View, Palo Alto, Santa Clara, Saratoga, and Sunnyvale), and the East Bay (Alameda, Albany, Berkeley, Concord, Danville, El Cerrito, Emeryville, Fremont, Hayward, Lafayette, Livermore, Newark, Oakland, Orinda, Piedmont, Pleasanton, Richmond, San Leandro, San Ramon, Sunol, Union City, and Walnut Creek); the Philadelphia edition includes Philadelphia and Aston, Delaware; the Seattle edition includes all of Washington and Oregon; the Washington, D.C., edition includes the District of Columbia, Maryland/Baltimore, Baltimore County, Frederick County, Montgomery County, Prince George's County; Virginia/Alexandria, Arlington County, Fairfax County, Leesburg, and Loudoun County.

TABLE 3.2

Selected Chinese Business Advertised in Twelve Regions

	Boston	California–Northern	California–Southern	California–San Diego	Chicago	Houston	Nevada–Las Vegas	New Jersey	New York	Philadelphia	Seattle	Washington, D.C.
Accounting	9	119	390	107	31	55	10	26	132	15	18	25
Media/Advertising	31	43	178	26	14	79	18	6	72	27	35	13
Law/Immigration Service	43	224	881	100	58	100	22	23	249	31	71	44
Beauty Salons	28	197	327	54	37	58	29	14	157	36	47	26
Cleaners/Laundries	5	16	26	0	4	2	0	2	6	0	11	9
Doctors/Dentists	97	970	2721	512	146	315	51	144	933	63	163	132
Chinese Medicine / Acupuncture	17	287	470	71	46	76	16	13	159	20	24	32
Education	60	526	988	187	28	221	49	24	241	19	64	7
Employment	6	11	21	0	29	18	9	0	33	0	5	0
Funeral	16	115	102	38	9	12	10	2	20	8	8	0
Furniture	18	86	173	49	22	53	8	8	30	16	12	19
Insurance	22	154	423	52	29	124	22	28	144	38	48	32
Real Estate	59	383	595	107	65	270	71	87	213	23	85	56
Restaurants (Chinese only)	455	472	620	233	533	239	81	226	607	293	299	126
Travel	30	112	291	30	18	48	9	16	127	18	32	32

SOURCE: *Chinese Yellow Pages* (titles vary), Boston, 2005; Chicago, 2006; California (northern) 2006; California (southern) 2006; California (southern/San Diego), 2005; Houston, 2007; Philadelphia, 2005; Seattle, 2007; Nevada / Las Vegas, 2005; New Jersey, 2006; New York, 2006; Washington, D.C., 2007.

of servicing ethnic consumers even if they do not live inside the few remaining ethnic neighborhoods. The services and markets created by the entrepreneurs have become a powerful force that has kept those who have long settled outside Chinatowns connected with the community.

The variety and extent of the services available in Chinese America has set this ethnic economy apart from all others. In his 1995 study of Monterey Park, California, John Horton finds that in the 1980s, the

Chinese were already "selling every conceivable service and product."[68] A decade after Horton's study, when more available data were compiled, this became even more apparent. The scope of the ethnic businesses, shown by the Chinese-language yellow pages in the twelve metropolitan regions in 2005 and 2006, is large and comprehensive (see table 3.1). While Chinese telephone books for the Chicago area listed 104 types of businesses, those from northern California and southern California each advertised services in more than six hundred different categories. Ethnic entrepreneurs are active in just about every imaginable trade or specialty, from finance, insurance, real estate, law, and medicine to construction, wholesales, personal services, grocery stores, and restaurants (see table 3.2). In 2006, a total of 21,005 Chinese business establishments were listed in the Los Angeles area and 10,004 in northern California, reflecting the existence of a huge commercial and service market along ethnic lines. The Chinese American economy, previously concentrated in a few niches like the restaurant, grocery, laundry, food processing, and garment industries, now includes almost every trade, business, and profession. Entrepreneurs who want to remain within the community in banking, education, real estate, law, financial planning, health care, computer technology and many other fields require not only knowledge of ethnic culture and practices, but also the skills and standards shared by the mainstream sector.

The shape of the original niche economy has changed, too. The owners of some Chinese supermarkets have renovated, redecorated, and adopted up-to-date planning, store financing, central accounting, and cooperative advertising practices. They clearly understand that middle-class Chinese American shoppers are looking not only for produce, seafood, meat, and other food products that cannot be found anywhere else but also quality service in pleasant surroundings.[69] The stores of the 99 Ranch Market chain, for example, stand in sharp contrast to the crowded grocery stores in old Chinatowns. Equipped with huge parking lots, long rows of tall shelves, specialized lighting systems, and large refrigeration and freezer units, the spacious, high-ceilinged 99 Ranch Markets set the standard for contemporary Chinese supermarkets and have become the centerpiece in suburban Chinese malls in California, Arizona, Nevada, and Washington. According to the company's official Web site, the rapid growth of the 99 Ranch Market chain since the 1990s has had much to do with efforts of "absorbing new business concepts and management techniques," "updating equipment and technology," and offering "the best service with professionalism."[70]

Some new immigrants are still interested in the traditional laundry business, but the laundries operated by the Chinese today show little resemblance to the hand-laundry businesses created before World War II. One entrepreneur, for example, installed more than a hundred washers and dryers in his 6,000-square-foot self-service laundry in Brooklyn, New York; all are computer programmed. Inside the store is an ATM machine, a self-serve coin machine for laundry detergent, five money-changing devices, five television sets, and a desk-top computer with internet access.[71]

But upgrading services according to mainstream standards is hardly enough. To attract more than local consumers, ethnic entrepreneurs have to offer what is unavailable elsewhere. For businesses selling products and services associated with the ancestral homeland, this is not much of an issue. In nontraditional trades, however, entrepreneurs have to tailor the services to suit the tastes of their potential consumers. One needs only to glance at the advertisements placed in Chinese telephone books and Chinese-language newspapers to get a sense of what these entrepreneurs are capable of offering. In construction, for example, Chinese builders and renovators offer expertise that combines modern Western architecture with elegant touches of the East, with specialties in building Chinese restaurants, Oriental entrances and doorways, Japanese gardens, pavilions, rockeries, fountains, and fish ponds. Ethnic travel agencies, often well connected with airlines and hotels in China, Taiwan, Hong Kong, and nations in Southeast Asia with large ethnic Chinese population, provide significant discounts to Asian American travelers. Taking into account their clients' age group, regional and dialectic background, and budget, they provide a great variety of domestic and overseas vacation packages.[72] Wiring money, exchanging currency, and conducting international business transactions are made easy by ethnic banks and financial institutions, and the flexibility of some loan programs is especially appealing to immigrants who have yet to establish legal residence or credit records in the United States. Computer technology companies sell both English and Chinese software. In addition to individual users, they specialize in designing programs to cater to the needs of the restaurant, wholesale, import and export, manufacturing, international shipping, food processing, clothing, and medical industries.

In the early 2000s, the New York law firm of Ross, Legan, Rosenberg, Zelen, and Flaks, LLP, appointed Lantao Sun, a former PRC diplomat who was still in law school at the time, head of its Chinese division and launched an advertising campaign with the catchy slogan "Serve the People" (*wei renmin fuwu*). Attributed to Mao Zedong, the phrase "serve the people" was frequently quoted by millions in China after the Communists came to power. Appearing in big red characters in Chinese-language newspapers, telephone books, and television ads, this popular line, along with a photo of a smiling Sun, became the firm's selling point to immigrant clients, many of them from the Chinese mainland.[73] Taking an apparently humble approach, one that has been historically effective, the law firm extended a bridge to potential clients who found the American legal system intimidating. The message it sent was clear: American-trained ethnic lawyers are here to help Chinese immigrants.

Legal professionals in the community have diligently focused on what concerns the Chinese the most: immigration. They provide special services for visa seekers of every type, from investors, merchants, and managers of transnational enterprises to skilled laborers, chefs, nurses, artists, foreign adoptees, and spouses of citizens or permanent residents. Some asylum lawyers advertise that they know "special tricks," informing potential clients that they might gain legal status by invoking China's one-child policy or claiming to be victims of religious persecution or domestic violence. The personal injury lawyers are most accessible; their services are free if their clients are not awarded money, and twenty-four-hour hotlines take calls in English, Mandarin, and Cantonese regarding car accidents, falls at subway stations, lead poisoning, property damage, and medical malpractice. There are also labor law specialists who represent laborers who are paid below-minimum wages, who do not receive overtime payment, and who do not get to keep their tips.

It is the intimacy they offer and the specific knowledge they possess about their potential clients' circumstances that set ethnic businesses apart from those in the mainstream. One ad reaches out to the undocumented: "Have you been in America for very long? Are you single or divorced? Have you lost your status and have no one to turn to? We are here to help you overcome these obstacles. We will help you find a marriage partner, get legal status, and realize your American dreams!" "Your emancipator is one phone call away!" an immigration lawyer announces in the yellow pages. Among the people she says she has rescued are female newcomers from China, Taiwan, and Hong Kong whose legal status was in jeopardy because of marital problems with U.S. citizens. She has helped male clients to secure legal status, as well, including undocumented clients and a Vietnamese Chinese who had previously been arrested.[74]

Ethnic firms target both middle-class and working-class clients and consumers. The investment and marketing strategy firms, for example, provide consultation on business development and market expansion both in the United States and overseas; many of them boast about their expertise in doing business with China and Taiwan.[75] Schools and educational institutions are most appealing to middle-class Chinese Americans who want to give their children an edge in getting into prestigious colleges. As advertised, these institutions offer classes taught by instructors who had scored nothing short of 800 (the highest possible) on every SAT subject; their educational consultants are distinguished alumni of the most prestigious universities. Working closely with Chinese-language media, these institutions have organized lecture series and published many essays and study guides.[76] A variety of other educational services are geared toward immigrant workers, such as bilingual (or multi-dialectic) classes to help newcomers pass a driving test or learn special skills for future employment.

In San Gabriel, California, more than 500 Chinese business establishments cover a mile-long strip on Valley Street, between New Avenue and San Gabriel Avenue. They include luxury hotels, high-end restaurants, jewelry stores, beauty salons, car dealerships, special fashion boutiques, and many medical and financial service offices. This ethnic commercial district attracts tens of thousands of Chinese consumers and clients from all over southern California every weekend: it contributed 14 percent of the city's $400-million revenue in 2003.[77] Such expanded ethnic economic activities bring together Chinese Americans of different class, regional, and generational backgrounds. At 99 Ranch Markets owned by Chinese from Vietnam, sale items are broadcast in English, Mandarin, and Cantonese. "On the Gold Mountain of Beijing," a once immensely popular song in the PRC, is often played in Taiwanese-owned music and book stores. Matchmaking services work closely with new immigrants, including those who are undocumented, but they would not be able to function without the participation of citizens and green-card holders. One bridal shop owner in New York said that to stay in business she had to think ahead and take into consideration clients of all backgrounds: "It is not wrong to say that many of my clients are Fujianese, but I also work with many young people who were born here or have been here for a very long time—not to mention the fact that they marry people of all kinds of background. Our service packages are designed for customers of different traditions and tastes. They can have a Chinese-style (*zhongshi*) wedding or a Western-style (*xishi*) wedding, and they can have something in between. If the parents want it one way and the young couple argue for another, we can help them compromise or accommodate both. We are ready to serve everyone."[78]

The majority of the more than 1.5 million Chinese who immigrated to the United State in the last few decades of the twentieth century came for better economic opportunities. Many of them have realized the American dream by creating entrepreneurships that involve ethnic capital, labor, and consumers, and some of those are now marketing their products to Chinese on the other side of the Pacific. Gift stores in ethnic business districts are packed with iPods, digital cameras, electronic games, cosmetics, medicine, wine, and other goods for travelers to take to China, and even before the United States officially opened up its tourist industry to Chinese mainlanders in June 2008, ethnic travel agents, hoteliers, restaurateurs, realtors, and other business and professional service providers had already begun looking for ways to advertise directly to consumers in China. A newer generation of ethnic business and service providers, many of them products of the American higher education system, are ready to reconnect with investors, workers, and consumers in China.[79] The effects of globalization on economic development along Chinese ethnic lines are just beginning to appear.

CHAPTER 4

The "Spirit of Changle"

CONSTRUCTING A REGIONAL IDENTITY

MOST OF THE SIGNS for the Chinese American associations in New York's Chinatown are permanently carved on stone walls or tiled on huge buildings with Chinese architectural touches, to signify their long history and prominence in their community as well as their control over land and buildings. The eye-catching awning of the Changle American Association (CAA) on Chatham Square, at the tip of East Broadway, in contrast, points to the organization's youth—it was established in 1998—and suggests that the office space is leased. Located on the second floor of 2 East Broadway, the headquarters of the CAA is a busy place. Men and women go in and out of the small office and the adjourning meeting room, speaking loudly in the Fuzhou dialect. The door of the office is also open to visitors: the association takes public relations seriously. More than anything else, the leaders of the organization want their people to be known to the world.

American Chinatowns were the worlds of Cantonese immigrants in the past. Starting from the late nineteenth century, the Cantonese immigrants, an overwhelming majority of the ethnic community, built extensive district- and clan-based networks with the Chinese Consolidated Benevolent Association (CCBA) as their highest representative body. For many decades, the CCBA was recognized as the community's spokesperson by both the larger American society and the nationalist government in China. It launched communitywide actions against local and federal discriminatory laws in exceedingly effective ways during the years of exclusion; its efforts to crack down on political opponents within the community between the 1930s and the 1960s are also well known. Since 1965, however, the power of the CCBA has declined significantly. More profound than internal factionalism and the CCBA's alienation from labor and youth groups are rapid changes of demographic composition of the community. In New York, for example, Cantonese residents of the old Chinatown in Manhattan were gradually surpassed in number by immigrants from Hong Kong and Taiwan in the 1970s. And in the 1980s, thousands of new immigrants turned Flushing in Queens into one of the city's fastest-growing ethnic neighborhoods. Beginning in the early 1990s, Manhattan's Chinatown got yet another facelift, as latecomers from Fujian province in China emerged as a dominant force. Meanwhile, ethnic neighborhoods in Flushing and Brooklyn have become worlds of Fujianese, Wenzhouers (from Zhejiang province in China), and Northeasterners of the Chinese mainland. This chapter is a case study of this development. It examines the ways that recent Chinese immigrants from the Changle (pronounced Chang-le) region of Fujian province negotiate power within the Chinese American community. In their struggle against discriminatory stereotypes, the leaders of the CAA attempt to create a distinctive image for immigrants from their native place.

Immigrants from the Changle region are no strangers in the minds of the American public. Beginning in the 1990s, they have been the subject of a number of headline stories: they were targets of the U.S. government's crackdown on human trafficking from China. While the mass media and the general public focused on the tragedies that often accompanied this type of smuggling, the immigrants were working hard to create a new image for themselves. As the fastest-growing Chinese American regional group, the Changle immigrants exemplify the new dynamics and power relations in post-1965 Chinese America.

Changle and the Image of the Changle Immigrants

Located along the Min River in Fujian Province on the southeastern coast of China, across the strait from the island of Taiwan, Changle is the homeland of a majority of the new Chinese immigrants in New York. With a population of a little over 672,000 in 2001, the county (which acquired cityhood in 1994) is not as big as most of its neighbors, largely because a significant portion of its natives have emigrated. A 2001 census compiled by the Fuzhou municipal government, which has administrative jurisdiction over Changle, revealed that about 400,000 Changle natives and their descendents were living outside China, in such places as Hong Kong, Taiwan, Macao, the United States, and Europe.[1]

Nineteenth-century Chinese immigrants in the United States came primarily from the coastal districts of the southeastern province of Guangdong, where the Chinese have had frequent contacts with outsiders since the First Opium War (1839–1842). Some natives of Fujian emigrated to California during the Gold Rush that began in 1849, but before 1965 the vast majority of the Chinese population in the United States was Cantonese. During the last two decades of the twentieth century, however, Fujian replaced Guangdong as a major base for U.S.-bound emigration. A majority of the new Fujian immigrants have come from the region around Fuzhou, the provincial capital, about 80 percent of them from Changle, one of the ten cities or counties under the administrative jurisdiction of Fuzhou. Because all the people from Fuzhou share the same dialect, the Changle people (*Changle ren*) often address themselves or are referred to as Fuzhou people (*Fuzhou ren*), even though the relatively few immigrants from the Fuzhou metropolis do not like to be associated with immigrants from rural areas like Changle, nicknamed the Village of Smugglers (*toudu zhi xiang*).

Because of its location, Changle has had a long history of maritime activities and overseas migration since the Song Dynasty. Some of its natives settled in Taiwan, Hong Kong, Southeast Asia, Britain, and Holland. Not until after 1980, however, did their numbers in the United States begin to grow. This wave of immigration was stimulated by the normalization of U.S.–China relations and economic reforms in China that began in the late 1970s. Inspired by those Chinese Americans who built big brick houses for their families and donated money to the village schools, going to America instead of going to college became the dream of young people, but at that time the number of Changle natives in the United States was very small, which meant that the 1965 Immigration Act—and in particular, its family unification provision—could not be utilized by Changle ren who wished to emigrate to the United States. Those eager to leave had to seek alternative means to do so.

In the 1980s, groups of Changle natives began to leave their home villages through arrangements made by individuals the Chinese call snakeheads (*shetou*). At first some were able to travel to the United States with falsified or fake documents. When obtaining these papers became difficult, many individuals and families tried to go to the United States by crossing the open sea without the required passports and visas. The media coverage of intercepted boatloads of people from Fujian, alive or dead, captured the fascination of the world.

Their story, as told in the American mass media, began with the *Golden Venture*. In the summer of 1993, this run-down freighter registered in Honduras ran aground on the Rockaway peninsula in Queens borough, New York. The smugglers had promised to send small boats to pick up the passengers, but in the midst of a bloody battle among members of the Fuqingbang, a Fuzhou natives' gang that was responsible for the task, no one showed up.[2] The 286 Chinese on board were reportedly forced to jump off the ship and swim to shore; ten drowned. It was soon revealed that most aboard were from Changle, which gained the region undesired international fame. The *Golden Venture*, as Peter Kwong points out, has "defined the discourse" of contemporary Chinese immigration. In the months and years that followed, the cruel exploitation of illegal immigrants would make headlines in many nations and became the topic of several U.S. government reports and scholarly works. In December 1998, thirty-five people were charged in an immigrant-smuggling operation that investigators said made $170 million in two years by bringing 3,600 Chinese across the Canadian border through the St. Regis Mohawk Indian reservation into the United States. The Chinese were said to be from three Fujian counties, including Changle. In 1999 and 2000, U.S. and Canadian authorities intercepted several boatloads of undocumented immigrants. On June 18, 2000, another tragedy captured international attention: a customs officer working at the English port of Dover discovered in a truck, under a cargo of tomatoes, sixty Chinese, fifty-eight of whom had already suffocated. Twenty-three of the dead were later identified as emigrants from Changle.[3] Such sensational stories made Fuzhou immigrants in general and Changle immigrants in particular a synonym for smuggled Chinese. An Internet search on Changle immigrants in September 2004 resulted in 175 entries; almost all of them concerned smuggling activities.

It cost in U.S. currency about $20,000 per person in the late 1980s and $30,000 in the early 1990s to be smuggled into the United States. By 2004, the price had risen to $80,000, a 300 percent increase over twenty years. As the per capita income for urban residents in Fujian province was only about $1,400 (11,175 yuan) in 2004, very few individual families could afford to pay such an exorbitant amount.[4] As with the early Chinese immigrants, families and relatives in the villages pooled money from various sources and some took out high-interest loans. Once a deposit of half of the fee was paid, the snakeheads would provide the prospective emigrants with fake documents to travel to Hong Kong. From there, they would go to other countries before entering the United States. The remaining payment would be due once these people arrived in the United States.[5]

According to U.S. media reports, the majority of Fuzhou immigrants were lured to the United States by snakeheads who minimized the dangers of the smuggling process. Some of the snakeheads, however, were highly respected members of the community because they provided opportunities otherwise not available in their villages. When Cuiping Zheng, known as *Pingjie* (Sister Ping), was on trial in New York in 2005, many immigrants from Fujian expressed their sympathy and concerns for her. According to the *Shijie ribao*, the majority of the villagers in Changle thought that Zheng was a *da hao ren* (great person) who helped her fellow villagers search for opportunities overseas.[6] Although economic reforms in the 1980s and 1990s brought significant improvements to the villages, the income of the peasants was far lower than those in China's big cities. If U.S. dollars were converted to Chinese yuan, the amount of money a dishwasher in a Chinatown restaurant could make would be very large by village standards.[7]

In the early 1990s, the Chinese government lifted its special exit permit policy, making it relatively easier for people to leave the country. Young and middle-aged men left in large numbers; those who stayed were seen as people with no promising future (*mei chu xi*). A twenty-six-year-old restaurant worker in New York City explained why he decided to leave in 1998:

> At that time everyone thought America was the place to get rich. My situation was not bad at home; I had an iron rice-bowl—a job paid by the city government. But my prospects were not so good. My uncle, my cousin, and my sister's husband were all in New York. My uncle built a very nice house in the village, and my

grandfather's grave was the one everybody admired. My mother never said that I had to leave, but she kept on telling me so and so had left and so and so had found a job in the United States. For my own future and the future of my family, I decided that going to America would be the best thing to do.[8]

If the emigrants were not completely ignorant about the risks involved, they were not overly concerned. For some, the ordeal was a test of will and ambition. One of them said, "I was young and physically strong. The question was whether I was brave enough to make the crossing. So many of my villagers had done that; why couldn't I? Once I had announced that I wanted to go, everyone started to save money for me. Of course people whispered about the tragedies. A classmate of mine died, and we were all saddened. But I did not want that to stop me; I did not let that shatter my dreams. When I was about to leave, no one in my family talked about those things; everyone wished the best for me."[9]

Some scholars estimate that between 1986 and 1996, over 100,000 Chinese entered the United States illegally.[10] People in New York's Chinatown believe that out of a total of 200,000 Changle immigrants in the United States, 80 percent were either smuggled or trafficked into the country. That number may be exaggerated; most of those who got caught, however, were indeed from Changle. The number of people who disappeared en route is unknown.

The new arrivals started working in the United States in restaurants, garment shops, or construction companies. Many of them used family networks to find jobs, working mostly for business owners who spoke the Fuzhou dialect. Qingming Chen, a takeout restaurant owner who came to New York in 1997 at age twenty-five, was picked up by "big brother Lin," a distant cousin on his mother's side, when he first arrived. Two days later, Chen started working at a Manhattan restaurant owned by a friend of Lin's: "I made $40 that day and was very excited about it! I called my family and they were all very happy. Most people would have to work for at least two weeks to get $40 in Changle."[11]

If the new immigrants found that money was easy to make, they also learned that it was hard to save if they wanted a comfortable place to live. In the village visitors could stay at their relatives' houses, but in America the newcomers were on their own even if they had relatives. "It is better this way, I guess," said a man in his late thirties, now a homeowner himself, "but it was hard for me to understand at the beginning when my relative said he had found a place for me. I had just started to work and had borrowed a lot of money. Why couldn't he let me sleep on the couch? All I needed was a place to sleep!" Eventually he took a job in Georgia. "I did not want to leave New York," he said, "but that restaurant owner provided shelter."[12]

Another man, a new business owner, described the four years he lived in an apartment shared by many laborers as the most difficult part of his life: "I didn't mind hard work. If I stayed healthy and there was work, I was thankful. But those long nights were hard. I watched videotapes on my bed and chatted with my roommates, also on my bed—that's the only space that I had. To beat homesickness I played cards with friends, sometimes all night. And I drank a lot."[13]

The new immigrants were subjected to social prejudice. "I would not rent any of my apartments to those *Fuzhou lao* [guys from Fuzhou], even if they pay cash in advance," said one woman from Hong Kong. "I would not let them stay in my apartment either—they are too loud," said another, who is also from Hong Kong. "Besides, they borrowed too much money to get here. How can they pay off debt by working in Chinatown? Some of them became ill, mentally ill [pointing at her own head]. I don't want to see this kind of people in my place." Some landlords or business owners do not want to deal with Fuzhou people, saying simply that they do not want to be bothered by the gangs.[14]

THE CHANGLE ENTREPRENEURIAL STYLE

About 80 percent of the Changle immigrants live in the New York area, where Chinatown encompasses more than twenty blocks on Manhattan's Lower East Side. The new immigrants have brought new life to Chinatown. East Broadway and Eldridge Street, once quiet, are now filled with shops, restaurants, vendors, and employment services. Instead of Cantonese or Mandarin, the Fuzhou dialect is now the language of the neighborhood. As Jane Lii, who reported for the *New York Times*, pointed out, the "new blood" of the Fujianese in Chinatown began to play an increasingly important role in the community in the mid-1990s, posing a real challenge to the old Cantonese population and the more affluent immigrants from Taiwan.[15]

In early 2004, Tsang Wai-Yin, a reporter for the Chinese-language newspaper *Shijie ribao*, interviewed twenty prominent businessmen from Changle in New York. Her three-part special report, "Changle ren zai meiguo" (Changle people in the United States), appeared in the paper's weekly magazine, *Shijie zhoukan*, from late September through early October, and provides the first in-depth coverage of the experiences of a young immigrant group. According to Tsang, the early arrivals made their living by relying on "three knives"—one for chopping meat and vegetables, a second for sewing clothing, and a third for mixing cement. By early 2004, however, the Changle immigrants dominated the small takeout restaurant business in the New York area, had opened some of the largest buffet restaurants in the United States, and had entered a variety of economic activities. Relying on connections from home, they have also built an extensive business network utilizing market, labor, and financial resources among themselves.[16]

The typical Changle immigrant begins working in the United States at a Chinese restaurant. Once the person has paid off his or her debt and saved some money, he or she tries to go into business, usually borrowing money from friends and using family members as labor. If the person succeeds, he or she expands the business a few years later or moves to a better location. Beyond the New York area, restaurants operated by Changle immigrants may now be found in Washington, D.C., Baltimore, Boston, Cleveland, Houston, Denver, and various cities in California, as well as in Toronto and Vancouver. One immigrant interviewed by the author recalled his early experiences: "I was an all-purpose restaurant worker (*dazade*) for two years before I started out on my own. Don't laugh at me—I had never cooked a grain of rice before coming to the United States. At home my mother would not allow her only son to work in the kitchen! But everyone I knew here made money in the restaurant business, and I figured that's what I would have to do. I had a partner and we bought a place together. I was the chef—can you imagine? I don't think any of the customers who came during the first week ever returned [laugh]! But I got help from friends and some of them taught me how to cook."[17]

To cut down the cost and avoid competition, Changle immigrants opened businesses in run-down neighborhoods or other less desirable locations. Quandi Chen, who served as the first president of the Changle

American Association, started a takeout place in Harlem in 1987. "In those days gunshots were heard just about every day," he recalled. "I made a living under gunfire." One day, Chen's restaurant was hit by eight bullets, and one of them went through the supposedly bulletproof glass window and lodged deep in the stove. "I was a little scared by that incident," Chen admitted.[18] A fellow Changle immigrant had a similar experience: "When that restaurant was up for sale, a friend told me that the location was bad: there were gangs in the neighborhood. At that time I just saw the good deal. I was in my early thirties and what would people think they could get from me? I did not have the money to be choosy anyway. One day someone broke into my car. A little later the window of the storefront was smashed. After that, I decided to move."[19]

To expand business, many of these takeout restaurants provide delivery service despite the risk. In areas where few places offered delivery, the residents welcome affordable food brought to their homes. Owners of these establishments do not have to compete with bigger and fancier restaurants for customers. However, the delivery people, who carry only a small amount of cash, are often the victims of robberies or even homicides. From December 1998 to early 2004, six Chinese restaurant workers were killed while delivering food. On October 15, 2002, thirty-six-year-old Jianchun Lin was shot in Brooklyn while bicycling to deliver food for the Happy House Restaurant. At the time he was killed, Lin was still $10,000 in debt, and his ten-year-old son was left behind in Changle. In the late evening of February 13, 2004, eighteen-year-old Huang Chen, whose parents owned the Ming Garden restaurant in Queens, fell prey to a group of teenagers looking for cash to buy athletic shoes. The young Chen, who had left Changle as a ten-year-old, had just graduated from high school. Although he offered the attackers the forty-nine dollars he carried as well as the dinner they ordered, the young men hit Chen's head repeatedly with a baseball bat before stabbing him to death with a knife. His body, wrapped in a garbage bag, was discovered the next day in a lake in Brookville Park near Kennedy Airport.[20]

To some extent, the success of a Changle immigrant can be measured by the grandeur as well as the number of restaurants he or she owns. The smallest takeout places, where customers order food through a small hole in a bulletproof window, are operated by immigrants who had moved up from being laborers not too long before. After a few years, the owner might open another establishment or move to a more desirable area. The highest standards have been set by such giant restaurants as Jingfeng in Manhattan and the luxury eateries operated by the East China Buffet Restaurant Corporation. Jingfeng can seat 1,500 patrons, and the East Buffet restaurants in New York, Long Island, and Connecticut can each serve 800 to 2,200 customers at a time. With 120 employees on its payroll, Jingfeng operates like a medium-sized company. It is the place of choice for formal community gatherings and banquets in New York's Chinatown.[21]

Zhonggao Zheng, a major shareholder of Jingfeng, served as the director of a business board that runs several other eateries and a real estate company. He is active in community affairs in both the United States and China and is no doubt one of the most respected community leaders in New York's Chinatown. Zheng's personal achievement has a symbolic value among the immigrants as they pursue the American dream. In February 1995, when a group of labor union activists picketed Jingfeng, local establishments backed the restaurant. At the "Thousand Plate Dinner Party in Support of Jingfeng," attended by notables of New York's major Chinese American organizations, Lin Song, the head of the labor union that had organized the picket line, was labeled a "devil" who wanted to destroy the community's economic prosperity. Although union organizers had raised legitimate concerns, Jingfeng did provide its employees with working conditions and benefits that many smaller eateries could not match.[22]

Their concentration in the restaurant business has allowed the Changle immigrants to develop other types of businesses as well. One of the three owners of the East Buffet Restaurant Corporation, Tianming Zheng, came to New York in 1982 after living in Hong Kong for a few years. He opened Flushing's first Chinese restaurant, Ming Yuan, and later sold it for a good profit. Over the next decade, he purchased one restaurant after another. Each time he would remodel the place thoroughly, open the business, and then sell it and move on. At a certain point in his business expansion, Zheng decided to display restaurant menus by projecting colorful slides of the dishes in lighted frames. He deposited $2,000 on an order of twenty slides. When the advertising company failed to deliver the product on time, he went to its office and waited until the job was completed. There Zheng learned that the advertising business was less labor intensive than the restaurant trade, so he soon opened the New Generation Advertising Company in Chinatown. As a large portion of the approximately fifty thousand Chinese restaurants in the United States at the time were operated by Changle immigrants, and many of them wanted similar slides, he never had to worry about getting customers. Within a decade, the company had accumulated $2 million in assets, and its workspace had expanded from 700 square feet to 5,800 square feet.[23]

Chuanshu Wang, another prominent member of the CAA, moved up by remodeling restaurants as well. Arriving in New York in 1990 by "jumping the airplane" (tiaoji), Wang took three years to pay off his debt to the snakeheads before starting out on his own. His first business was to remodel a takeout restaurant in upstate New York, near the Canadian border. At that time, he had no office space, no car, no cell phone, and he could not speak English. As he soon found out, shopping for building materials was very time consuming and difficult because most suppliers did not carry what was needed for Chinese restaurants, and preassembled or ready-to-use materials were even harder to find. Wang eventually started a retail supply business to serve Chinese restaurants only. Making one stop at his 100,000-square-foot company, Yongxin, one can find all the construction tools, building materials, dining sets, kitchen cabinets, and other materials needed to put together a Chinese restaurant. Over the years, Wang's business received orders from all over the United States, Canada, and even Changle. By 2004, it had its own iron and woodworking shops to make customized furniture and restaurant signs; the company also carried lights and lamps, as well as other decorative accessories.[24]

Centered in the restaurant business, the Changle immigrants have built a network of entrepreneurship that utilizes their own resources and markets. They make business deals among themselves. In the words of one of the leaders of the CAA, the idea is to "let no fertile soil be washed into the land of others" (feishui bu ru wairen tian). Business owners provide services to one another; a market base supported by the large Changle immigrant population assures their success. Dohua Chen, the owner of the 999 Florist in Flushing, New York, started in New York by selling soft dofu drinks (dohua) from a cart on the street. Over eight years, especially on cold winter afternoons, Chen recalled, many people from his native place purchased drinks so that he could go home earlier. Some even brought him hot coffee to keep him warm.[25]

The trust built on ties to their place of origin plays an important role in the economic activities of the Changle immigrant community. It is not easy for newcomers to secure bank loans; however, lending money to each other is common among relatives and fellow villagers. Some companies even let their customers purchase goods on credit. Such practices certainly make it more convenient for Changle people to do business within their own group, even if they might also create problems. Tianming Zheng, for example, eventually gave up his advertising company because too many of his acquaintances made purchases on credit, and it was difficult for him to collect from friends and fellow villagers even when the company was having cash-flow problems.[26]

The expanding businesses created a huge job market for new immigrants. The restaurants owned by Fuzhou people provide some 400,000 jobs. "There are lazy Changle immigrants," said one business owner, "but I have never heard about anyone from Changle who could not find a job in New York."[27] Chuanshu Wang feels good about being able to provide jobs for the new immigrants. The more than seventy employees of Yongxin all speak the Fuzhou dialect, and each worker receives a starting wage of $70 a day. Experienced workers are paid up to $100 a day.[28] By 2000, Changle immigrants had entered a variety of businesses. In addition to restaurants, garment shops, and construction companies, there are real estate agencies, employment services, beauty salons, discount stores, family-run motels, bridal shops, and cell-phone booths. A long-distance bus service operated by Fuzhou immigrants along the East Coast poses a real challenge to the Greyhound monopoly.

The purchasing power of the new immigrants is a big factor in the Chinatown economy. Luxury wedding ceremonies traditional among the people of Fuzhou, for example, have given rise to a number of lucrative businesses. During Chinatown's wedding season, which runs between late September and Chinese New Year, immigrants speaking the Fuzhou dialect host about 1,500 banquets and generate $20 million in restaurant business. A location for a wedding banquet over the Thanksgiving weekend has to be reserved at least two years in advance. The biggest winners, of course, are the bridal services. In the late 1980s, there were no specialized bridal shops; only a few clothing stores carried wedding dresses. In 1995, the *Chinese Yellow Pages* listed four bridal shops, all operated by Cantonese or Taiwanese entrepreneurs. By 2004, the number of bridal shops had increased to thirty-two, many owned by Fujianese. Moreover, the services of these bridal shops have expanded to meet the demands of those planning elaborate weddings. In addition to formal Western-style suits and both Western- and Chinese-style dresses, a complete package includes hair styling, facial treatments and makeup, manicures, and photographic services. During the wedding season, each establishment might cater to as many as a hundred clients each month. Employees of these shops work around the clock during the Thanksgiving weekend, for each store might have as many as twenty weddings in a single day. Florists, jewelers, and the owners of specialty gift shops all enjoy expanded businesses opportunities at this time of year. Newly arrived performing artists from China are hired to sing or perform magic at these celebrations.[29]

The new immigrants have not only revitalized the economy of New York's Chinatown; they have also pushed up real estate values in other areas of the city. Housing prices that had been declining in the late 1980s picked up quickly in the 1990s. Apartments vacated by Cantonese or Mexican tenants were rented by immigrants from Fuzhou, generating twice as much income for landlords in Chinatown and in Flushing, Queens. In the late 1990s and early 2000s, about 80 percent of the luxury housing development units in Queens were purchased by Fuzhou immigrants.

THE CHANGLE SOCIAL NETWORK

Historically, immigrants from Guangdong province dominated the Chinese American community in New York. As late as mid-2004, the ability to speak Cantonese was still a prerequisite for leadership positions in community organizations; most organizations used the dialect at public events. Because the Fuzhou dialect is quite different from Cantonese, immigrants from the region were underrepresented in leadership positions within the community even though after 1980 they emerged as the majority group in New York's Chinatown. Moreover, new immigrants from Fuzhou, especially Changle and its neighboring county Lianjiang, were looked down upon by other Chinese Americans: even natives from other parts of Fujian Province did not want to be identified with them.

Instead of working through the existing hierarchy of the community power structure, the new immigrants organized among themselves. With support from the old Fuzhou Countrymen's Association, the expansion of Fuzhou business entrepreneurship led to the formation of the Fuzhou-America Chamber of Commerce and Industry; meanwhile, immigrants from Changle and other regions formed numerous smaller groups based on family or village ties. In 1998, a group of businessmen pulled together these small and informal alliances and officially established the Changle American Association. In just a few years, the association has emerged as a powerful force in Chinatown, posing a direct challenge to the existing community establishment.

To a large extent, it was the desire to combat social prejudice, to change their "twisted image," that brought the Changle immigrants together. They did not want to be seen as lawless people. As more and more gained legal status and financial stability, they demanded social recognition and political rights. The association's publications stated that its members had suffered more than any other immigrant group from China because they had been subject to social prejudice within the ethnic community itself. Such prejudice not only had a psychological impact on the new immigrants and imposed hardships on their social life but it also made it difficult for them to find work and shelter. Human smuggling, the CAA pointed out, was not an invention of the Changle people: It has been well documented that many early immigrants also had various tactics to circumvent the laws of the United States. Urging the Chinese American community to reassess the quality of this regional group, the association emphasized the cultural heritage of Changle and the accomplishment of its people.[30]

The campaign to create a positive image brought the new immigrants together, for Changle natives are a proud people. Despite the fact that they are looked down upon by other Chinese Americans, few Changle immigrants are ashamed of their regional identity. "I am proud of where I came from. Wherever I go, I tell people loudly that I came from Changle," said one business owner. "We are loud. If you see a group of people talking loudly, that's us. That's our Fuzhou people," said another with a big smile. Almost every leader of the CAA can recite memorable anecdotes about his or her place of origin as they remind others that they came from the same region where some of China's most distinguished historical figures were born.[31]

Members of the CAA understand prejudice in class terms. They believe that they are looked down upon mainly because most have had to start at the very bottom of the social ladder, so they emphasize their economic achievements in the United States. Starting low is not something to be ashamed of, they argue. The fact that Changle immigrants have already taken steps toward success ought to be seen as a clear indication that they possess unusual courage, strength, and talent. Individuals who project a positive image, usually successful entrepreneurs, have been selected to lead the group to exemplify their native-place pride. "We have many outstanding people in our community. My duty in the organization is to identify these people and persuade them to come forward to serve the community," said a leader of the association. "We need these people to provide leadership. We need to show others that these are our people, not the smugglers or gang members."[32]

Almost every president, vice president, director, or board member of the CAA has been an entrepreneur. Being financially stable allows these people time for public service. Zhonggao Zheng, the owner of a number of restaurants, including Jingfeng, and the Fuxing Real Estate Company, has gained social recognition from his career in the restaurant business. A member of the Fujianese Association's board of directors in 1973, he served as the association's president from 1981 to 1985. In 1988, he represented New York's Chinese Americans at George H. W. Bush's inauguration. In 1993, he received the Distinguished Asian American Award from the mayor of New York. Zheng has also been recognized for his charity work and praised for his generosity in raising funds for his native place. When the CAA was established, it created a special position just for Zheng: as permanent chief advisor, he was ranked above the president.[33]

Although it is not an official requirement, holders of prominent positions in the CAA have all been recognized for their monetary contributions. Names of donors at major fundraising events are posted in the association's office and printed in its publications. Those who hold the highest positions have usually donated the largest sums. "I gave money at every annual meeting and fundraising event. We [the leaders] all did," said one leader of the CAA proudly. In his opinion, those who have succeeded have an obligation to the community: "I am lucky to have gotten to where I am. The more capable you are, the more you should give (*neng zhe duo lao*)."[34]

To reach its members effectively, the CAA utilizes family and kin networks based on place of origin. Quandi Chen, the association's first president, worked for years to form village- or town-based alliances among fellow Changle immigrants. Leaders of twenty-six such alliances have served as president, vice president, or on the board of directors. Because these people are at the center of their own alliances and have probably played an important role in assisting their fellow immigrants, the CAA has been able to build a substantial network through them. "The only way to make our association strong is to organize from the bottom," said Chen. "My goal is to form more village groups. I want immigrants from every village (*cun* and *xiang*) or town (*zhen*) to have an alliance of their own so that every Changle immigrant can be mobilized."[35]

This effective network building has enabled the CAA to become a major factor in New York's Chinatown. At the celebration of the fiftieth anniversary of the People's Republic of China (PRC), in the parade celebrating the handover of Hong Kong to China, and at other major events, the largest crowds have followed the banner of the CAA. Although most of its members are laborers who have to work long hours, the association can send thousands of people into the street at any given time, something that even the Chinese Consolidated Benevolent Association (CCBA), which had long claimed to be the spokesperson of the community, can no longer do.

Regardless of its extraordinary energy and strength, the CAA is by no means a part of the community establishment. Its newness and its pro-PRC stance make the association look like an oppositional force to the CCBA. Maintaining its independence, however, has been important to the leaders of the CAA, and they have their own take on community power relations. Shuimei Shi, who served as the president of the association from 2000 to 2004, feels very comfortable with the position of his association. He said: "It is our duty to show the world who we are and what we can accomplish, and it is up to them [the establishment] to decide what to do with us. I am not concerned whether they are going to accept us or take us seriously. Our association is still young.

On the other hand, the growth of our association does not depend on the recognition of others. The question is what they can do without us. How many people can they gather without the participation of our Changle immigrants? We don't need them; they need us!"[36]

THE CHANGLE SPIRIT

In the campaign against social prejudice, the CAA attempts to publicize a new image for its own people. It urges its members to keep up what they call the Changle spirit. According to the official publications of the association, the Changle spirit reflects three distinctive characteristics of its people. First, they are very loyal to each other, value the sentiments of their native place (*xiangqing*), and have a strong commitment to group solidarity. "In my village," said one community leader, "if one person were in trouble, support would arrive from everywhere" (*yiren you nan, sifang zhiyuan*). "People often ask how *Changle ren* overcome seemingly insurmountable difficulties to come to America. My answer is very simple: we help each other along the way." The Changle immigrants see themselves as being different from the Cantonese, who arrived in the second half of the nineteenth and early twentieth centuries: "Money to the Cantonese people is like a wife to a man; he would not lend money to anybody, even to his own brothers. If we Changle people were like that, none of us would have made it to America."[37]

Strong native-place sentiment is manifested as mutual support among the immigrants in the United States. One leader of the CAA who came to New York in 1983 as a teenager made this point, referring to the people in his group as members of his extended family, calling them "big brother Shi," "big brother Chen," or "big sister" so and so. He declared: "Every elder villager here is a big brother of mine, and I have many big sisters too. Once I left the village, I depend on these members of my extended family for help. When I bought my first takeout place, I did not know how to run it. But this big brother [pointing at an elder person in the room] came to help. He basically held my hand and showed me how to run the place. I would not starve in New York with all these big brothers and big sisters around."[38]

The fact that most business owners have hired workers from their home villages is seen as another distinct characteristic of the Changle people. "It is easy to work with those who can speak the Fuzhou dialect," said one employer, "but that's not the only reason that I prefer them over others. A newcomer from Changle understands his situation, he appreciates the opportunity to work, and he tries to work twice as hard." Being able to provide jobs for fellow villagers who needed work has given the greatest satisfaction to many business owners, for it is presented as a service to their own community: "I gave jobs to more than forty people who started at the bottom of society. Nothing makes me happier than watching them paying off their debts and then getting settled," said one CAA leader. Shuimei Shi, who jumped ship in 1971, especially values native-place sentiment: "I knew absolutely nobody in New York when I arrived. On my first day here, I wandered the streets thinking, 'Where am I going to sleep tonight?'" In Chinatown, Shi asked whether there was anyone from Fujian, and someone pointed him to a barbershop. He was very relieved when he finally heard the Fuzhou dialect. "Nowadays we have so many native-place people (*tongxiang*) in New York. We should not let the newcomers suffer the way I once did."[39]

Forging group unity is the main concern of the CAA. According to its leaders, the Changle people understand the importance of group solidarity: they want to "twist" themselves into "one rope." In community gatherings, the immigrants are urged to see each other as equals, which helps ease tensions between employers and their employees. Newcomers toil long hours in small restaurants, often juggling two or more jobs, but they rarely complain about their bosses in public. Most new arrivals from Changle do not have the legal status or the language skills necessary for better jobs. It is necessary for a new immigrant to work hard for a living. At the same time, "helping" a relative or fellow villager can also give a laborer a sense of satisfaction. A forty-year-old business owner did not see fairness as an issue when working his first job in a restaurant: "When I first got here I did the job of two people. The boss was my second cousin. He had borrowed a lot of money and could not afford to hire another hand. When I finished work in the evenings, he and his wife still had more work to do and her health was not good. It was not easy for them. How could I complain? They were nice enough to give me that job, and they were the only family I had in New York. They would say now that I helped them in those years. Well, I am glad that I did."[40]

The close-knit network also functions to set rules for work ethics as well as labor relations. One woman who has become a business owner spelled out how the unwritten rules work:

> Laziness is not accepted here. Some newcomers had easy lives in China and they do not understand the concept of working hard. They will have to change because no one in America will spoil them the way their parents did at home. If they can't figure that out and refuse to work hard, they will lose their jobs. Business owners, on the other hand, are not completely free to do what they want. There is a common understanding about the minimum sum a person should be paid. Some restaurant owners take advantage of those who have no work permits and pay these people as little as possible. Things like that do happen. But usually people don't treat fellow villagers like that; they do not want to gain bad reputations. It is true that the newcomers do not always have the resources to seek help, but their friends or whoever introduced them to their jobs understand what is fair and what is not. Word spreads quickly if one treats his fellow villagers poorly.[41]

Another business owner who had more than twenty people on his payroll in mid-2004 said he rarely advertises available jobs in the newspapers: "People would contact me when they need jobs for their relatives. A friend would call to say that his nephew was looking for a job, something like that. If it was a close friend I would have to give him face (*gei mianzi*) and offer the nephew a job right away even if I was not looking for extra help. Once my mother in China called and asked me to hire so and so. What could I do? I couldn't turn away people from my own village. I sometimes had to find work for them to do."[42]

Mutual obligations within the group, as stressed by community leaders, make the organization of laborers along class lines difficult, if not impossible. When union workers picketed Jingfeng restaurant in a dispute over how tips should be divided, no employees of the restaurant, almost all of them from the same region, talked to reporters. The workers even organized their own counterdemonstration to show their support for their bosses—in this case, their native-place fellow immigrants.[43]

The second element of the Changle spirit, as articulated by leaders of the CAA, is the immigrants' ability to endure hardships and their willingness to take risks. If most other immigrants started with little to nothing in the United States, they argue that the Changle immigrants started from a negative point, as most of them were heavily in debt when they first arrived. Members of the community, however, are encouraged to develop a rather philosophical attitude about such disadvantages: "Only the ones who have tasted the most bitterness could command others" (chi de ku zhong ku, fang wei ren shang ren). Or, quoting another popular Chinese expression, they often say, "The sweetest taste comes after bitterness" (ku jin tian lai). Following such logic, enduring hardship is just a way to anticipate success. The Changle immigrants have certainly endured more hardship than most. In order to pay off debts and support their families, it has been common for the newcomers to work sixty to seventy hours a week. Although life in the United States is much harder than they had imagined, they are proud of the fact that very few have returned home without having earned a good amount of money. It takes at least three to four years of hard labor to pay off a typical debt, but very few have reneged. The trust they have in one another, one leader of the CAA said, made it easier for families to borrow money to finance trips to the United States.[44] Asked by a reporter from the Shijie ribao what he thought about the criminal charges against Cuiping Zheng, the snakehead who allegedly hired gang members to collect debts, one Mr. Zheng (no relationship to Cuiping Zheng) said, "Everyone knows smuggling is a business—you pay to go to America. If you refuse to pay what you have agreed to pay after your arrival, of course you would be in trouble."[45]

Although the snakeheads did not inform their clients about the risks involved, few immigrants see themselves as victims. "We come from a fishing community," one of them said. "You don't give up fishing because of the storms." The immigrants are fully aware of the tragedies, but they do not think the relatively small number of deaths resulting from human smuggling is statistically significant compared with the tens of thousands who have successfully made the journey. Bravery and courage, argue the CAA leaders, are the keys to the success of their people. "Our people are not afraid of taking risks," one of them said. "We go to the mountains knowing full well there are tigers (mingzhi *shan you hu, pian xiang hu shan xing*). That's why we could quickly establish ourselves in the United States. Very few others would dare to open restaurants in neighborhoods controlled by street gangs. Without doing that, however, many of us would not be able to have businesses at all." Although a few Changle immigrants have been shot or killed while delivering food and many more have been robbed, the practice of starting businesses in high-crime areas did not stop. Since the death of Huang Chen in February 2004, however, leaders of CAA have been cautious, and advocate not taking excessive risks; they suggested that takeout restaurants give up delivery service.[46]

The third element of the Changle spirit, according to the CAA, is their people's flexibility. It is a tradition for the people of Changle to leave their overpopulated home villages in search of new opportunities. Adjusting to life in a strange land, however, has not been easy. The immigrants came from all walks of life: they were peasants, fisherman, factory or construction workers, teachers, government officials, and business operators. Once in the United States, however, all of them have had to start at the very bottom of society. They have had to work as menial laborers and to accept very low wages. Being flexible, to the Changle immigrants, means being able to move up and down the socioeconomic ladder (*neng shang neng xia*) regardless of one's previous social status. Ronghua Chen, a prodigy who started publishing poems in China when he was twelve, personifies such flexibility. After an airplane trip and a sea voyage, he crossed mountains and rivers on foot, passing through more than ten countries before being instructed to swim ashore near New York six months later. In Chinatown, Chen started by laboring in restaurants and delivering food by bicycle. Once he was arrested by the police while distributing flyers on the street. In a television interview, a tearful Chen said, "Not a single day I did not regret. I often worked for more than ten hours a day. Even though I couldn't go to bed until one o'clock in the morning, I had to rely on sleeping pills to get two or three hours of sleep each night. I worked the lowest job in the restaurant; anyone could boss me around and anyone could bully me."[47]

But Chen did not return to China. Being a Changle native, his responsibility to his family is more important than his own pride. He learned to be humble and flexible, and that allowed him to find ways to survive and use his talents. In time, he worked as the manager of a big restaurant before entering into a partnership with a florist and opening his own restaurant. After his wife joined him, Chen picked up his pen again; he first served as the secretary of the Fujianese Association and later became the secretary of the CAA. He also found opportunities to lecture on Chinese calligraphy at American University in Washington, D.C. In 1997, during the historic handover of Hong Kong to China, Chen's poem "Greetings, My Homeland!" appeared in several major newspapers and magazines in China. "I became famous overnight," said a joyful Chen.[48]

From the viewpoint of CAA leaders, being flexible has allowed the Changle immigrants to grasp new opportunities, and they have been willing to start with the very smallest business available. By mid-2004, about 70 percent of the Changle immigrants were involved in the food businesses, ranging from street carts stocked with drinks and steamed pastries, to mom-and-pop takeout places serving fast and affordable food, to large restaurants geared to formal dining and social gatherings. Their restaurants are not limited to Fuzhou cooking. Large eateries such as those operated by the East Buffet Restaurant Corporation hire chefs specializing in traditional Chinese regional dishes as well as Japanese, Korean, Thai, and Western cuisines. Business owners operate according to market demand, and their entrepreneurship has expanded at a remarkable speed.

Their insistence on solidarity, willingness to endure hardships, and flexibility has enabled the CAA to utilize group resources and help members to adjust to new lives. In mid-2005, a third of the 200,000 Changle immigrants still had not attained legal status; many are still toiling in restaurants and garment shops and on construction sites. It has been the spirit of Changle, spread through stories of those who have succeeded, that has kept their American dreams alive, and it is this spirit that the CAA wants its members to carry forward.

COMBATING PREJUDICE: THE YIDONG MARKETPLACE INCIDENT

Although a significantly large number of Changle immigrants own businesses, most of their establishments are small. Manhattan's East Broadway is bursting with small vendors and shops run by Changle immigrants. Most single-unit shop spaces are divided for multiple business operations. To make ends meet, these businesses rely on the labor of family members and stay open for very long hours.

In the summer of 2004, the shareholders of the Yidong Shopping Mall on East Broadway, who held a fifty-year lease from the city government, announced a rent increase that would double or triple the amounts that its tenants had paid earlier. In addition, each new lease would be subject to a deposit of six months' rent plus another two months in advance. This drastic increase would no doubt have imposed grave hardships on the small vendors who have little capital. In response, the vendors of the shopping mall, many of them members of the CAA, organized the Yidong Mall Small Vendors Alliance in late July and staged a three-day demonstration in front of the Emperor's Seafood and Hui Shi Jia restaurants, which are owned by the major shareholders of the mall, Yanming Chen and his wife Liuzhen Huang. The landlords, however, did not take the vendors seriously. Given the high demand for business space in Chinatown, they believed that finding new tenants would not be difficult. In a heated exchange with the tenants, Huang called Fuzhou immigrants "trash" and threatened to "clean them out," and her son was seen videotaping the demonstrators during their first street rally on July 28.[49]

Agitated, about one hundred vendors scheduled another three-day demonstration to start on August 7. Before the rally and picketing took place, however, the local police, invited by the vendors' alliance to come to the event, were informed that the demonstration had been canceled. Similar rumors also reached the vendors. As a result, some of them went home after work. Only about one hundred demonstrators showed up that evening as scheduled. The picket line attracted many onlookers, and some sympathizers donated large amounts to support the demonstrators, who soon noticed that their actions were again being videotaped. They suspected that the man holding the camera had been hired by the Yidong landlords. When confronted, the Spanish-speaking cameraman began to shout at the demonstrators and was soon taken away by the police.[50]

To win support from the community, the protestors situated their struggle within the broad context of the city's economic difficulties. Arguing that the terrorist attack of September 11, 2001, had slowed down Chinatown's economy, they urged the city government to support small businesses as a means of speeding up recovery. Drastic rent increases, they reasoned, would force many small vendors out of business, which would further slow down Chinatown's commercial activities. They wanted the government to interfere because the property belonged to the city. A flyer written in both English and Chinese was distributed on the streets, asserting that "the shareholders of the Yidong Mall want to destroy our community harmony and prevent the reconstruction of Chinatown's economy." "What Chen and Huang tried to do," the flyer continued, "was no different from the terrorists. If the rent increase cannot be stopped, Chinatown's economy will be destroyed."[51]

The Chinese text of the flyer spelled out the demonstrators' cause in clear class terms. Calling Chen and Huang "vampires" who would grow bigger by "sucking the blood of Fuzhou immigrants," the alliance stated:

> Chen Yanming and Huang Liuzhen use their wealth to oppress small vendors, sabotage community solidarity, and prevent the economic growth of Chinatown. To double or triple our rent is to completely ignore the sluggishness of the economy and the hardships of small businesses; it is to bring our livelihood to an impasse. . . . Compared with the rich and arrogant shareholders we are small and vulnerable. For the dignity of us Fuzhou fellow immigrants, for our right to survive, for a stable and healthy development of the Chinatown community, and for harmony, unity, and peace, we are going to fight for our cause to the end.[52]

Moreover, the protestors also defined their struggle as one against social prejudice within the Chinese American community. "We are not trash! Say 'No' to Discrimination!" one of their signs read. The protestors viewed Huang's attitude toward the Fuzhou immigrants as a reflection of the prejudice of more established Chinese Americans against the new immigrants, which is deeply rooted in the class structure of the new Chinese American community. Huang certainly did not want to be identified as a hater of the Fuzhou immigrants. Denying that she had ever used the word "trash" to describe the Fuzhou people, she now claimed that her ancestors were also from Fujian Province. Nevertheless, she and her husband would not let the small vendors have their way. They hired lawyers and forced individual vendors to sign new leases.

To further intimidate those who had participated in the demonstration, they reported unauthorized sales of telephone cards in the mall to the local police. In late August and September, police raided Chinatown and searched the merchandise of more than one hundred small vendors. Thousands of dollars' worth of telephone cards were confiscated.[53]

A combination of class oppression and social prejudice finally generated overwhelming community support for the protesters. The picketing of the two restaurants was a huge success, and the idea of a vendors' alliance, originally organized to protest the rent increase by the Yidong shareholders, now appealed to merchants throughout the East Broadway commercial district. In October, the leaders of the first small vendors' alliance announced the establishment of the East Broadway Vendors' Alliance and took legal action against the local police for the attack on the small business owners. The Consulate of the People's Republic of China in New York immediately announced its support of the group, as almost all its members were immigrants from the Chinese mainland.[54]

The struggle between the small business operators and the landlords who controlled the commercial space at Yidong is part of a larger struggle between new immigrant groups and the community establishment. Although they controlled fewer resources, the CAA pointed out that the new immigrants had become an indispensable force in the community's economy. The newcomers might have a lower standard of living, they said, but compared with the American-born Chinese, they are more likely to spend their money in Chinatown. As one of the leaders of the CAA noted, "Many large business owners still believe that they can run Chinatown the way they want because they control community resources. What they ought to understand is that their numbers are few. Without us as business operators and consumers, Chinatown would have to be shut down."[55]

BACK TO CHANGLE

The media coverage of human trafficking has painted a darker picture of the country that Chinese immigrants have left. To the American public, the circumstances these Chinese left behind must be extremely harsh in both political and economic terms. Nevertheless, as some scholars have pointed out, relatively few post-1965 immigrants left China for political reasons. Neither was absolute poverty a consideration for the natives of Changle. Stimulated by economic reforms in China since the late 1970s, Fujian has been especially successful in attracting foreign investments, which allowed the province to establish thousands of new business enterprises and significantly increase its volume of foreign trade. The living standard of Fujian natives is now higher than that in other areas of China. For the peasants in Changle, however, opportunities to earn money are fewer than those in China's large cities, let alone those in developed countries in the West.[56]

To a large extent, a negative image of China generated sympathy toward the new immigrants, which has led to more generous U.S. policies. Many Changle immigrants have tried to attain their legal status by claiming political asylum, arguing that they are victims of China's one-child policy. Thousands of successful petitioners have obtained legal residency in the United States, which not only allows them to work but also to qualify their family members for legal entry. Few individuals with legal status are interested in challenging China's government policies; neither do they want to be identified as political dissidents. Having legal status makes life in the United States easier; claiming asylum is just a practical path to take.

During the last two decades of the twentieth century, some established community organizations shifted from a strong anti-Communist stance to one that accepted both China and Taiwan. The Changle American Association has always been known as a pro-PRC group. The constitution of the CAA states that the central goals of the association are to advance the spirit of patriotism, to promote friendship between the United States and China, and to push for a united China. Patriotism in this case implies loyalty to both the United States and China. Not only do the immigrants value their ties with China; they also understand that social prejudice against them in the Chinese American community has much to do with China's status within the international community. Shuimei Shi, the former president of the association, was a seaman in Hong Kong and had traveled around the world before coming to the United States in 1977. "In those days, Chinese people were discriminated against because China was backward," he said. "Not until 1979, when China formally established diplomatic relations with the United States, did the situation begin to improve." The immigrants could have blamed China for their low social status in the United States, but more often than not, that has not been the case. One leader of the CAA explained his sentiments toward China in a vivid way: "America is my boss; China is my mother. I would not disown my mother because she is poor."[57] The CAA displays flags of both the United States and the PRC in its office, and it has offered strong support to the PRC consulate in New York. On August 15, 2004, when Shi completed his term as president of the association, he delivered a formal speech entitled "My Heart Is Still Chinese."

Although CAA does not have any formal political connections with the PRC, its members have cheered every Chinese achievement as though it were one of their own. In the parade celebrating Hong Kong's return to China on June 30, 1997, the CAA and many other new immigrant groups from Fujian, such as Fuqing and Lianjiang, sent huge floats and banners bearing the names of their native places. As one young immigrant put it, "We were looked down upon by old-timers as well as immigrants from Taiwan and Hong Kong mainly because China delayed its economic reform for three decades. But the Chinese people are now standing up." In other words, the development of China's economy can change the power structure within the Chinese American community.[58]

For that reason, the immigrants want China to be stronger and stronger, and they want to do whatever they can to speed up that process. Support for China's economic reform is the most recognized activity of the CAA. Earlier immigrants built big houses for their families and elaborate graves to honor their ancestors, and their donations went to the construction of pavilions and the refurbishing of schools and temples. Beginning in the late 1990s, money earned overseas has been invested in building apartments, factories, and hotels, and in many other economic enterprises as well.

The remittances the immigrants have sent to Changle have helped increase commercial activities in their native place. Although some scholars in the West are concerned about the importance of preserving rural economies, those who left Changle do not share such concerns. They have no intention of maintaining the rural traditions built by their ancestors; they want their fellow villagers to grasp every economic opportunity available. If an earth-shaking change (*tian fan di fu*) were needed to bring prosperity immediately and improve people's standard of living, the immigrants would definitely like to see that happen.

At the beginning of the twenty-first century, Changle is moving in the right direction, in their view. Old fishing and rice-farming villages have been moving away from self-sufficient agriculturally based economies, and old dusty, sleepy towns are being taken over by bustling areas that feature broad streets, high-rise apartments, elaborate gated single-family residences, fancy hotels, and new stylish stores. In addition to developing highly commercialized agricultural products, each of the eighteen towns under the jurisdiction of Changle City has built its own business infrastructure. The town of Wuhang, for example, operates twelve hotels, and its two industrial centers occupy about forty-one acres of land (250 *mu*). The 139 factories in Hangcheng produce a wide range of merchandise, including machinery, plastics, electronics, textiles, crafts, foodstuff, bottled drinks, and construction materials. Although most towns or villages have developed their own grassroots industries utilizing local resources, it is the nontraditional industrial establishments that have made the immigrants most proud. "No iron ore has ever been found in Changle, but our people built a four-billion-yuan steel plant; the soil is not suited for growing cotton, but we developed a one-billon-yuan textile industry. We can do anything we want," said one of the leaders of the CAA. Even an international airport has been built in Changle, allowing travelers to fly directly to or from Hong Kong and countries in Southeast Asia.

To business-minded entrepreneurs from Changle, China is an enormous market with great economic potential that has provided many opportunities for investment, and the government of the PRC offers various incentives to attract money from overseas. But money is not the only return available. One businessman put it this way: "I could have stayed here to make more money. I could expand my business here. But I do not want to have another restaurant in New York. If you have the money you can do so many things in China. It is very exiting to do something new in my hometown. Besides, our native place (*jiaxiang*) needs money and appreciates the investment. It's hard for me to describe this, but doing business there makes me feel great."[59]

Attracting investment from overseas has been an important part of the Chinese government's agenda. During his visit to New York in May 1999, the mayor of Changle, Baochu Lin, met with about three hundred immigrants at the Jingfeng restaurant. He presented the immigrants with a detailed plan for the city's economic development and laid out opportunities for them. In late September of the same year, the CAA sent a delegation of more than sixty people to Beijing to celebrate the fiftieth anniversary of the PRC. When the delegation arrived in Changle, it was warmly welcomed by the heads of the city. The once-ordinary peasants and workers who had sneaked out of the country illegally and given up their Chinese citizenship not too long before were now guests of honor at banquets hosted by local and provincial government officials. "My goal," said Chuangshu Wang of the CAA, "is to pull the capital of our immigrants together and invest it in large projects. In our native place we can rely on people we know to do business."[60]

The immigrants have made an impact on their native place: Changle has become one of the fastest-growing regions in Fujian Province, even though a large portion of its working population is abroad. The improved economy means that more people can afford the $80,000 smuggling fee currently being charged to come to the United States. Family members and relatives already in the United States can help find jobs for prospective immigrants. The rapid growth of the local economy, however, has also offered more options at home, while a significantly improved living standard has made staying more desirable. More jobs have become available in both local businesses and the larger steel and textile factories, and some Changle natives have found business opportunities in Shanghai and Beijing. Relatively few young people in Changle are left working in the rice paddies; most of them today are wage earners or business operators who frequent restaurants, coffee shops, and karaoke bars. Migrants from Sichuan Province are now hired to cultivate the farmland; they also perform domestic chores for well-to-do families. Some young Changle people, products of China's one-child policy, own motorcycles and automobiles. When the first shipment of sixty Mercedes Benzes was delivered to Changle, it sold out the first day.[61]

On September 9, 2003, a reporter from the *New York Times* revealed that the attractions of America that had lured thousands of Chinese from their home villages were no longer strong because at present not as many Changle people were desperate enough to seek the opportunity to come to America. "I won't say that young people do not want to come to America anymore, but they would only if they could board a flight to New York. They would not [want to go] unless the trip is safe," said

Chuangdi Chen. The villagers now have a more realistic picture of the United States. From those who have returned home, they have learned that America is no paradise. Zheng, a college graduate who returned home to Changle after seven years in the United States, told a news reporter that he never laughed or smiled while he was there. "It was the same routine every day," he said. "Get up. Work for sixteen hours. Go to bed. Get up again. I was a fool. A machine." In his hometown, Zheng's job generates a modest income even by local standards, but his life is less stressful and he enjoys hanging out with friends and spending time with his wife and son. Moreover, going to America is no longer the only way to pursue a good life. "Our home village (jiaxiang) is moving forward at a fast pace," said a CAA official proudly. "Many people can see there are more opportunities at home, and the situation will only get better every day."[62]

If the Changle immigrants view their low status in the United States as a reflection of the failure of China's socialist economy after 1949, the emergence of China as a new world economic power at the beginning of the twenty-first century gives them courage and inspiration. To some extent, the immigrants see the improvement of China's status in the global economy as a primary reason for a reorientation of power relations in the Chinese American community.

CHAPTER 5

Surviving Poverty in an Ethnic Social Hierarchy

BAOSHAN LI, A STOCKY, SELF-EMPLOYED construction worker in his mid-thirties, gained permanent resident status under the 1992 Chinese Student Protection Act. Nevertheless, he has not gathered the courage to apply for U.S. citizenship: the thought of being questioned by non-Chinese immigration officials is too intimidating. After twenty years in the United States, Li knows very little English, and he speaks Mandarin with a strong Cantonese accent. For that reason he is not entirely independent. Highly skilled in wood floor and ceramic tile installations, he gets work through Bob, the owner of a company selling carpet, wood flooring, and ceramic tiles. Like Li, Bob is also from China. Having immigrated to the United States from Guangdong province with his family as a teenager, he finished high school in California and graduated from a community college. His American education and the ability to communicate with people in English, Cantonese, and Mandarin give him the versatility that Li lacks. Starting as a construction worker himself a decade ago, Bob was able to get a job as a salesman for a building material company before going into business for himself. "You can say that I have been in the trade for a long time," he said. "To do well one needs to know the materials, the labor involved in installation, and the clients. Not everyone has that kind of knowledge; I had worked with all types of materials with my own hands."[1] In Diamond Bar in Los Angeles County, Bob's flooring materials have been in high demand since the boom of the housing market in the late 1990s. He is not Li's employer, but rather a labor contractor. Most of his merchandise is sold to homeowners, with labor performed by crews of construction workers like Li, and these workers give Bob a share of their earnings. Li thinks it is a fair arrangement; it saves him the trouble of finding the work himself, and because he is a little shy, Li does not feel comfortable bargaining with the customers. The money Li makes is not bad, especially because most of it comes in cash. He lives in a rented room, goes to work in the morning in an old Toyota truck, and picks up take-out Chinese food for dinner in the evening. He sends money regularly to his parents in China and is saving more so that his brother there can get married. After that, Li said he might go home for a visit—his parents are eager to find him a bride.[2] That Li has a green card makes him a very eligible bachelor in China.

Li works at his customers' job sites, moving from one to another with his apprentice Lao Wu (old Wu), a former factory worker from Tianjin. The apprentice is about ten years Li's senior, but he treats Li with unquestionable respect, addressing him as "master" (*shifu*). The skinny Wu likes to talk, if the subject is not about himself; up to now, he is not sure whether the move to the United States was a wise one. To finance their trip, Wu and his wife Fei sold their own apartment and that of her parents, and they borrowed a substantial amount of cash from friends and relatives.[3] The travel documents they purchased to gain entry to the land of opportunity have long expired. With neither marketable skills nor work permits, they depend entirely on jobs within the ethnic community. The couple went to New York City first, where Wu worked in restaurants. By the time they moved to Los Angeles two years later, he had made up his mind to never go back to restaurant jobs again. "Hardship I can endure," he said, "but at my age, being bossed around and bullied day after day is difficult, mentally. So here I am, learning a trade from Master Li, humbly."[4]

Wu's wife, Fei, is a *yuezi gong*—a live-in nanny for women with newborn babies. Chinese tradition requires women to be confined in bed for a whole month to recover after they deliver their babies. Middle-class women whose parents or in-laws are unavailable in the United States often hire domestic workers during this period, and undocumented women like Fei come in handy. A yuezi gong gets paid twenty percent more than a regular nanny and receives room and board for free. Even though she has to work around the clock seven days a week taking care of both the mother and the infant, Wei continues to do it because she needs the money badly. The main problem is that each job she gets lasts for only a very short period of time, forcing her to move often.

Fortunately, there is a high demand for her service in southern California. The employment services sometimes call her for interviews for new jobs before she finishes the previous one. However, Fei does not have job security of any kind. Once she took a job in an affluent neighborhood in Orange County. The pregnant woman was expecting in two weeks and promised to hire Fei for at least three months. But less than a week after Fei started, the employer's mother came from Hong Kong. The old lady was not happy about Fei's receiving a yuezi gong's wage before the baby was born, and she persuaded her daughter to hire an hourly paid maid instead. Fei was given a day's notice to leave.

It is ironic that Fei works as a yuezi gong taking care of other people's children, while she cannot even afford to take care of her own baby. A year after Fei came to America, she got pregnant unexpectedly with her second child; her twelve-year-old daughter was still in China with Fei's parents. Eager to go back to work, she paid a traveler $1,000 to carry her then three-month-old son to board an airplane in Los Angeles, to be picked up by Fei's parents at Beijing International Airport. Three years after their arrival to the United States, Wu and Fei are still deeply in debt.

Li, who lives not too far away from Wu and Fei, has become the couple's closest contact. He offers Wu rides to work, and hands his own cell phone to Wu when Fei calls. He loaned the couple money when their son arrived. And when Fei gets fired, it is Li who comes to console Wu. "Don't worry," he said in a soft tone. "She has worked too hard. She deserves a break. I will drop her off at the employment service before we start to work tomorrow. It won't take her long to find another job. Don't worry too much; things will get better."[5]

The belief that things will get better keeps Wu and Fei going. Wu has good reason to anticipate improvement, but he also understands the limited possibilities and sets his goals practically and realistically. His dream is to become a master of his trade with a license like Li, to gain legal status in the United States (both he and Fei are waiting for asylum hearings), to clear all his debt, and to bring their children over. "As my wife put it," said Wu, "we would ask for nothing more if our children could attend colleges in the United States."

Wu and Fei's experiences, as well as Li's, are shared by hundreds of thousands of Chinese immigrants. Although many of them have already improved their situation, middle-class status remains beyond their reach. The 2000 census calculates a national poverty rate of 12.4 percent. Although the 12.6 percent rate for Asian Americans is close to the national average, it is significantly higher than the 8.1 percent rate of non-Hispanic whites. Though more and more Chinese Americans have achieved social mobility, a decline in the poverty rate is yet to be seen.[6] The Taiwanese American population in America has perhaps the highest rate of well-educated and well-off individuals among ethnic Chinese groups, but at the same time, the percentage of Taiwanese immigrant families below the poverty line is still much higher than that of non-Hispanic whites.[7] Moreover, the actual poverty rate of the Chinese American population would probably be higher than the census reflects if all undocumented immigrants were counted. Though it is a rising tide full of opportunity, the Chinese ethnic economy clearly does not lift all boats equally.

The central concern of this chapter is the role of the ethnic economy in social mobility. Are individual Chinese Americans of various socioeconomic and legal backgrounds allowed the same opportunities to work within the system? If not, does the economy actually determine Chinese Americans' opportunities and encourage social hierarchy? I argue that the unconditional dependencies of laborers on their coethnic middle-class employers isolate the laborers from the mainstream job market. Instead of promoting mobility for everyone and narrowing class differences, the Chinese ethnic economy actually works to further polarize members of the community.[8]

Housing and Poverty

Researchers have defined poverty in different ways. The U.S. Bureau of the Census calculates the poverty rate based on family income in relation to the size of the household. This measurement is quite reliable for documented individuals and families with recorded income, but does little to include undocumented immigrants or reflect activities in the informal economic sector. Homeownership and neighborhood location offers an alternative measurement to differentiate middle-class Americans from impoverished ones. As Stephan Thernstrom discovered in his study on mid-nineteenth-century Newburyport, Massachusetts, middle-class families lived in their own houses, while the laboring-

class families rented.[9] In *Class and Community*, Alan Dawley also found
that nineteenth-century shoemakers in Lynn, Massachusetts, could not
afford to purchase homes. With supplemental income from three older
children and his wife, for example, one worker rented a seven-room
house in a town of small and large factories.[10] The development of
urban neighborhoods along class or ethnic lines in late-nineteenth- and
twentieth-century America has drawn much attention from researchers
on race and poverty. In these studies, Chinatowns in San Francisco and
other American metropolitan areas are described as filthy urban slums,
similar to African American communities in New York's Harlem and
Chicago's South Side.[11]

Although still more urban than average Americans, the vast majority
of Chinese Americans are no longer residents of inner-city ethnic
enclaves. New York, San Francisco, Los Angeles, Honolulu, and San Jose
are cities with large Chinese populations, but their proportion of Chinatown residents has declined significantly. New York City's Chinatown
accommodates 14 percent of the Chinese population in the city, but
only 8 percent of San Francisco's Chinese and 2 percent of Los Angeles'
Chinese reside in Chinatowns.[12] More and more Chinese Americans are
apparently suburban dwellers. Even the new Chinatowns developed since
the 1980s, as some scholars have argued, are strikingly different from
the old ones. No longer urban slums, these ethnic neighborhoods have
suburban and middle-class outlooks, and they are an integral part of the
multicultural and multiethnic American society. Geographer Wei Li terms
these ethnic clusters "ethnoburbs" to make exactly this point.[13]

The geographic distribution of the contemporary Chinese American
population allows scholars to reassess the new Chinese America in terms
of its class compositions. Most amazing is the fact that a large number of
new immigrants are able to disappear into the suburbs as soon as they
arrive. Although the process of suburbanization of middle-class Chinese
Americans began before 1965, immigrants' bypassing traditional primary
centers of initial settlement is a relatively new phenomenon. Some scholars
are quick to conclude that because the proportion of immigrants who
have made their first homes in Chinatowns has shrunk over the years,
most of the newcomers must have possessed sufficient resources to bypass
the inner city and settle in affluent middle-class suburbs.[14]

Although housing and area of residence are important indicators of wealth or lack of wealth, neither homeownership nor residential location permits quick judgment of economic status for a population of complex backgrounds and social relations.[15] It takes time for newcomers to purchase homes. A market of overpriced real estate properties in the late 1990s and early 2000s made the American dream of homeownership beyond reach for many middle-class families, while the instability of the American economy in more recent years probably encouraged some potential buyers to wait. In other words, it is not unusual for middle-class Chinese American individuals or families to rent their homes. Although it is logical to assume that poor Chinese Americans are less likely to own homes or rent in upscale residential areas, drawing conclusions along neighborhood boundaries overlooks the intricate ways that immigrant laborers find shelter. The multifarious relationships between middle-class Chinese Americans as employers and landlords on the one side, and their coethnic laborers and tenants on the other, require an exploration of the economic status of individuals and families beyond a quick glance of where they reside, for the realities of living patterns of immigrant laborers are far more complicated than they appear to be.

Individuals and families decide where to live for different reasons. For many newcomers, finding affordable housing is as important as finding a job. The income of a Chinese immigrant laborer at the beginning of the twenty-first century is not sufficient to cover rent for an entire house. In many areas, laborers are not making enough money to rent a whole apartment. Although middle-class families find suburban living more desirable, others are probably driven away from Chinatown housing simply because they cannot afford to live there. Government-subsidized housing units are so few in old Chinatown neighborhoods that even in the late 1970s qualified applicants would remain on the waiting list for five to six years before they could move in.[16] To view old Chinatowns as urban slums is itself problematic, as the amenities of such ethnic neighborhoods have pushed real estate values up drastically in recent decades. Across the bay from San Francisco in Oakland's historic Chinatown, for example, modern apartment complexes erected since the late 1980s have attracted middle-class buyers who prefer to live in urban Chinatown than in the suburbs. Meanwhile, even as their middle-class neighbors drive up the cost of renting in Chinatowns, easy access to jobs is still the main draw for Chinese laborers, so many live in overcrowded, old buildings.

The high cost of Chinatown housing compels laborers to share their living space with unrelated individuals or families. Baoshan Li, the master flooring installer, rents a bedroom in a small house. He has a television in his room with satellite cable to watch Chinese-language programs, and he shares the kitchen and bathrooms with two other families. "I snore loudly; nobody can stand it when I sleep," he said. Even so, until he paid off his debt he did not have a room of his own.[17] To Jenny Yi, a hotel clerk who also holds a part-time job in a restaurant, having a room to herself is a big luxury: "I like to read a little in a peaceful place or talk to my mother privately. In my room, no one bothers me." Although the $800 monthly rent consumes about half of her income, after working for twenty-five years in the United States, Yi felt it was important to enjoy a different lifestyle than the one she had in her early years in this country.[18]

To many laborers who do not have a stable income, the luxury of having their own room is beyond reach. A day laborer in his mid-thirties in Flushing, New York, shares a bedroom with another immigrant in a three-bedroom apartment. The other two bedrooms are taken by two unrelated families; each of them has a young child. He said, "My wife and son are not here so I don't need much space. I share a room with a guy from Dongbei (northeast China), which is not that bad. I don't cook much and rarely use the living room. It is better to make some room for the children. I am not eager to go home after dinner because it is noisy there until late at night."[19] Ping, who works in two Los Angeles Chinese restaurants for sixty-five hours a week, makes about $2,000 a month, but she tries to put some money aside just in case: "I got sick last spring and worked very little for almost three months. I almost had a mental breakdown at the time because I still had to pay $400 rent each month. In L.A., no one in my shoes would pay $1,000 for rent."[20]

Working at two part-time jobs in southern California, a woman slept on the couch in the living room of a one-bedroom apartment for two years. The couple who rented the apartment paid $1,100 each month and charged her $450. That was about the cheapest housing she could get in a town of affluent middle-class Americans. Because the rental agreement did not allow the couple to add additional tenants, she was told not to talk to the neighbors, and she was not allowed to have visitors. She knew she would have to move out once her husband and son came to the United States. Not knowing how much her husband would be able to make, she was horrified by the thought of having to pay rent by herself, and tried to get into a homeless shelter. She did rent eventually, but a few years later, after she and her husband were divorced and she moved to Arizona to start a new job, her seventeen-year-old son ended up in a homeless youth shelter.[21]

The worst living conditions are found in family motels. In Monterey Park, Los Angeles, Lao Wu and Fei take long-term shelter in a motel converted from a two-story single-family house. The owner of the property, a Chinese from Vietnam, resides two blocks away; the motel tenants are mostly from mainland China. For ten dollars a day, the couple gets a room that is big enough to squeeze a double-size mattress and a small television into, and they share a kitchen and two-and-half bathrooms with two dozen other tenants. At one point, Wu recalled, the house was occupied by thirty-two individuals. On his day off and when Fei is away, Wu likes to purchase a pound of shrimp. He waits for his turn to cook and enjoys his dinner and wine sitting on his bed; the bedroom is so small there is not even room for a chair.[22]

According to an investigation by the *Shijie ribao*, there were many family motels in the Los Angeles area, especially in San Gabriel, Monterey Park, and Alhambra—areas that are considered suburban. Most managers of the motels were Chinese immigrants. They leased the properties, installed partitions, and built bunk beds for short-term tenants. Some were hired by property owners to do so. Flyers advertising these motels were posted on the walls of supermarkets and community centers, and on lamp posts and telephone poles, but most tenants learned about their services from friends, employment agencies, tourist bus drivers, immigration lawyers, and sometimes smugglers.[23]

Family motels are especially popular in Los Angeles and New York, although these unlicensed businesses do not advertise officially. From the outside, a motel looks just like any single-family dwelling or apartment in the neighborhood. However, one homeowner in Monterey Park said that the house next door sometimes accommodates as many as twenty tenants:

These people must be new to this country. They are loud and they smoke. There are men and women, new faces all the time. Some will sit on the steps of the porch or simply squat there. Do you know in which part of China people squat like that? One day a stranger came knocking on our door holding a piece of paper. My husband looked at the address written on the paper; it was our neighbor's house. I peeked through a window of a room of the house once and saw four bunk beds. It's illegal, but my husband said we shouldn't bother them. He said we don't report on our neighbors.[24]

In August 2004, police raided a family motel in Los Angeles and found that the 1,500-square-foot, three-bedroom and one-bath residence was partitioned into six rooms. Besides the kitchen and the bath, every room was filled with mattresses and bunks. In a complaint filed with the city government, the neighbors said that a few dozen people lived in the house and their cars took up all the parking spaces on the street.[25]

Complaints against family motels have been especially loud in San Gabriel. In 2003, Ken Moy, a Chinese American, promised that if elected to city council, he would close the motels and bring peace to these neighborhoods. For more than a year after he came to office, Moy conducted several investigations with the cooperation of the city police and shut down a number of family motels. In August 2004, under pressure by local residents, the city of Monterey Park also launched a campaign to crack down on family motels. The mayor of the city and a number of council members visited several neighborhoods; they called the operation of family motels a violation of the rights of local residents and a disruption of municipal peace. To encourage people to come forward, the city installed a police hotline and solicited tips regarding illegal residential activities. Several family motels were exposed, and the police also went to some targeted areas and issued parking tickets for unclaimed cars. The locals, however, wanted more decisive measures. Some residents stormed a city council meeting and urged the government to report illegal business operations to immigration authorities. Alarmed, several family motel operators quickly evicted their tenants, and a few homeowners put their houses on the market.[26] The language used by local residents against the operation of family motels reminded Chinese Americans of a citywide effort to halt Chinese business expansion in the 1980s.[27]

The persistence of family motels reflects the fluidity of the immigrant laborers. These motels are especially patronized by short-term
visitors. Although Lao Wu and Fei have lived in the same room for two
years, this is unusual. Because neither of them has job security, they are
unwilling to sign a lease.[28] Deng Hong, an immigration lawyer in Los
Angeles, said that many of his clients who come to Los Angeles to file
petitions cannot afford to stay in regular motels. A tourist bus driver in
New York said that he also referred young students visiting the city to
family motels: "If they could save money, why not? Why should they
pay over $60 a night when they can get by for $10 or $20?"[29] But most
tenants of the family motels are newcomers or laborers returning to
the city in search of new jobs and medical treatment. Without access
to cars, these individuals have to stay close to employment and ethnic
services, and most family motels are in convenient locations near ethnic
business clusters.

Although extremely crowded, family motels provide services unavailable elsewhere. In addition to shelter, motel operators help newcomers
get started. Airport pickups and rides to employment services are crucial
to the survival of immigrants who have no family or relatives in the
United States. Sharing living spaces with people in a similar situation is
both comforting and rewarding: some tenants gain critical knowledge
from each other on how to make it in the United States.[30] The motel
operators or managers are often recent immigrants themselves. With little
capital investment, they can have a business of their own and draw a
good income from rent, chauffeuring, and kickbacks from immigration
lawyers and other ethnic service providers.[31]

While the possibility of sharing living spaces and the availability of
family motels continue to attract immigrant laborers to urban ethnic
neighborhoods in Los Angeles, New York, San Francisco, and Oakland,
the search for more affordable housing also drives many newcomers
away from these areas. To attract laborers to more remote areas or areas
with a small Chinese American population, Chinese restaurant owners
and employers of domestic helpers usually provide room and board for
their employees. Jerry, who runs a big buffet restaurant in a small town
in Wyoming, said that the only way for him to attract and keep his
Chinese employees, including two chefs, one manager, and four waiters
(the dishwashers and busboys are Mexican immigrants), is to provide

them with housing: "Why would they come here otherwise? If they have to pay rent, they would have preferred New York."[32] As a busboy in his early years in America, Xiao Wen shared a house with his co-workers in Nevada. The two rooms upstairs were occupied by the chefs and their family members, while Xiao Wen and seven or eight others had their beds on the first floor.[33] One college graduate from Shanghai said that she worked as a live-in nanny for a female attorney who had a newborn baby so that her husband could finish graduate school. She stayed with the same employer for more than two years because housing was provided for both her and her husband.[34]

Liying, now a factory operator in San Jose, was a housemaid for several years in Lafayette, California. After her husband died of liver cancer it became especially important for her to provide a safe home for herself and her school-age daughter: "I took that job out of concern for my daughter. There was no other way I could possibly have afforded housing in a nice neighborhood like that. My late husband probably would not have approved of my working as a maid, but I think he would be happy to know that we were living in a safe place and that our daughter went to a good school."[35] It must be pointed out that although she lived under the roof of a mansion owned by her employers, Liying's living standard and lifestyle were anything but middle class. Neither she nor her daughter was allowed to spend leisure time outside their living quarters in the basement, which consisted of a bedroom with a bath and the adjacent laundry area, where they cooked meals with an electric hot plate and a microwave oven. Although their living conditions were still better than that of most of the laborers cramped in inner-city Chinatown areas, residing in an upscale neighborhood was by no means an indication of their wealth. On the contrary, it is the level of their poverty that prevents laborers like Liying from paying rent in the city, and pushes them to seek alternatives in the suburbs.

WORKING AND POVERTY

Newcomers who have no personal connections often find jobs in restaurants, garment shops, construction, and domestic service in the ethnic economy through network services. Forgoing the eye-catching bilingual or multilingual signs popular with banks, restaurants, markets, beauty salons, hotels, and other businesses in ethnic business clusters,

Chinese employment services advertise mainly in Chinese, and they work closely with immigrant laborers who have no access to the mainstream job market.

Those who cannot afford to be choosy have to start at the bottom, and sometimes in remote areas. When Tommy Tang first arrived in 1996, he visited an employment office in Los Angeles and was sent to work in a restaurant in Indiana. He recalled:

> It took me only one trip to the employment office to find my first job. The agent said that I arrived at the right moment, for some restaurant in Indiana was looking for a guy to wash dishes for $1,000 a month. Five or six people were hanging around in the office at the time; everyone seemed to be surprised: "Wow! Washing dishes for $1,000 dollars! What a deal!" The agent handed me the phone and I talked to the restaurant owner. He told me that I could make an additional $100 if I was willing to clean the bathrooms. The people in the office again showed their surprising faces. They said bathrooms in Chinese restaurants are tiny so the cleaning job ought be easy. I couldn't figure out why I was so lucky and wondered why those who seemed to envy me didn't jump at the opportunity ahead of me. It took me years to understand that only a person fresh off the boat would accept a job thousands of miles away.[36]

It turned out that Tommy was sent to a huge buffet restaurant: "I had never seen that many dishes in my life. My hands are fast, but no matter how quickly I put them away, there were always more to come. The bathrooms were big too, and I had to clean them several times a day for about $3."

But Tommy was able to move up, one step at a time.[37] As sociologist Min Zhou argues, the new ethnic enclave not only provides opportunities for newcomers to find work and get started but it also allows them to learn entrepreneurial skills from employers of a similar ethos. In that sense, Tommy's first job was his first step toward social mobility.[38] Twenty-five years old at the time, Tommy was healthy, strong, and hard working. He later was promoted to busing the tables and performing other tasks. It was in that restaurant that Tommy began his education in running a small business. When he returned to Los Angeles three years later, he waited tables and learned to cook. He also made a short trip to China and returned with an immigrant visa, because by then his mother, who had remarried to a U.S. citizen, was eligible to sponsor him. Six years after he first arrived in the United States, at age thirty-one, Tommy and two friends bought a fast-food Chinese restaurant. And after he got married, he and his wife bought all shares from the other partners and operated their own business. He and his wife worked long hours to make ends meet and hired two part-time employees. "Look at the scars on my hands," he said, rolling up his sleeves. "Look here, and at the burns here! That's nothing in our trade. When I cut myself, all needed was a paper towel to stop the bleeding and I would go right back to work."[39]

About a quarter million Chinese immigrants find jobs at fifty thousand Chinese restaurants scattered throughout the United States. A newcomer often starts as a dishwasher or simply a *dazade* (a worker who does everything). If promoted, he might move up to wait tables, which is considered skilled work. A dishwasher can receive $1,000 a month working seven days a week, while a dazade might make as much as $1,500. The income of a waiter/waitress is usually higher; when business is good the person might get $100 in tips in a single evening. "I would not say that I liked the work," said one former waitress, "but counting tips in the evenings made me happy. I worked hard every day for that moment."[40]

For some individuals, passing the initial test was difficult. Lao Wu, who came to the United States at age forty, for example, found it hard to adjust from being a factory worker in China to a restaurant worker in America. He said that he didn't mind hard work, but having someone always looking over his shoulder made him nervous: "Just as I finished mopping the floor—before putting away the mop—I could tell she [the boss] was right there to tell me to do something else. She would yell at me for the smallest mistake I made—like not picking up a tiny piece of paper on the floor or breaking a glass. And I was told constantly to speed up. In the factory, I operated the machines. In the restaurant, I was the machine."[41] Eventually he got fed up and switched to construction.

Most construction workers have worked in restaurants before. In construction, they also have to start at the bottom, as day laborers. In New York, the San Francisco Bay Area, and Los Angeles, the day laborers gather on a particular street of ethnic business clusters in the mornings, waiting for those who would employ them for the day. In Flushing, New York, one man from northern China said that he could not make it in a restaurant because most of the businesses in the city were operated by Fuzhou people who spoke a different dialect. Standing against a wall with a group of guys, his eyes fixed on the far end of the street, he was hoping the next approaching car would bring him a chance to work.[42]

Standing next to this man was Xiao Liu, a young man wearing glasses and a baseball cap and carrying a backpack. Inside the backpack he said were gloves, masks, and first-aid gear. "I asked for gloves one day and the contractor looked at me as though I came from a different planet. Can you imagine they don't provide gloves for this type of work? These guys [his fellow day-laborers] do not care about their own lives any more, but I'm still in my twenties and I don't want to ruin my health. If I don't provide myself with some kind of protection, who will? Have you heard about the guy who was killed by a falling wall? No one even knows his name! That's extremely scary!" The subject brought silence to the group. Everyone looked away as if they had heard nothing. Asked what he had done for a living before coming to the United States, however, Xiao Liu dropped his head and paused. Pacing back and forth on the sidewalk, he became somewhat emotional:

> I won't tell you what I did for living back in Shenyang [a city in northern China]. Why should anyone even ask? All I can tell you is that nothing I had done in the past was anywhere near what I am doing now, not a bit! I wielded a pen—you know what I mean? I made a living using my pen! How did I end up here on the streets of New York like this? Of course I was frustrated with my job. I needed to do research, but they didn't give me money to travel to Beijing. I thought I was treated unfairly. I was fed up and jumped at an opportunity to come here.[43]

In the United States, Xiao Liu started in a restaurant and worked there for three months. One night after work he helped his boss clean and close up. "Just as I was about to say goodbye," he recalled, "he [the boss] told me that I didn't need to come back the next day. He said it in a low voice in such a casual way, as if he was telling me where I should go for dinner. It really hurt!" Since then, Xiao Liu has been a day laborer. The job was hardly better, he said, but at least he was no longer worried about getting fired.[44]

Being a day laborer means looking for work constantly, almost on a daily basis. On the street these workers gather in small groups of five to ten people. They share information about housing, and they talk about how much they were paid for their previous tasks. In the years of the housing market boom, these day laborers were in high demand by building contractors and homeowners with various building or remodeling projects. On a good day a lucky worker could pocket $120 in cash after ten to twelve hours of work; and most thought they should not accept anything less than $100 a day. One late morning in August 2005, a middle-aged building contractor stopped at Prince Street near Roosevelt Avenue in Flushing where about twenty-five men were still waiting. Two of them stood up immediately to greet him. "Master Wang (Wang *shifu*), what's up?" one of them asked hopefully. Wang said that he was looking for someone to demolish the interior of an old house and help install new drywall. The man who first approached him nodded and left with him. The other man lit a cigarette and sat down. Within minutes the guy who went with the building contractor returned to the group. "How come?" someone asked. The man shook his head: "$90 a day. Not me. I am ready to take the day off!" Master Wang showed up again. He borrowed a cigarette from someone to light up his own. He didn't say a word, as if nothing had happened. A tall man who was sitting on the curb rose slowly and nodded at Wang, and the two left together. No one commented. It was after 9:00 am; obviously some of the workers would not be able to find work for the day.[45]

Asked whether it was difficult to find work, Guang Wu, who was in construction for more than two years, said that it had to do with supply and demand. Whenever there was a surplus of labor, it was difficult to bargain for higher wages. "If you insist on getting paid no less than $100 a day, some days you just can't get hired. If you don't mind getting as little as $60, there will be plenty of work."[46] "Every day I come here telling myself I will not work for less than $100 a day," said Xiao Liu. "But after sitting around for two or three days, you look at things differently. That's the way it is."[47]

Construction work is dominated by men, while garment shop and domestic service work fall on the shoulders of women. Due to international trade agreements and the increasing domestic pressure to improve working conditions in garment factories, the number of Chinese-operated factories has declined significantly since the late 1980s.[48] Some of the small garment shops, however, still operate outside government or union regulations. Chinese novelist Bing Ren, who came to Los Angeles to research the lives of Chinese immigrants, found that women who remain in the trade work in conditions much worse than those in garment factories in China.[49] At the same time, the demand for domestic service has increased significantly since the late 1990s, and employment agencies offer middle-class employers a variety of choices. One can request a house maid who cooks a particular type of regional food, a nanny who speaks a particular Chinese dialect, or a care provider who comes from a particular region of China, Hong Kong, Taiwan, Indonesia, or the Philippines.

When Yamei first arrived in Los Angeles, an employment agent tried to talk to her into taking a domestic job after learning that she was alone, and she was told that people from Shanghai were not considered desirable for restaurant work because they had a reputation for being too clever to follow orders. Yamei hesitated, but she gave in after waiting for two weeks without work. She was called in to meet a prospective employer, a middle-aged man looking for a maid to work in his house. Yamei followed him to his house in a hilly neighborhood overlooking city streets. Her main duty was to take care of the man's eighty-two-year-old father, who was terminally ill. Yamei was expected to feed, bathe, and dress him and administer his medicines. The elderly man's legally blind wife needed assistance as well. Yamei's responsibilities would include cooking and cleaning for the household. She would be paid $1000 a month, plus free room and board. Yamei needed to work desperately, but she did not take the job. More troubling than the heavy work load was realizing how vulnerable she would be in that type of working environment. "What could I do if this man [the middle-aged employer] tried to take advantage of me? If something happened to me, no one would ever find out. My husband would not be happy if he knew that I was living in the same house with a single man like that."[50] To Yamei, safety was the main concern, since she had no family or friends. Her fake travel documents not only made her ineligible to work but they also prevented her from seeking assistance from law enforcement agencies.

The only protection available to her would be offered by the ethnic community. For that reason, she wanted to work in a restaurant where other workers would be around.

The demand for domestic servants is so high that employment agencies have to push female job seekers to take such positions. One agent in New York said that she talked many women into these jobs: "People are careful about whom they will hire to work in their houses; they like women who are neat, capable, honest, educated, and have no family around. I have good eyes for these women. Some of them were former teachers, office clerks, or nurses back in China. I understand it is hard for them to think of themselves as servants. But when they are new to this country they often have few other choices."[51]

Some domestic care providers chose the work because the people they take care of depend on them. A woman in her late thirties said that her employers were usually kind to her because they wanted her to take good care of their children: "When the lady of the house is away at work, I am the one in charge. As long as I take good care of the small children, I can do whatever I want."[52] Lanlan, a yuezi gong, felt her job was important to her employers: "When the lady came back from the hospital, she was tired and her body was weak, and she needed me around to help her and take care of the baby. I gave her advice on how to take care of the baby, and both she and her husband respected my suggestions. Even the visitors are nice to me."[53] Yuanmin, who has taken care of an elderly woman in Los Angeles for more than four years, said that she did not look for other jobs because the woman's children wouldn't know what to do if she quit. "They are all busy with their work and families," she said. "They basically begged me to stay. The old lady's hands and legs do not work well. She needs help with cooking and washing and she cannot go out by herself. When I told the lady that my son was coming [from China], her daughter-in-law immediately said that he could stay in the house too. I can't say 'no' to them; they knew they wouldn't be able to keep me otherwise."[54]

But others have had different experiences. Some women said they had to swallow their pride and often endured insults, which is not always easy to do. Liying, for example, said that after each grocery shopping trip, her employer would go over every item on the receipt before paying her back. "She never trusted me. She always acted as if I would steal," she said.[55] Another domestic worker, who was a former government official in China, said that her mistress, whose husband owns a car dealership in Los Angeles, was simply rude. "Let me give you an example. Once she was angry at me because I gave her seven-year-old son orange juice before dinner. I explained that the child asked for it, but she snapped, 'Would you give him shit if he asked for it?' You see, this is someone who has not had a good upbringing. No one ever talked to me like that."[56]

POVERTY AND MOBILITY

Most immigrant laborers try hard to make as much money as possible and save more whenever they can, but moving up is easier said than done. For people who live in poverty, there seem to be many obstacles that prevent them from improving their economic status, and wages in the informal sector of the ethnic economy have not increased much in the past two decades. Betty, a domestic worker, blamed new immigrants, especially undocumented immigrants, for bringing down wages: "There are too many of them, which makes it impossible to bargain."[57] As domestics, the workers are never paid by the hour. Betty's day starts at 6:30 in the morning, when she gets up to cook breakfast and pack lunch for her employers. She takes care of two preschoolers during the day, in addition to cleaning the house and cooking meals. Her chores will not be finished until after 8:30 in the evening. In 2007 she received a flat payment of $1,800 a month, which was considered very good for a domestic worker within the Chinese American community at that time. Counting the hours that she puts into the work, her pay was much lower than the minimum wage. "I can take a break when the family goes to visit friends over the weekend. Families take vacations too, but in that case they usually send the nannies home and find a replacement when they return."[58]

Within the ethnic economy, wages increase at a very slow rate. One factory operator in Houston said that she gets an hourly wage increase of twenty-five cents each year.[59] It is common for restaurant workers to be paid below the minimum wage because their employers are counting the tips. Undocumented workers have to accept less than those with work permits, "Not that I don't know there is such a thing as minimum wage," said one of them. "Giving me a job is a huge deal because there is a risk on his [the boss's] side. Whether I am happy about what I am getting is irrelevant. I am sensible enough to not bring this up."[60]

Even though they tried hard to spend as little as possible on rent, food, and other necessities, saving money seems almost impossible for many immigrant workers because of unexpected expenses. Lao Wu and Fei, for example, thought they could be debt free after working for two years in America, but because of Fei's pregnancy and the birth of their son, they had accumulated even more debt by that time. In addition to their low income, unemployment and illness (most of those working within the ethnic economy do not have health insurance) are major obstacles when it comes to making ends meet. Many newly arrived undocumented immigrants are deeply in debt because the cost of purchasing travel documents has gone up significantly in the past few years. Meanwhile, the higher cost of living in the United States has made it even more difficult for these individuals to advance. Therefore the undocumented immigrants are most likely to remain at the bottom of the social ladder.

Laborers receive very little protection, not only from their jobs but also from the services they get from the ethnic economy. To use the services of an employment agency, a laborer is subject to a fee of 10 percent of his or her estimated first-month's wage, which is due before the person starts the job. If the worker gets fired any time during the month, he or she is not entitled to a refund from the employment agency. In early 2000, as more and more undocumented immigrants were looking for jobs, and job security become a serious for many, some employment services began to charge a piece rate of $45 for each job recommendation. Although the fee was lower, many noticed that some agents were no longer finding long-term jobs for them. Sometimes the workers were sent to jobs that lasted only a couple of days, putting them in a more tenuous situation. According to one news report, on June 20, 2004, the Singapore Employment Service in New York's Chinatown referred a woman named Gao Xiaoqing to a restaurant job in Alabama. Gao, who had just arrived in the United States, accepted the job and agreed to leave for the South that afternoon. Within ten minutes of her taking the offer and paying the $45 fee, the restaurant owner called back to say she was no longer needed. However, the employment agent refused to give her a refund, arguing that she had already entered into a contract. Several people who witnessed the situation had had similar experiences and expressed sympathy for Gao.[61]

The lack of security and protection causes tremendous stress and frustration in the laborers, who often have no place to go to file their grievances. In early 2002, a young man named Zhao Yongding was sent by an employment agent in New York to work at the Lucky Wok restaurant in Florida. He moved to Florida at his own expense, but the owner, upon learning that Zhao did not possess a work permit, told him he would be paid $200 less each month. The two got into an argument and the owner's wife, who was from Malaysia, called the police and immigration authorities. According to a report in a Chinese language newspaper, the immigration officer was sympathetic to Zhao and sent him back to New York. There Zhao learned from his lawyer that he had little chance of winning his asylum appeal. With $40,000 of debt and no way to get out, Zhao jumped in front of a fast-moving subway train.[62]

Although legal status is crucial to social mobility, attempts to change status can be difficult, expensive, or even dangerous. A lucky asylum petitioner might win a case within a few months for as little as $5,500. But should the petitioner's credibility become an issue of concern at any stage of the process, he or she can be arrested and deported. Some asylum cases are pending for many years, even over a decade at times. After failing two interviews, a twenty-five-year-old asylum seeker named Peter had no confidence of winning his final appeal. He said his attorney made a strong case, claiming he was a victim of religious persecution in China, but Peter performed poorly during the hearings because he was uneasy about the situation: "How could I not fail? I couldn't find the courage to make eye contact with the official when I was lying. He [the official] could see it, and the judge was no fool either." Peter appealed again, but only to avoid immediate deportation; he can work legally as long as his case is pending, and he wants to save enough to return to China. Even though he holds two jobs and works almost eighty hours a week, saving money is extremely hard because he has to pay high legal fees.[63] Widespread rumors about police arrests outside immigration courts have also stirred up so much fear that some individuals simply cannot gather enough courage to go to the hearings, which means they have completely given up hope of gaining legal status.[64]

Some individuals also question the morality of filing for political asylum, which requires them to denounce the Chinese government by portraying themselves as victims of various persecutions. Restaurant manager David said he would rather go back to China than make false accusations against his homeland. First arriving as a short-term worker from Sichuan province in China in 1991, David and the majority of his group did not return after their contracts expired. In Los Angles he progressed from dishwasher to waiter and then to a managerial position in a big Chinese restaurant. He could save more than $1000 a month because the restaurant owner provides free housing and food, but instead he lets a large part of his hard-earned money disappear during his monthly trips to Las Vegas. He now has a girlfriend and wants to settle in the United States permanently, but seeking asylum is still out of the question. He said: "I am staying here for personal reasons. I had no home to go back to at the time [his contract expired] because my wife and I were divorced. I am not a political person; the truth is that China had done me no harm. To make false accusations against the country would be against my nature and my religion. I am a big man, I can't do that."[65] The company that hired David when he first arrived is willing to help him out by putting his name back on the company's payroll, but the lawyer, who charged him $6,000 in fees, did not manage the case properly. David eventually switched to another lawyer and paid additional fees, and he is still waiting anxiously to find out how his fate will be determined.[66]

Successful asylum seekers are not always proud of what they have been able to accomplish. Those who are open enough to share their stories often say they simply followed the advice of their lawyers and did what needed to be done to win their cases, which is crucial to their survival in America. The asylum program was established to give aliens who are "refugees," as defined by law, permanent resident status. Those that build a case for refugee status try to show that they have suffered from persecution or fear persecution if returned to their native country. What is regarded as grounds for granting asylum is discretionary; the criteria, which change from time to time, are determined by the attorney general of the United States through asylum officers and immigration judges. This means that it is not enough for someone to simply convince the government that he or she is unwilling to return to his or her home country due to prior ill-treatment or a well-founded fear of future persecution; to win a case the petitioner's claim has to fall into a category for which asylum would be granted. Assistance from those who know the process is crucial under the circumstances, and legal service advertisements in Chinese-language newspapers and other sources keep their potential clients informed of what works and what does not, depending on policies and practices of the government. In the early 1990s it was relatively easy for individuals to obtain asylum based on claims against China's one-child birth-control policy. Many petitions were rejected by the courts in the late 1990s, however, as the U.S. government realized that pursuing such a policy would make an entire generation of Chinese from the PRC eligible for asylum. Legal experts have since explored new avenues for their clients within the framework of the legal system, and many petitioners file their claims accordingly.[67]

As discussed in chapter 1, the dubious actions of individual petitioners are often taken because of some of the problems with the asylum program. For example, Yamei, who claimed religious persecution, would have felt more comfortable claiming that she was a victim of China's one-child birth-control policy, but had she done so, her petition might have been denied. For that reason she felt fortunate that she had followed her lawyer's advice. Some immigrants feel there is nothing wrong with using the asylum provision to gain legal status, even though they have made false claims. One asylum seeker told a news reporter that using the efficacious petition, instead of the accurate one, showed the person's wisdom (*zhihui*) and knowledge of the United States. Huang Keqiang, the president of the Lin Zexu Foundation in New York, sharply criticizes American immigration policies. He points out that the system itself is to blame: "All one has to do is to make up a false but touching story. Even if the immigration officer knows it is a lie, asylum may still be granted, while honest people are often treated in the opposite way."[68]

To get legal status through a false marriage, an alien, documented or undocumented, has to pay a standard fee of $30,000, half of which goes to the citizen partner as soon as the marriage certificate is issued; the remaining is due when the alien partner gets a permanent resident status, which requires the couple to stay married for at least three years. Should the citizen partner decide not to fulfill his or her obligation, which happens often, the other partner would lose the money and probably face deportation. In recent years immigration authorities have tightened their control over such cases. A marriage involving an alien and a citizen is subject to investigation, and the couple would be asked to present joint bank accounts and photos, as well as evidence indicating that they are indeed living together. Investigators sometimes also check each partner's associations outside the marriage to see whether any of them continue to have bank accounts with others who might be their actual girlfriend or boyfriend, or whether anyone is still listed as single in their Facebook profiles, or whether the citizen partner has received money from the alien partner. If a marriage is found to be fraudulent, the alien partner might be arrested when the couple go for the scheduled interview, but the citizen partner can still keep the money.[69]

In most cases, the struggle to escape poverty does not end with gaining legal status. Many years of working within the ethnic economy have hindered such individuals from entering the mainstream job market. Jenny Yi, who came from Shanghai in 1988 at the age of nineteen, has never found the time to go to school because she works such long hours. As a motel clerk in New York, she makes $8 an hour and receives no benefits. Although the motel serves free continental breakfasts, the employees are not allowed to eat it. She spends about half of her income to rent a room in a three-bedroom apartment and another quarter of it to pay a Christian therapist after breaking up with a boyfriend of five years. But Jenny does not think of herself as being at the bottom of society. The fact that she has legal status (gained under the 1992 Chinese Students Protection Act) makes her feel good. She emphasized the fact that she did not share a room with anyone—a luxury not many laborers in New York can afford. The decision to see a therapist also makes her feel special; in a way she is spending money like middle-class Americans. Although Jenny does not think she will become rich, she said she was not too concerned about saving money because as a U.S. citizen she would be entitled to social security and medical benefits in the future.[70]

Like many immigrant laborers, Jenny finds consolation in religion. She considers the church she joined when she first came to New York as the only home she has in the United States. Every Friday evening she shares her own thoughts with God and her Bible study group, where she hangs out with several laborers, half of them undocumented. She believes strongly that God created her for a reason and put her where she is for a purpose. The greatest thing about having a Christian faith, she and her Bible study classmates said, was to have the power not to think much about what they could or couldn't acquire, for material possession is a very small aspect of one's life: "I gave myself to God; God will take care of me."[71]

Of those immigrant laborers do gain social mobility, most climb up slowly within the ethnic economy and remain in the trades where they started on the bottom rung. A day laborer may become a self-employed skilled worker, a garment shop worker may become a subcontractor, and a restaurant worker may attain mobility by purchasing a business of his own. More often, however, small business owners who rise from their position as manual laborers cannot make ends meet without utilizing the unpaid labor of family members. Although the children of these immigrants have more opportunities to advance into the mainstream job market through education, because many of them grew up working in their family's own business, they too remain disproportionately concentrated in the occupations of their parents.

POVERTY WITHIN AN
ETHNIC SOCIAL HIERARCHY

The large impoverished immigrant population within Chinese America has become a solid foundation upon which the ethnic social hierarchy is built. To some extent this factor offers some not-often-mentioned answers to a frequently asked question: Why are the Chinese in America able to advance so rapidly? The economy and the supporting networks are built to benefit middle-class entrepreneurs and employers. With the assistance of ethnic networks, Chinese business owners and middle-class families throughout the United States are given easy access to immigrant laborers and immigrant clients, allowing them risk-free opportunities to maximize business profits and improve the quality of their lives.

The operation of employment agencies offers a good example of how the ethnic networks serve clients of different classes simultaneously. The laborers have to pay fees to get the service that is provided to their potential employers free of charge. Even though the income of the employment service comes entirely from the job seekers, the agents are completely oriented toward supplying what the employers are looking for. Acknowledging that her fee was determined by the wage scale of her labor clients, one agent specializing in domestic service in New York said that the success of her business depended on the employers' satisfaction rather than that of the nannies, because the former were the ones who provided the jobs. For that reason she often finds herself trying to persuade immigrant women to accept low wages. "Most employers come to us because we give them cheap labor, although most would say that they are looking for someone who could cook Chinese food or speak a certain dialect," she said. "We would have no business if our workers asked for what American domestics are getting. I will tell a client the going rate for a certain type of work and let them know higher pay is expected if the nanny doesn't get weekends off, but I do have to be flexible because if I'm not, they can go to other agents. Not many people can afford full-time domestics these days."[72]

Although a hire is not completed until the two parties reach an agreement through an employment agent, the employers are not obliged to keep their promises. The agent will ask only the employee to sign a piece of paper stating that the fee is not refundable, while the employer does not have to sign anything. It is common for the laborers to find out after they start work that they have to do more than they agreed. When the employers find excuses to reduce their wages, there is little room for the laborers to negotiate. Asked whether he worried about workers quitting their jobs, one restaurant owner said this happened all the time, and he was only concerned when replacements were hard to find. However, he did say that the problems could not be solved by increasing workers' wages: "We keep the business going by offering quality food at a low price. More money paid to the workers means we have to raise prices, which would drive the customers away." In any case, he does not worry about not being able to find enough people to work at low wages: "If not enough Chinese are willing to work for us, I can go for Mexican laborers."[73]

To business owners or middle-class families, the employment services are simply magic. One restaurant owner said she always got what she wanted. Once when she was looking for a waiter and called in advance, she arrived to find five guys waiting to be interviewed. During another trip to Los Angeles for a medical appointment, she and her husband stopped by an employment office to see if they could find a good chef.

The agent asked them to wait, and two candidates came in within twenty minutes.[74] Jennifer, an accountant who was confined to her bed for two years due to an illness, recalled a similar experience. "All I wanted at the time was someone who could help with household chores and administer shots, but the agent asked a number of questions: 'Do you want a Mandarin speaker or a Cantonese speaker? What type of cuisine do you prefer? Do you mind if the person is young?' They are very thoughtful. My husband went to the office over the weekend and returned with Xiuhua. She was only twenty-eight years old, and a nurse back in China."[75]

Paying only a fraction of what their non-Chinese compatriots would have to pay, middle-class Chinese Americans can enjoy a lifestyle that not many Americans in a similar financial situation can afford. For $1,000 a month, Jennifer had her own nurse who gave her shots, baths, medicine, and massages, on top of doing daily chores such as cooking, cleaning, and laundry.[76] Paying her only $600 a month because her daughter also needed to live in the house, Liying's former employers gained a lot of leisure time and used their residence for parties and gatherings. When the husband was away at work, the lady of the house would spend most of her time taking care of her own skin, exercising, shopping, and socializing with friends. She hosted mahjongg games at home twice a week, and the guests were served tea and hors d'oeuvres during the break, along with dinner after the game. Bigger parties were held on weekends, and Liying was responsible for all the cooking and cleaning. When the family had house guests, Liying baby-sat young children and did everyone's laundry in addition to her regular duties. Sometimes she would be asked to wash the guests' cars. She was never paid extra for doing extra work (she was hired to take care of a two-person household) and was told not to accept tips from the guests. "They would have to pay thousands of dollars to get what I did for them if they got a non-Chinese service provider. But what can I say? All I heard before we moved out was that they found a Chinese nurse to replace me; that the woman could give the lady massages on top of all the tasks that I performed. There are too many desperate people looking for jobs and housing. I was not surprised by what they could find."[77]

Business owners often take advantage of the fact that some of their immigrant laborers are well educated and have various skills. Few well-educated individuals would work as menial laborers or domestics, but downward mobility is a common experience shared by many Chinese immigrants. One waitress who has a science degree from a college in China said that her boss often took her home to tutor his teenage son: "I overheard that he used to pay $20 an hour for tutoring, but now he gets away with paying me only $8."[78] Timmy, an artist, was often asked by his boss to teach painting to her and her children. "She told everyone she did not have the heart to watch me use my hands to do the dishes. She asked me to teach them drawing once or twice a week, as if it was a favor to me, but she paid me a dishwasher's wages."[79]

Dealing with clients who have no permanent residences or stable income, ethnic businesses often require payment in cash before the service is provided. A simple asylum petition case, for example, is paid in three installments. The lawyer will not start to work on a case until he receives the first payment. Once the case is prepared, the second payment is due. The third payment is due when a hearing is scheduled. The outcomes of these cases have a huge impact on the future lives of the petitioners, but the lawyers are paid regardless of the results. In the late 1990s and early 2000s, asylum petitions—a very small portion of the legal services immigration lawyers provide—generated about one hundred million dollars each year, attracting more and more legal professionals to work for their coethnic clients.

This is the case in just about every sector of the ethnic economy that involves the participation of both immigrant laborers and middle-class Chinese Americans. As long as a substantially large number of Chinese immigrants remain at the bottom of the ethnic economy, middle-class Chinese Americans are going to have a much higher quality of life than their compatriots of other racial or ethnic backgrounds. They can maximize their profit margin by utilizing low-cost immigrant labor; they can benefit from offering services to these laborers; and they can enjoy affordable goods at the market and gain access to child care and other domestic service at a cost way below the market value. The end result is the image of Chinese Americans as a "model minority" group, yet the countless individuals who make this possible are all but invisible.

To outside observers, the Chinese are doing well and manage to get ahead by sticking together. The growing number of ethnic banks, shopping centers, supermarkets, eateries, real estate agencies, accounting offices, law firms, and other businesses in American metropolitan areas as well as nearby suburbs show the vigor of the Chinese ethnic economy; their ability to attract laborers, entrepreneurs, and consumers of various socioeconomic backgrounds is more than impressive. Although one can hardly deny the fact that the ethnic economy is mutually beneficial to all parities involved, and that many immigrant newcomers simply cannot survive without the assistance of their ethnic networks, equal opportunities for all participants have yet to be developed. This is not to blame the Chinese American middle class; most Chinese American business owners, employers of domestics, and professional service providers are ordinary Americans who work hard to improve the quality of their own lives and get ahead. If many middle-class Chinese Americans indeed have done well for themselves, their success also contributes to the economy of the United States. But certain aspects of the ethnic economy, upon which the ethnic social hierarchy is built, have also worked to perpetuate poverty and widen the gap between rich and poor. As Chinese Americans continue their struggles for equality and civil rights in the United States in the twenty-first century, a critical examination and reevaluation of economic activities and social relations within their own community is urgently needed.

Conclusion

INCLUSION OR EXCLUSION?

NOVEMBER 2008 WAS UNUSUALLY COLD. New York was hit by a heavy snowstorm, adding extra chill to the economic downturn. The nation's job market suffered the largest one-month drop since 1974 with the loss of a staggering 530,000 positions.[1] A recession, which had started in the prior year, would soon be declared by the National Bureau of Economic Research. The national economic crisis, however, did not seem to have had a direct impact on the influx of undocumented Chinese immigrants. At least one thousand newcomers arrived in Manhattan's Chinatown before Thanksgiving, forming large crowds in front of employment agencies on East Broadway Avenue. According to reports from Chinese-language newspapers, many recent undocumented newcomers first traveled from southern China to South America. From there they were sent to Mexico or Canada through underground channels before crossing U.S. borders.[2] During the Thanksgiving weekend, the U.S. border patrol officers intercepted a beer truck and a Dodge van in Sasabe, Arizona, near the Mexican border and arrested fourteen Chinese on board along with several Mexicans.[3] Those who crossed successfully, escaping border inspection, often went straight to ethnic business centers in New York and California in search of jobs.

The timing of their arrival, says one news report, caused grave concerns for the Chinese American community. The unemployment rate among Chinese Americans was on the rise, and some restaurants and firms in remote areas were expected to go out of business. Some thought the presence of large numbers of undocumented workers could worsen the situation and drive down wages.[4] More worrisome was the potential damage to the image of the community. As the federal government linked border control efforts to national security, some were afraid of unwanted attention.

Such concerns surface when Chinese border crossers intercepted by government authorities make the mainstream news. It is no secret that undocumented immigrants are everywhere, but few in the Chinese American community like to discuss the issue in public. In the spring of 2006, the immigration issue took the center stage of American national politics as hundreds of thousands of undocumented immigrants and their supporters participated in organized mass rallies and protests, but representatives of the Chinese American community were largely absent.

The silence of Chinese Americans on immigration reveals the considerable ambivalence within the community. The public outcry for more restrictive policies brought back bitter memories of a time when all Chinese laborers were denied legal entry to the United States. Some observers noted that the arguments against immigration presented at the congressional debate in 2005 were reminiscent of those made 129 years before, at a special joint congressional committee investigating Chinese immigration in San Francisco.[5] Details of the 1876 committee hearing are published in a huge volume of congressional records that exhibit the era's strong anti-Chinese sentiments; the hearings laid the ideological foundation for the enactment of the Chinese Exclusion Act of 1882.[6] Though much of the current debate over immigration appears to be focused around costs and benefits, racial sentiments have come out in the open from time to time. There are concerns about the fast-growing Hispanic and Asian populations, as some believe that the rise of new minority groups will deplete already limited resources for existing minority groups.[7] Fears that American culture is fragmenting beyond repair and that American national identity is being challenged are also rooted in race.

The issue of undocumented immigrants is particularly delicate for Chinese Americans because of the pervasive negative image of the smuggled Chinese. As the public is preoccupied with tragedies of human trafficking and sensational stories of exploitation, academic researchers have also tended to confirm such fears by using language that treats unauthorized immigrants as criminals and portraying their existence as totally undesirable. One study, for example, reached back to the misleading language of nineteenth-century anti-Chinese immigration

debates and used "coolie system" to describe the ways that Fuzhounese
from the Chinese mainland were smuggled to the United States in the
1990s. Arguing that illegal border crossing is closely connected to kid-
napping, enslavement, and even murder, the study calls for laws to halt the
"indentured migrant labor trafficking" and advocates efforts to investigate,
arrest, and prosecute "suspected human smugglers."[8] More daunting is the
attempt of a few scholars to link illegal entrants to the historical networks
established by the Chinese immigrant community to circumvent exclusion
laws.[9] Some scholars suggest that the only way for the government to
effectively terminate the inflow of unauthorized Chinese immigrants is
to seek cooperation from a few illegal entrants: in exchange for amnesty,
these individuals would have to provide law enforcement officers with
details of the smuggling process, names of the smugglers, and serve as
witnesses.[10] Such tactics are similar to those of the Chinese Confession
Program during the Cold War era.[11]

But those who are familiar with the Chinese American community
know that accounts of smuggled Chinese have been sensationalized and
exaggerated, and that most of them hardly apply to the general undocumented Chinese population. Although the involvement of gangs and
criminal activities has been apparent in some cases, there is little evidence
to suggest a connection between undocumented immigrants and forced
labor.[12] Many Chinese living in this country without legal status are
not conscious lawbreakers either, especially those who gained entry as
temporary visitors. The line between documented and undocumented
immigrants can also be ambiguous because some undocumented individuals are family members of permanent residents or citizens. Moreover,
some currently legal immigrants were undocumented not too long ago,
and others have not yet adjusted their status only because of "errors and
delays by immigration bureaucrats."[13]

Sentiments toward undocumented immigrants are mixed within the
ethnic community. A woman who volunteered her time in a Chinese-
language school on Saturdays seemed to be primarily concerned about
public image: "They [the smuggled immigrants] have created a bad
impression not only for China but also for all of us in the United
States."[14] In neighborhoods where family motels operate, residents
expressed their frustrations and blamed the undocumented immigrants
for the problem.[15] Even the undocumented do not necessarily want

more company, for fewer people also mean less competition. As one said, "Too many newcomers. We are fighting for each other's rice bowls."[16] However, acknowledging that low-cost labor is crucial for their businesses, some entrepreneurs worried about not being able to find affordable employees. "I can't raise prices or my customers would walk away," said one restaurant owner. "What else can I do to keep the business going?"[17] Economic benefits aside, many who have hired or worked with undocumented laborers find it very hard to see these immigrants as criminals. "These are good kids," said one business owner who claimed to be a friend of several young workers in a neighborhood restaurant. "These are honest, hardworking, and respectful human beings. They could have had a lot going for them if legal status was not the issue. My heart goes out to them."[18]

The legal criminalization of unauthorized immigrants, however, has pressured many to keep a distance from them in public. Even immigrant advocates sometimes find it unwise to include the undocumented in their pursuit of social justice because the very existence of these "illegals" contradicts the positive image of Chinese Americans as law-abiding citizens. Since denouncing the undocumented is not easy, it is almost a blessing for the community that many individuals remain hidden. As the Hispanic community takes much of the heat in the national debate, silence seems to be the best option for Chinese Americans. After all, lack of organization among the undocumented means that this group of individuals is less capable of making collective demands, and that they are likely to accept their unrecognized existence.

The Chinese American community has experienced significant changes since the 1960s. The struggles against exclusion and for racial equality that provided the momentum for ethnic solidarity in the past are no longer of primary importance in community life. By publicizing its very best and brightest, the community has improved its own image, which has perpetuated a successful stereotype of the ethnic group as a model minority. It is understandable that some do not want undocumented immigrants to ruin the celebratory mood and hard-earned triumph many share. However, maintaining a silence on the issue of undocumented immigrants is to see some fellow immigrants as "others," which also helps conceal inequality within the community between the more privileged and more disadvantaged groups.

It is ironic that the Chinese American community of the twenty-first century would choose to stay quiet on the issue of immigration, and that some Chinese American scholars would use the legal and illegal dichotomy in their academic endeavors. A look back at history reminds us of a time when the Chinese were legally inadmissible to the United States; even family members of immigrants, including wives of U.S. citizens, were denied entry at America's gate. History also reminds us that during the long and dark six decades of exclusion, at the height of nativist sentiment, the ethnic community utilized all of its resources and mounted legal and legislative campaigns to challenge discriminatory laws. Many of the early immigrants spoke little English, but they were able to see the limitations of the laws. They achieved impressive success largely because the entire community was mobilized, because no opportunity was missed, and because no one was excluded. The community's ability to negotiate with law-enforcement officials and legislators under difficult circumstances marks an important chapter in Chinese American history, one that should not be forgotten too soon.

Today, the majority of Chinese Americans are immigrants. Most immigrants, documented or undocumented, embarked on a long journey to America for similar reasons. Yamei, Lao Wu, Fei, Lily, and hundreds of thousands of other undocumented immigrants came to the United States because they were attracted by the freedom, democracy, and greater opportunities that this country has to offer. Their dreams to build a better future for their children in America are similar to those of the middle-class Chinese American parents who attended college admissions programs in Los Angeles. Today, the nation continues to struggle with the old subject of inclusion or exclusion. As most Chinese Americans can now comfortably claim to be part of the mainstream, we in the community must ask some tough questions: do we really want to set a boundary between "us" and "them" and deny rights to those "illegals," as had been done to all Chinese in the past?[19] Is racial equality and social justice possible without tearing down the wall that separates members of our own ethnic community? Do we, as middle-and upper-class Chinese Americans, have any moral obligations to the laborers who have served us food in restaurants, packed fruit and vegetables in grocery stores, remodeled our homes and mowed our lawns, and taken care of our young children and aged parents so that we could enjoy more leisure and move more swiftly up the social ladder? Is preserving a positive image of the community more important than such obligations?

What direction Chinese immigration will take in the years to come is yet to be seen. A worldwide economic downturn could affect Chinese migration in complicated ways and could pull it in opposite directions. China's declining rate of growth due to falling exports may push more of its unemployed citizens out of the country, and some may try harder to come to the United States. But an economic recession in the United States may reverse the trend, making prospective emigrants wonder whether America still provides better opportunities. The recession will force many companies to go out of business, and ethnic enterprises are not immune to such pressure. The shrinkage of Americans' purchasing power, however, may also mean that consumers have to shop more carefully, making the good bargains offered by ethnic businesses even more attractive and demand for low-cost labor more persistent.[20] In any case, international migration is caused by many factors. Inflow of Chinese immigrants, authorized and unauthorized alike, will probably slow down, but the economic recession will not bring it to an abrupt end. What we have to confront is the reality that undocumented immigrants are far more integrated into the Chinese American community than has been publicly acknowledged, and that to continue to marginalize them is to ignore the history of Chinese immigration in the United States and the historical contributions of the Chinese to American society.

NOTES

1. *Shijie ribao* (World Daily, commonly known in English as *World Journal* or *Chinese Daily News*), April 25, 2008, C10; April 28, 2008, B3.
2. A large number of studies have addressed these issues. The term "ethnoburb" was coined by Wei Li. See Li, "Spatial Transformation of an Urban Ethnic Community" (1997) and "Anatomy of a New Ethnic Settlement" (1998). Also see Shenglin Chang, *The Global Silicon Valley Home* (2006); Wei Li, Gary Dymski, et al., "Chinese-American Banking and Community Development in Los Angeles County" (2002); Jan Lin, *Reconstructing Chinatown* (1998); and Zhou Min, *Meiguo huaren shehui de bianqian* (2006). On suburban China-towns, see Timothy Fong, *The First Suburban Chinatown* (1994); and John Horton, *The Politics of Diversity* (1995).
3. U.S. Census Bureau, Census 2000 Brief, *The Asian Population: 2000* (Washington, D.C.: U.S. Census Bureau, February 2002), 9; Min Zhou, "Once Excluded, Now Ascendant" (2003).
4. The concept of Chinese America has been challenged as many scholars abandoned the term "community" and used "communities" instead. Several scholars have viewed Chinese Americans as a heterogeneous group. Most revealing are the studies focusing on Taiwanese Americans. See, for example, Hsiang-shui Chen, *Chinatown No More* (1992). Peter Kwong and Dušanka Miščević see the differences among Chinese Americans today as "staggering" and argue that one can hardly talk of Chinese America as one community. See Kwong and Miščević, *Chinese America* (2005).
5. Ivan Light and Steven J. Gold think that in place of socialism and inclusive nationalisms, ethnicity has emerged as a prominent and acceptable base of personal identity and collective action. See Light and Gold, *Ethnic Economics* (2000), ix.
6. In his study on Chinese Christianity in the United States, for example, Fenggang Yang finds that the Christian faith of Chinese churchgoers in Washington, D.C., is often built upon traditional Chinese values. See Yang, *Chinese Christians in America* (1999).
7. See, for example, Chiou-Ling Yeh, *Making an American Festival* (2008). Also see Elionne L. W. Belden, *Claiming Chinese Identity* (1997); Shehong Chen, *Being Chinese, Becoming Chinese American* (2002); and Gloria Heyung Chun, *Of Orphans and Warriors* (1998).
8. Some Asian American scholars have framed Asian labor migration in the context of the worldwide expansion of capitalism, but research conducted to support such a theory is limited. See Lucie Cheng and Edna Bonacich, eds., *Labor Migration under Capitalism* (1984). Renqiu Yu's study provides insight into the struggle between Chinese laundrymen and the merchant-

dominated community power structure. See Yu, *To Save China, To Save Ourselves,* (1992).

9. Political scientist Peter Kwong is one of the very few scholars who have explored class relations of contemporary Chinese America. See Kwong, *Forbidden Workers* (1997) and *The New Chinatown* (1986). Also see Kwong and Miščević, *Chinese America* (2005). Also see Ko-lin Chin, *Smuggled Chinese* (1999) and *Chinatown Gangs* (1996).

10. See Nicholas B. Dirks, Geoff Eley, and Sherry B. Ortner, "Introduction," in *Culture/Power/History* (1994); Sherry B. Ortner, "Identities: The Hidden Life of Class" (1998); Joan Scott, "On Language, Gender, and Working-Class History" (1988).

11. This interview was conducted in December 2003.

12. Nathan Glazer, "Concluding Observations," in *Debating Immigration,* edited by Carol M. Swain (2007), 265.

13. Essays in Carol M. Swain's volume provide good references on the current debate about undocumented immigrants. See *Debating Immigration.*

14. Ivan Light, *Deflecting Immigration* (2006), 53.

15. Although the poverty rate of the Asian American population is lower than the national average, it is much higher than that of the non-Hispanic white population. The existence of a large number of undocumented immigrants within Chinese America suggests that the census might have underestimated the poverty rate of Chinese Americans. See chapter 5 for details.

16. Several scholars have shown the economic disadvantages of Chinese workers in ethnic businesses and emphasized the aspect of economic exploitation in the ethnic economy. See Donald Mar, "Chinese Immigrant Women and the Ethnic Labor Market" (1984); Paul Ong, "Chinatown Unemployment and the Ethnic Labor Market" (1984); Jimy Sanders and Victor Nee, "The Limits of Ethnic Solidarity in the Enclave Economy" (1987).

CHAPTER 1   CONTEMPORARY CHINESE AMERICAN POPULATION

1. Interview with the author, February 15, 2004. Two follow-up interviews were conducted on June 2, 2006, and January 30, 2008.

2. Ko-lin Chin, *Smuggled Chinese* (1999); Willard H. Meyers, "Of Qinqing, Qinshu, Guanxi, and *Shetou*" (1997); Peter Kwong, *Forbidden Workers* (1997).

3. Sucheng Chan, "The Exclusion of Chinese Women" (1991); George Anthony Peffer, *If They Don't Bring Their Women Here* (1999); Madeline Y. Hsu, *Dreaming of Gold, Dreaming of Home* (2000); Xiaojian Zhao, *Remaking Chinese America* (2002).

4. John W. Caughey, *Their Majesties the Mob* (1960); Roger Daniels, ed., *Anti-Chinese Violence in North America* (1978); Eugene Hollon, *Frontier Violence,* especially chapter 5; Rose Hum Lee, *The Growth and Decline of Chinese Communities in the Rocky Mountain Region* (1978); Craig Storti, *Incident at Bitter Creek: The Story of the Rock Springs Chinese Massacre* (1991); Priscilla Wegars, ed., *Hidden Heritage* (1993); Marie Rose Wong, *Sweet Cakes, Long Journey* (2004); Liping Zhu, *A Chinaman's Chance* (1997). See also Elmer C. Sandmeyer, *The Anti-Chinese Movement in California* (1973), and Alexander Saxton, *The Indispensable Enemy* (1971).

5. An additional 100 ethnic Chinese were allowed to enter from outside China.

6. 59 Stat. 659, Act of December 28, 1945.
7. Zhao, *Remaking Chinese America*, 78–92.
8. The United States and the PRC had not yet established diplomatic relations in 1965. The Chinese quota was allotted to immigrants from Taiwan. The annual quota for each nation was increased to 25,600 in 1990.
9. INS Act of 1965, Public Law 89–236.
10. See Edward Park and John Park, *Probationary Americans* (2005).
11. Him Mark Lai, "The United States" (1999), 267.
12. U.S. Department of State, *U.S.-Hong Kong Policy Act Report*, April 1, 2005, 8.
13. "Executive Order 12711—Policy Implementation with Respect to Nationals of the People's Republic of China," April 11, 1990 (U.S. President, *Weekly Compilation of Presidential Documents*, 26: 1–26, 558–559).
14. 106 Stat. at large, 1969, October 9, 1992.
15. Him Mark Lai, "The United States," 267.
16. Jeffrey S. Passel and D'Vera Cohn, *Trends in Unauthorized Immigration* (2008), 11.
17. U.S. Immigration and Naturalization Service, Office of Policy and Planning, "Estimates of the Unauthorized Immigrant Population Residing in the United States: 1990 to 2000" (2001), Table B, "Estimated Unauthorized Resident Population, Top 15 Countries: 1990 and 2000," 9.
18. For the rules regarding census collection, see U.S. Census Bureau: *United States: 2000, Summary Population and Housing Characteristics*, Part II (2002), C–1.
19. In a more recent incident, Census Bureau staff helped a Department of Homeland Security enforcement unit access publicly available data on ethnicity by zip code. Some scholars are concerned that such incidents might have a negative impact on participation of foreign-born individuals in census surveys. One report finds that most large-scale surveys do not include sufficient numbers of foreign-born respondents, and undocumented immigrants are less likely to cooperate with census takers. See U. S. Government Accountability Office, *Estimating the Undocumented Population*, 29.
20. See Joanne van der Leun, *Looking for Loopholes* (2003), 31.
21. Ronald Skeldon, *Myths and Realities of Chinese Irregular Migration* (2000), 7.
22. M. J. Miller, "Illegal Migration" (1995), 537.
23. Zai Liang and Wenzhen Ye, "From Fujian to New York" (2001), 205. Several other scholars have made similar arguments. See Kwong, *Forbidden Workers*; Meyers, "Of Qinqing, Qinshu, Guanxi, and *Shetou*"; Ko-lin Chin, *Smuggled Chinese*. A detailed description of a Fujianese smuggling operation ran by Sister Ping is found in Patrick Radden Keefe, "The Snakehead" (2006).
24. Ronald Skeldon offers a comprehensive summary of irregular Chinese immigration; see Skeldon, *Myths and Realities of Chinese Irregular Migration*. Also see Kwong, *Forbidden Workers*, 19–46.
25. Keefe, "The Snakehead," 70.
26. Kwong, *Forbidden Workers*, 2, 6.
27. Chin, *Smuggled Chinese*, 4.
28. See Skeldon, *Myths and Realities of Chinese Irregular Migration*, for example.
29. Interview with the author, August 12, 2005
30. Interview with the author, April 22, 2005.
31. Interview with the author, June 3, 2006. Two follow-up interviews were conducted in 2008.

32. This is apparent from sources in Chinese-language newspapers. Most legal consultation inquiries are from undocumented individuals from mainland China, but immigrants from other regions also seek legal advice from their community newspapers.

33. Jerry Seper, "Homeland Security Says 11 Million Illegals in U.S.," *Washington Post*, August 19, 2006.

34. Liang and Ye, "From Fujian to New York," 191; Liang and Morooka, "Recent Trends of Emigration from China," 149.

35. Skeldon, *Myths and Realities of Chinese Irregular Migration*, 13; Chin, *Smuggled Chinese*, 6. Another researcher, however, believed that as many as 100,000 Chinese made it to the United States illegally each year in the early 1990s; see James K. Chin, "Reducing Irregular Migration from China" (2003), 50.

36. Pew Hispanic Center, *Modes of Entry for the Unauthorized Migrant Population* (2006), 2.

37. Ibid.; Anna Gorman, "Staying Put When Visas Expire," *Los Angeles Times*, May 22, 2006, B1, B8.

38. Pew Hispanic Center, *Modes of Entry for the Unauthorized Migrant Population*, 3–4; U.S. Government Accountability Office, *Estimating the Undocumented Population*.

39. The rate of visa overstayers from European nations is much lower. Pew Hispanic Center, *Modes of Entry for the Unauthorized Migrant Population*, 3–4.

40. INS Office of Policy and Planning, *Estimates of the Unauthorized Immigrant Population Residing in the United States: 1990 to 2000*, 2.

41. China has refused to take back those who were smuggled out the country. To avoid deportation, some undocumented individuals intentionally destroyed their passports upon arrival.

42. Nancy F. Rytina, *Estimates of the Legal Permanent Resident Population and Population Eligible to Naturalize in 2004* (2006), 2.

43. Public Law 99–803, Act of November 6, 1986.

44. U.S. Immigration and Naturalization Service, *Statistical Yearbook of the Immigration and Naturalization Service* (1989), 46, Table 22.

45. John Pomfret, "Smuggled Chinese Enrich Homeland, Gangs, Villagers Work, Chase Dreams in U.S.," *Washington Post*, January 24, 1999, A19.

46. U.S. Immigration and Naturalization Service, *Statistic Year Book of the Immigration and Naturalization Service* (1993).

47. Many individuals consulted ethnic immigration law firms after the deadline; some remain undocumented to this day. This is apparent in many discussions in the legal consultation pages of *Shijie ribao*.

48. *Shijie zhoukan*, February 12, 2008.

49. Keefe, "The Snakehead," 82.

50. Ibid., 85.

51. Public Law 104–208, 110 Stat., 3009–546, September 30, 1996, amended on November 1, 1996 (Immigration and Nationality Act); Connie G. Oxford has written an excellent analysis of this topic. See Oxford, "Protectors and Victims in the Gender Regime of Asylum."

52. Interview with the author, February 15, 2004.

53. Ibid.

54. Alejandro Portes and Rebén G. Rumbaut, *Immigrant American* (1996), 23.

55. Interview with the author, June 3, 2006; April 25, 2008.

56. Applying Passel's method, the size of unauthorized Chinese would be greater than six hundred thousand. This estimate includes individuals in semilegal status. See Jeffrey S. Passel, *The Size and Characteristics of the Unauthorized Migrant Population in the U.S.* (2006), 16.

57. Both situations are discussed often in Chinese-language newspapers.

58. In a *Los Angeles Times* essay, Xiao-huang Yin also estimates that about half a million illegal Chinese immigrants are in the United States. See Yin, "The Invisible Illegal Immigrants," *Los Angeles Times*, April 2, 2006, M6.

59. 2000 population statistics are from Terrance J. Reeves and Claudette E. Bennett, *We Are the People: Asians in the United States* (2004); Min Zhou, "Once Excluded, Now Ascendant" (2003), 38.

60. George Lipsitz, "Abolition Democracy and Global Justice" (2005), 5.

CHAPTER 2   DRAWING LINES OF CLASS DISTINCTION

1. Interview with the author, December 20, 2004. Remarried, Min was a licensed accountant when the interview took place.

2. See, for example, Renqiu Yu, *To Save China, to Save Ourselves* (1992); Peter Kwong, *Forbidden Workers* (1997).

3. There is a large body of literature on class. The classic definition of class is based on a Marxist framework that emphasizes the material possessions of individuals. In *The Communist Manifesto*, Karl Marx conceptualized class as embodying the individual's relationship to the means of production. Accordingly, there are basically two classes in a capitalist society: the owners of the means of production and the workers. See Karl Marx and Friedrich Engels, *The Communist Manifesto* (New York: Penguin Books, 1998). To some scholars, classes can be defined in terms of relationship that changed over time; see E. P. Thompson, *The Making of the English Working Class* (1966); Herbert G. Gutman, *Work Culture, and Society in Industrializing America* (1976); Richard Sennett and Jonathan Cobb, *The Hidden Injuries of Class* (1972); Benita Eisler, *Class Acts* (1983); Sherry B. Ortner, *New Jersey Dreaming* (2003).

4. The Chinese are not unique in this regard. See the special news series that appeared in two top U.S. newspapers in May and June of 2005: "Class Matters" (*New York Times*, May 15 to June 12, 2005) and "Moving Up" (*Wall Street Journal*, May 13, 20, 27 and June 2, 2005).

5. K. Scott Wong, "Cultural Defenders and Brokers" (1998), 4.

6. See Xiaojian Zhao, *Remaking Chinese America* (2002), 95–104.

7. Jade Snow Wong, *Fifth Chinese Daughter* (1950).

8. Zhao, *Remaking Chinese America*, 53.

9. About this organization, see Renqiu Yu's award-winning book, *To Save China, to Save Ourselves*.

10. Sucheng Chan, *Asian Americans* (1991), 34.

11. Min Zhou and Rebecca Kim, "Formation, Consolidation, and Diversification of the Ethnic Elite" (2001), 235; Bernard P. Wong, *Patronage, Brokerage, Entrepreneurship and the Chinese Community of New York* (1988).

12. The Boxer Protocol was imposed on China by Western nations on September 7, 1901, ending an anti-West uprising known as the Boxer Rebellion. The protocol forced China to pay an enormous indemnity and give many concessions to Western powers. The United States turned part

of the Boxer indemnity into scholarships for Chinese students to study in America.

13. Chen Chao, *Jindai liuxueshen* (1998), 40–46; Pei Chi Liu, *Meiguo huaqiaoshi shu bian* (1981), 419–428.

14. Peter Kwong, *The New Chinatown* (1986), 16.

15. Ji Chaozhu, *Cong 'yangwawa' dao waijiaoguan* (2000) 11. Ji was a translator for Chairman Mao and Zhou Enlai. He later was appointed as China's ambassador to Britain and deputy secretary of the United Nations.

16. Some scholars use the term "elite unbound" to emphasize the fact that the students and scholars had little contact with the Chinese American community. See Zhou and Kim, "Formation, Consolidation, and Diversification of the Ethnic Elite," 242–244.

17. Him Mark Lai is perhaps the only historian who has tried to link this educated elite to progressive student groups in the Chinese American community. According to him, a handful of the students did participate in community activities, especially in newspaper publishing. See Him Mark Lai, "To Bring Forth a New China, to Build a Better America" (1991).

18. Interview with the author, August 14, 2003.

19. One author, for example, introduces her great-grandfather as "one of the richest and most prominent Chinese in the country." See Lisa See, *On Gold Mountain* (1995), xvii. A Canadian-based writer describes her home in Shanghai after the communist revolution as "an oasis of comfort and elegance in the midst of the city's drabness" and ranks her family as one of "only a dozen or so" that "employed a staff of servants." See Nien Cheng, *Life and Death in Shanghai* (1986), 3–4.

20. Interview with the author, August 12, 2002.

21. Interview with the author, April 5, 2004.

22. Interview with the author, August 11, 2002.

23. Interview with the author, May 1, 2003.

24. Interview with the author, July 21, 2005.

25. Interview with the author, September 5, 2003

26. Interview with the author, May 1, 2003.

27. Ibid.

28. Interview with the author, January 2, 2005.

29. Interview with the author, September 5, 2003.

30. Interview with the author, September 5, 2003.

31. Interview with the author, August 11, 2002.

32. Interview with the author, June 5, 2001.

33. Interview with the author, August 11, 2002.

34. Ibid.

35. Interview with the author, November 3, 2005.

36. Interview with the author, November 15, 2003.

37. Interview with the author, December 22, 2006.

38. Interview with the author, December 27, 2007.

39. Interview with the author, December 22, 2006.

40. Interview with the author, May 1, 2003.

41. Ibid.

42. Interview with the author, April 15, 2005.

43. Le Ye, "Zhu haozhai kuaile duo, shiqu gengduo" (Living in a mansion brings many happinesses, but one could lose much more), *Shijie ribao*, July 1, 2007, B6.

44. Interview with the author, August 12, 2004.
45. Ibid.
46. Interview with the author, August 30, 2000.
47. Interview with the author, June 27, 2001.
48. Interview with the author, May 12, 2004.
49. Interview with the author, August 11, 2005.
50. Interview with the author, April 15, 2005.
51. Telephone interview with the author, December 27, 2006.
52. Interview with the author, January 2, 2007.
53. Interview with the author, February 15, 2005.
54. Interview with the author, August 25, 2006.
55. Interview with the author, February 21, 2005.
56. Interview with the author, April 1, 2002.
57. Ibid.
58. Yu Renqiu, *Qing ke* (2007), 167–182.
59. Interview with the author, August 27, 1999.
60. Ibid.
61. Interview with the author, December 25, 2003.
62. Interview with the author, May 7, 2007.
63. Interview with the author, November 20, 2005.
64. Interview with the author, November 15, 1997.
65. Interview with the author, January 2, 2007.
66. Interview with the author, November 20, 2005.
67. Ibid.
68. Interview with the author, September 5, 2003.
69. Interview with the author, January 7, 2005.
70. Interview with the author, August 2, 2000.
71. Interview with the author, May 21,1994.
72. Interview with the author, February 2, 2007.
73. Interview with the author, August 19, 2007.
74. Interview with the author, December 27, 2002.
75. Interview with the author, December 27, 2002.
76. Interview with the author, July 9, 2006.
77. Interview with the author, July 29, 2005.
78. Cao Guiling, *Beijingren zai niuyue*, directed by Zheng Xiaolong (1993).
79. James N. Gregory, *American Exodus* (1989), 102–103.
80. Interview with the author, October 27, 2007.
81. Interview with the author, May 11, 2007.
82. William Julius Wilson, *The Truly Disadvantaged* (1987).
83. Michael B. Katz, ed., *The "Underclass" Debate* (1993), 21.
84. William Julius Wilson, "Social Theory and Public Agenda Research" (1990), cited in Katz ed., *"Underclass Debate,"* 21.
85. Douglas G. Glasgow, *The Black Underclass* (1980), 3–8; Katz ed., *"Underclass" Debate*, 17.
86. David M. Heer, *Undocumented Mexicans in the United* States (1990), 3.
87. Liu Yueliu, "Xiang jian he tai ji" (Why do you kill your own people so harshly?), *Shijie ribao*, June 22, 2007, F1.
88. Zhu Wenhan, "Niuyue, zhian bian haole" (New York: public order improved), *Shijie ribao*, July 27, 2007, A3.
89. Han Jie, "Xun meimeng, shenfang yimin gongsi zhapian" (2007).

90. Yang Qing, "Ta, paoqi faqi; ta: gongli he zai?" (After being abandoned by her husband, she asks, where is justice)?" and "Jiashi fating baohu heishenfen dangshiren" (Family court will protect those with black status), *Shijie ribao*, June 28, 2007, B2.
91. See, for example, Bao Guangren, "Bufa lushi lieji duo, dangxin shoupian (Many unlicensed lawyers have bad records, be careful not to get cheated), *Shijie ribao*, June 28, 2007, B2.
92. He Fang, "Huaren shequ guai xianxiang" (A strange phenomenon in the Chinese American society), *Shijie ribao*, March 6, 2007, B1. The report is accompanied by an analytical essay by the same author.
93. Ibid.
94. Interview with the author, June 9, 2006.
95. Interview with the author, June 9, 2006.
96. Interview with the author, May 3, 2006.
97. Interview with the author, April 27, 2007.
98. Interview by Maria Gonzales under the supervision of the author, December 20, 2004. Several acquaintances of the author, single and middle-age professional Chinese American men and women, have been offered opportunities to profit from their citizenship through fake marriages.
99. Interview with the author, November 23, 2003.
100. Tommy Huang was legalized in 2004 with the assistance of a former employer. Interview with the author, November 23, 2003.
101. Interview with the author, August 12, 2004.
102. Apparently Zhen Ling's sister is a U.S. citizen. Through her, Zhen Ling's mother came to the United States as a nonquota immigrant and became a citizen, as well. Zhen Ling, however, would have had to wait for many more years because of the quota limit. Instead of waiting in Taiwan, she and her daughter came to the United States as temporary visitors and overstayed their visa. She gained legal status as a married child of a citizen over age twenty-one. Zhen Ling, "Nuer de luka" (My daughter's green card), *Shijie ribao*, February 24, 2007, F1, and "Nei hu bu kai ti nei hu" (What you want to keep as a secret, what gets talked about), *Shijie ribao*, July 20, 2007, F1.
103. Interview with the author, December 27, 2004.
104. Interview with the author, August 11, 2004.
105. Interview with the author, June 9, 2006.
106. Interview with the author, August 12, 2004.

CHAPTER 3 "SERVE THE PEOPLE"

1. Interview with the author, August 27, 1997.
2. This survey defines ethnic business ownership as firms in which individuals of a particular ethnic group own 51 percent or more of the stock or equity. U.S. "Revenues for Asian-Owned Firms Surpass $326 Billion, Number of Businesses up 24 Percent," *Census Bureau News* (Washington D.C.: U.S. Department of Commerce, May 16, 2006).
3. Ivan Light and Steven Gold, *Ethnic Economies* (2000), 24–25; Ivan Light, *Deflecting Immigration* (2006), 53.
4. Ivan Light and Carolyn Rosenstein, *Race, Ethnicity, and Entrepreneurship in Urban America* (1995); Eran Razin and Ivan Light, "Ethnic Entrepreneurs in America's Largest Metropolitan Areas" (1988).
5. Light and Gold, *Ethnic Economies*, 17–18.

6. Korean Americans also have had success in developing entrepreneurship, for example, but most of them are "petty merchants" who operate small corner markets, dry cleaners, or liquor stores in African American and Hispanic neighborhoods. Many depend on family labor or hire African American and Hispanic employees. See Nancy Abelmann and John Lie, *Blue Dreams* (1995), 122–138; Jennifer Lee, *Civility in the City* (2002), 53–62.

7. Howard Aldrich and Roger Waldinger, "Ethnicity and Entrepreneurship."

8. Researches of segmented labor market theories often see cheap immigrant labor as the key element for the development of ethnic entrepreneurship. For an analysis of the theory, see Eran Razin, "Entrepreneurship among Foreign Immigrants in the Los Angeles and San Francisco Metropolitan Regions" (1988), 284.

9. This issue has been addressed by some scholars. See Light and Gold, *Ethnic Economies*, 167–194.

10. See Pei Chi Liu, *Meiguo huaqiaoshi shubian* (1981), 297–300; Him Mark Lai, *Cong huaqiao dao huaren* (1992), 392–393. In 1959, for example, New York had 2,646 Chinese-operated laundries. The number was down to 1,300 in 1969.

11. Lai, *Cong huaqiao dao huaren*, 393–394.

12. According to Lai Him Mark, the Sacramento Chinese Food Dealers Association was established in 1953, with more than sixty members. And a year later, most Chinese shop owners joined the United California American Food Store (*Jiasheng meiguo shipin lianhe shangdian*), a registered organization that set prices and business standards. When many Chinese-operated dry goods stores in San Francisco were robbed or vandalized in the late 1960s, shop owners quickly organized the Golden Gate Neighborhood Grocer Association, which sought protection from the local police; Lai, *Cong huaqiao dao huaren*, 395–396.

13. Zhao, *Remaking Chinese America*, 95–99.

14. Ibid., 99–104.

15. These ideas are addressed in a number of studies; see, especially, Max Weber, "The Economic Relationships of Organized Groups"; and David L. Featherman and Robert M. Hauser, *Opportunity and Change* (1978).

16. Min Zhou, *Chinatown* (1992), 95.

17. Liu, *Meiguo huaqiaoshi shubian*, 264.

18. Ibid., 265.

19. Zhou, *Chinatown*, 95.

20. *Chinese Yellow Pages*, New York, 2006; New Jersey, 2006.

21. Zhao, *Remaking Chinese America*, 137.

22. Peter Kwong, *The New Chinatown* (1987), 33.

23. Interview with the author, June 30, 2001.

24. Tsang Wai-Yin, "Chengong Chanleren, xiao zhong you lei" (Successful Changle people, tears in their laughter), in Tsang, "Changle ren zai meiguo" (2003); interview with the author, August 12, 2004.

25. Victor G. Nee and Brett de Bary Nee, *Longtime Californ'* (1972), 256–259.

26. The other two laws are the Alien Fiancées and Fiancés Act (1946) and Chinese Wives of American Citizens Act (1946). See Zhao, *Remaking Chinese America*, 78–80.

27. Emphasizing exploitation, these scholars characterized jobs offered by the ethnic economy as having low wages and poor working conditions. See Kwong, *The New Chinatown*, 29–33; Paul Ong, "Chinatown Unemployment

and the Ethnic Labor Market"; Jimy J. Sanders and Victor Nee, "The Limits of Ethnic Solidarity in the Enclave Economy" (1987), 745–767; Donald Mar, "Chinese Immigrant Women and the Ethnic Labor Market" (1984).

28. Zhou, *Chinatown*; Xiaolan Bao, *Holding up More Than Half the Sky* (2001).
29. Peter Kwong found 500 garment factories in New York in 1984, while Min Zhou's study revealed 437 in 1988. See Kwong, *The New Chinatown*, 32; Zhou, *Chinatown*, 95.
30. Lucie Cheng and Philip Q. Yang, "Asians: The 'Model Minority' Deconstructed" (1996), 329–330.
31. Ibid., 331.
32. Milton M. Gordon, *Assimilation in American Life* (1964).
33. Nazli Kibria, *Family Tightrope* (1993), 57.
34. Among them is the so-called glass ceiling, which prevents Asian Americans from moving up to high-level positions in most occupations.
35. Razin, "Entrepreneurship among Foreign Immigrants," 284.
36. Min Zhou and Mingang Lin, "Community Transformation and the Formation of Ethnic Capital" (2005), 264.
37. See Zhou, *Chinatown*.
38. Light, *Deflecting Immigration*, 49–50; Light and Gold, *Ethnic Economies*, 39–44.
39. Interview with the author, April 25, 2003.
40. Interview with the author, August 12, 2004.
41. Interview with the author, August 28, 2001.
42. Interview with the author, October 24, 2004.
43. Interview with the author, November 12, 2004.
44. Interview with the author, November 12, 2004.
45. Tsang, "Chengong Chanleren, Xiao zhong you lei," 30.
46. Interview with the author, April 2, 2004
47. Interview with the author, October 18, 2001.
48. Interview with the author, June 20, 2004.
49. Peter Gregory, *The Determinants of International Migration and Policy Options for Influencing the Size of Population Flows* (1989), 17. A summary of the theory is found in Ivan Light, Parminder Bhachu, and Stavros Karageorgis, "Migration Networks and Immigrant Entrepreneurship" (1993), 28–29.
50. *Chinese Yellow Pages*, New York, 1990 1994, 2000, 2006; Han Jie, "Zhiye jieshao suo wei huaren yimin zhao gongzuo" (Employment services searching for jobs for Chinese immigrants), *Shijie zhoukan*, July 17, 2007, 14–21.
51. The relatively small number of non-Chinese clients are often related to Chinese individuals or grew up in a Chinese culture, or speak a Chinese language.
52. Han Jie, "Zhiye jieshao suo wei huaren yimin zhao gongzuo," 17.
53. Interview with the author, February 15, 2002.
54. Han Jie, "Zhiye jieshao suo wei huaren yimin zhao gongzuo," 16.
55. Interview with the author, August 12, 2004.
56. Ibid.
57. Interview with the author, October 12, 2006.
58. Interview with the author, December 20, 2005.
59. Interview with the author, July 15, 2002.
60. Interview with the author, August 10, 2004.
61. Interview with the author, December 28, 2003.
62. Interview with the author, February 15, 2002.

63. Interview with the author, July 12, 2001.
64. Interview with the author, February 15, 2001.
65. Bao Guangren, "Yiminju shaodang feifa yimin, ji xinzhao" (Immigration authorities found a new trick to crack down on the illegals). *Shijie ribao*, February 8, 2008, B1.
66. Ivan Light sees Chinese and Korean bankers, developers, and realtors as "place entrepreneurs" in Los Angeles and as immigrant growth machines because they are able to utilize ethnic resources to build new communities to house new immigrants. See Light, *Deflecting Immigration*, 126–128.
67. Interview with the author, December 20, 2005.
68. John Horton, *The Politics of Diversity* (1995), 29.
69. Horton notices that some Chinese-operated supermarkets in Monterey Park appear to "conform to familiar suburban styles in size and architecture" of the 1980s. Ibid., 30. For more information about Chinese supermarkets, see Alfred Yee, *Shopping at Giant Foods* (2003).
70. Official Web site of 99 Ranch Market, www.99ranch.com accessed on January 20, 2008.
71. Han Jie, "Wenzhou ren xiyidian, xi chu yipiantian," *Shijie ribao*, July 22–28, 2007.
72. Some agencies, for example, have designed special overseas travel plans to make it possible for people to leave the United States temporarily while waiting for their green cards.
73. The law firm handled a number of high-profile cases dealing with Chinese in the United States, including that of Yan Zhao, a tourist from Tianjing who was severely beaten by border patrol officers in Niagara Falls in July 2004. For information about the law firm, see *Shijie ribao*, August 10, 2004, I-1; Wang Jian, "Yue yang duihua Zho Yan lushi Sun Lantao xiangjie tianjin nu shangren bei ou an" (Transoceanic telephone interview with Zhao Yan's lawyer Sun Lantao regarding the case of a Tianjin business woman being attacked), *Chengshi kuaibao* (Metro Express), July 27, 2004, 1.
74. Based on *Chinese Yellow Pages* of southern California, 2007 edition, and advertising pages in *Shijie ribao*, August 2, 2004.
75. Ibid.
76. Min Zhou and Susan Kim call this an ethnic system of supplementary education. Min Zhou and Susan S. Kim, "Community Forces, Social Capital, and Educational Achievement" (2006) .
77. Yu Shengning, "Shenggaiboshi huangjinli yongji chaoza" (The Golden Mile in San Gabriel is crowded and noisy)," *Shijie ribao*, May 13, 2004, B2.
78. Interview with the author, September 12, 2006.
79. Don Lee, "Pitching L.A. to the Chinese," *Los Angeles Times*, March 9, 2008.

CHAPTER 4   THE "SPIRIT OF CHANGLE"

1. Changle American Association, *Changle American Association, Inc.* (2001), 37.
2. Testimonies of Lianqi Guo, the head of Fuqingbang, during the Cuiping Zheng trial, *Shijie ribao*, May 9, 2005, B10.
3. David Chen, "Exodus Slows from Fujian Province to U.S.," *New York Times*, September 7, 2003, 1; James K. Chin, "Reducing Irregular Migration from China" (2003); John Pomfret, "Smuggled Chinese Enrich Homeland, Gang Villagers Work, Chase Dreams in U.S.," *Washington Post*, January 24, 1999,

A19. There are many more such reports. According to the *New York Times* and the *Los Angeles Times*, 203 people were caught as container stowaways in Pacific Coast ports in 1999. Canadian and American authorities detained an additional 136 people on eight ships in the period between December 25, 1999, and January 14, 2000. On January 6, 2000, ten Chinese teenaged women about to cross the U.S. border were detained by Canadian authorities. U.S. border patrol officials further found a boatload of fifteen immigrants, along with three corpses, in Seattle on January 9, 2000. In December 1999, authorities found thirty immigrants in Long Beach, Los Angeles County, and arrested three men waiting near the ship. On January 5, 2000, another fourteen were detained in Seattle, while Canada intercepted one ship and caught twenty-five would-be immigrants. There were also reports of Chinese illegal immigrants caught in Guam and along the coasts of Australia and New Zealand. See also Ko-Lin Chin, *Smuggled Chinese* (1999); Zai Liang, "Demography of Illicit Emigration from China" (2001); and David Kyle and Rey Koslowski, eds., *Global Human Smuggling* (2001).

4. According to one report, the average income of urban employees in Fujian Province was 974 yuan. See "Introduction to China's Provinces, Municipalities, and Autonomous Regions," www.china.org.cn/English/features/ProvinceView/164868.htm (accessed September 30, 2007).

5. Xinjing yi re san (Arai Hifumi), "She zhi dao: Fuzhou–Xianggang–Niuyue," part 1, "Ershi wan ren hengyue taipingyang" (The Pacific crossing of 200,000 people), *Jiushi niandai*, July 1995, 34–40.

6. *Shijie ribao*, May 7, 2005, A3; Zheng was convicted in June 2005.

7. In Ko-Lin Chin's study, 86 percent of the three hundred people surveyed cited money as among the principal reasons for choosing to be smuggled into the United States. He noted that the average monthly income in China was around $100 compared with an average monthly income of $1,359 in the United States. See Chin, *Smuggled Chinese*, 14.

8. Interview with the author, August 8, 2004.

9. Ibid.

10. Chin, *Smuggled Chinese*, 6.

11. Interview with the author, August 10, 2004.

12. Interview with the author, August 8, 2004.

13. Interview with the author, August 12, 2004

14. Group interview with the author, August 13, 2004.

15. Jane Lii, "The New Blood in Chinatown: On the Eve of Hong Kong Takeover, A Revolution Takes Hold in Lower Manhattan," *New York Times*, June 22, 1997.

16. Tsang Wai-Yin, "Changle ren zai meiguo."

17. Interview with the author, August 12, 2004.

18. Ibid. See also Tsang, "Changle ren zai meiguo," part 1, "Shijie pa meiguo, meiguo pa Changle" (The world is afraid of the United States; the United States is afraid of Changle), *Shijie zhoukan*, September 21, 2004, 17.

19. Interview with the author, August 12, 2004.

20. Tsang Wai-Yin, "Zhongcan waimailang, beige he shi liao?" (2004). Chen's killer was convicted in March 2005, see *Shijie ribao*, March 17, 2005, B10.

21. *Changle American Association, Inc.*, 55–56.

22. Xinjing, "She zhi dao," part 3, "Niuyue tangrenjie qitan" (Strange tales from New York's Chinatown), *Jiushi niandai* (September 1995), 90–91.

23. Tsang, "Changle ren zai meiguo," part 3, "Chenggong Changle ren: xiao-zhong you lei" (The successful Changle people: tears amid smiles), *Shijie zhoukan*, October 5, 2003, 29.
24. Ibid., 34; interview with the author, August 12, 2004.
25. Tsang, "Changle ren zai meiguo," part 3, 34.
26. Ibid., 29.
27. Interview with the author, August 12, 2004.
28. Ibid.
29. Chinese business directories (titles vary), New York and East Coast editions, 1990, 1995, 1997, and 2004.
30. *Changle American Association, Inc.*, 52–53.
31. Interviews with the author, August 12, 2004.
32. Ibid.
33. *Changle American Association, Inc.*, 56.
34. Interview with the author, August 12, 2004.
35. Ibid.
36. Ibid.
37. Ibid.
38. Ibid.
39. Ibid.; Tsang, "Changle ren zai meiguo," part 1, 17.
40. Interview with the author, August 13, 2004.
41. Interview with the author, August 10, 2004.
42. Interview with the author, August 12, 2004.
43. Xinjing, "She zhi dao," part 3, 90–91.
44. Interview with the author, August 12, 2004.
45. *Shijie ribao*, May 17, 2005, A3.
46. Interview with the author, August 12, 2004; Tsang Wai-Yin, "Fangfan beiju zai fasheng, zi bao shouze laoji zai xin" (2004), 28–29.
47. Tsang, "Changle ren zai meiguo," part 3, 31.
48. Ibid.
49. "Yidong shanghu shiwei huodong xian zhao quxiao" (The Yidong vendors demonstration almost got canceled), *Ming bao* (Ming Newspaper), August 8, 2004.
50. Ibid.
51. "Shi ke ren, shu bu ke ren" ("If this can be tolerated, what cannot?"), undated flyer distributed in New York's Chinatown on October 8, 2004.
52. Ibid.
53. *Fazhi wan bao* (Legal Evening News), October 10, 2004.
54. *Ming bao*, October 15, 2004, A14.
55. Interview with the author, October 9, 2004.
56. Chen, "Exodus Slows from Fujian Province to U.S.," 1.
57. Interview with the author, August 12, 2004. See also, Tsang, "Changle ren zai meiguo," Part 3, 31.
58. Interview with the author, August 12, 2004.
59. Ibid.
60. *Changle American Association, Inc.*, 60.
61. Interview with the author, August 12, 2004.
62. Chen, "Exodus Slows from Fujian Province to U.S.," 1; interview with the author, August 12, 2004.

CHAPTER 5   SURVIVING POVERTY IN AN
            ETHNIC SOCIAL HIERARCHY

1. Interview with the author, June 25, 2002.

2. Interview with the author, July 8, 2002.

3. The concept of private homeownership is relatively new in mainland China. Until the 1990s, almost all real estate properties in urban areas were owned by the government. Peasants in the countryside could build houses in the villages for their own families, but they were not allowed to do so for commercial purposes. Residents in government-owned housing units in the cities were required to pay a nominal fee each month. Lao Wu and his in-laws never had any real estate properties; what they sold was the occupancy rights of these apartments.

4. Information about Li, Bob, Lao Wu, and Fei are from interviews with the author between July 5 and July 8, 2002.

5. Observations of Li and Lao Wu also took place between July 5 and July 8, 2008.

6. Roger Daniels, *Guarding the Golden Door* (2004),160.

7. U.S. Census Bureau Special Report, May 2003; the poverty rate for Taiwanese families in the United States was 11.2 percent in 1990. See Eric Lai, "A People of Their Own: Taiwanese Americans," in *The New Face of Asian Pacific America*, edited by Eric Lai and Dennis Arguelles (2003), 43–44.

8. Peter Kwong suggests this tendency in his study on New York's Chinatown. Other scholars also reveal the disadvantages of Chinese laborers employed in ethnic businesses. See Kwong, *The New Chinatown* (1987); Jimy Sanders and Victor Nee, "The Limits of Ethnic Solidarity in the Enclave Economy" (1987), 745–767; Paul Ong, "Chinatown Unemployment and the Ethnic Labor Market" (1984); Donald Mar, "Chinese Immigrant Women and the Ethnic Labor Market" (1984).

9. He found that the laborers were unable to accumulate enough surplus income to purchase a home. An ordinary worker often paid $60 to $100 a year to rent an apartment or a small house for his family. See Stephan Thernstrom, *Poverty and Progress* (1964), 28–29.

10. Alan Dawley, *Class and Community* (1976), 129.

11. Charles Nordhoff, *California, for Health, Pleasure and Residence* (New York: Harper & Brothers, 1873), 82.

12. Min Zhou, "Once Excluded, Now Ascendant" (2003), 41–43.

13. Wei Li, "Spatial Transformation of an Urban Ethnic Community" (1997) and "Anatomy of a New Ethnic Settlement" (1998). Also see Timothy P. Fong, *The First Suburban Chinatown* (1984).

14. Min Zhou and Rebecca Kim, "The Paradox of Ethnicization and Assimilation" (2006).

15. Zhou, "Once Excluded, Now Ascendant," 42.

16. Victor G. Nee and Brett De Bary Nee, *Longtime Californ'* (1973), 320.

17. Interview with the author, July 8, 2003.

18. Interview with the author, August 11, 2004.

19. Interview with the author, August 10, 2004.

20. Interview with the author, March 1, 2004.

21. This information is based on an email circulated within the community asking for help for the young student, who was kicked out of the shelter

due to regulatory policies. The youngster's mother is one of the author's interviewees.

22. Interview with the author, July 8, 2002.
23. *Shijie ribao*, August 20, 2004, B2.
24. Interview with the author, December 12, 2003.
25. *Shijie ribao*, August 19, 2004, B2.
26. *Shijie ribao*, August 20, 2004, B2; September 2, 2004, B1.
27. Fong, *The First Suburban Chinatown*, 62–67.
28. Interview with the author, July 8, 2002.
29. *Shijie ribao*, August 20, 2004, B2.
30. Interview with the author, February 15, 2004.
31. *Shijie ribao*, August 20, 2004; October 6, 2004 B2.
32. Interview with the author, July 7, 2008.
33. Interview with the author, December 2, 2004.
34. Interview with the author, April 15, 1994.
35. Interview with the author, December 26, 2003.
36. Interview with the author, February 20, 2004.
37. This interviewee did not want to talk about how he gained legal status.
38. Min Zhou, *Chinatown* (1992).
39. Ibid.
40. Telephone interview with the author, June 10, 2000.
41. Interview with the author, July 8, 2002.
42. Interviews with the author, August 12, 2004.
43. Ibid.
44. Ibid.
45. Based on the author's observations on August 12, 2005.
46. Interview with the author, August 10, 2005.
47. Interview with the author, August 12, 2004.
48. Him Mark Lai and Russell Jeung, "Guilds, Unions, and Garment Factories" (2008), 7–8.
49. Qi Ming, "Zhongguo nuren tiyan yixiang jianxin" (Chinese woman experiencing hardships in a foreign land) (2008) B6.
50. Interview with the author, July 8, 2003.
51. Interview with the author, August 12, 2004.
52. Interview with the author, May 3, 2006.
53. Interview with the author, December 28, 2006.
54. Interview with the author, December 1, 2003.
55. Interview with the author, December 26, 2003.
56. Interview with the author, June 21, 2002.
57. Interview with the author, September 20, 2004.
58. Interview with the author, December 15, 2004.
59. Telephone interview with the author, December 20, 2007.
60. Interview with the author, December 2, 2003.
61. *Qiao bao*, June 22, 2004 (www.tycool.com/2004/06/29).
62. *China Newsnet*, June 28, 2002.
63. Interview with the author, May 21, 2005.
64. *Shijie zhoukan*, October 19, 2008, 53.
65. Interview with the author, May 21, 2005.
66. Ibid.
67. For asylum regulations, see Ann Parrent, *Asylum Program* (1995), 17.
68. *China Newsnet*, June 28, 2002.

69. CaoYang Qinmin, "Fenbie miantan" (2008), 52.
70. Interview with the author, August 12, 2004.
71. Ibid.
72. Ibid.
73. Interviews with the author, July 8, 2008.
74. Interview with the author, December 28, 2005.
75. Interview with the author, May 11, 2004.
76. Ibid.
77. Interview with the author, December 26, 2003.
78. Interview with the author, October 5, 2003.
79. Interview with the author, July 7, 2003.

Conclusion: Inclusion or Exclusion?

1. Sudeep Reddy, Ray A. Smith, and Kris Maher, "Job Losses Are Worst Since '74," *Wall Street Journal*, December 6, 2008, A1.
2. Huang Weiyi, "Yuqian toudu ke yong ru huabu" (More than one thousand smuggled people emerged in NewYork's Chinatown), *Ming Bao*, December 1, 2008, A1.
3. Translation Center, "Huaren toudu, yazhou santian dai liangpi" (Smuggled Chinese, two groups were caught in Arizona in three days), *Shijie ribao*, November 29, 2008, B22.
4. According to one report, many Chinese restaurants outside the New York area have reduced the monthly wage of their workers from $2,000 to $1,800 or less. Huang, "Yuqian toudu ke yong ru huabu."
5. Lisa Friedman, "Immigration Debate Parallels: Historians See Similarities with 19th Century," *Daily News*, December 31, 2005, 1.
6. U.S. Senate, *Report of the Joint Special Committee to Investigate Chinese Immigration* (1877). The most detailed summary of the hearing is found in Elmer C. Sandmeyer, *The Anti-Chinese Movement in California* (1973).
7. This issue is included in conferences and edited scholarly volumes. See, for example, Carol M. Swain, *Debating Immigration* (2008); Nicolaus Mills ed., *Arguing Immigration* (1994).
8. Peter Kwong, *Forbidden Workers* (1997), 235–238.
9. Willard Myers, "Emerging Threat of Transnational Organized Crime from the East," *Crime, Law and Social Change* 24 no. 3 (1996): 181–222; Ko-Lin Chin, *Smuggled Chinese* (1999), 152–153.
10. Peter Kwong's solution is reminiscent of the government's Chinese Confession Program (1956–1965). See Kwong, *Forbidden Workers*, 238.
11. For the Chinese Confession Program, see Zhao, *Remaking Chinese America*, 176–181.
12. I have interviewed fifty-two undocumented immigrants and talked to a few dozens of others in restaurants, hotels, and day-labor job sites. None of these individuals was "indentured" or "enslaved."
13. Noah Pickus and Peter Skerry, "Good Neighbors and Good Citizens" (2008), 102.
14. Interview with the author, December 6, 2008.
15. *Shijie ribao*, August 20, B2; September 2, 2004, B1.
16. Interview with the author, December 24, 2004.
17. Interview with the author, May 2, 2007.
18. Interview with the author, January 24, 2003.

19. Nathan Glazer argues forcefully on this subject. See Glazer, "Concluding Observations" (2007), 265.
20. Some scholars have seen the movement of people crossing national boundaries as a response to a labor market demand in developed nations with segmented economic sectors. If there were no demand for their labor within the Chinese ethnic economy, the undocumented immigrants would not come, since they would have no access to mainstream job markets. See Douglass S. Massey, Jorge Durand, and Nolan J. Malone, *Beyond Smoke and Mirrors* (2002), 145.

Selected Bibliography

U.S. Government Publications

Reeves, Terrance J., and Claudette E. Bennett. *We Are the People: Asians in the United States.* Washington, D.C.: U. S. Census Bureau, December 2004. Census 2000 Special Reports.

Rytina, Nancy F. *Estimates of the Legal Permanent Resident Population and Population Eligible to Naturalize in 2004. Washington, D.C.:* U.S. Department of Homeland Security, Office of Immigration Statistics Policy Directorate, February 2006.

U.S. Census Bureau. *United States: Census of 2000.*

———. *The Asian Population: 2000.* Census 2000 Brief, 2002.

———. *United States: 2000, Summary Population and Housing Characteristics,* 2002.

———. "Revenues for Asian-Owned Firms Surpass $326 Billion, Number of Businesses up 24 Percent." *Census Bureau News,* 2006.

U.S. Department of State. *U.S.—Hong Kong Policy Act Report,* 2005.

U.S. Government Accountability Office. *Estimating the Undocumented Population: A "Grouped Answers" Approach to Surveying Foreign-Born Respondents.* GAO-06–775, September 2006.

U.S. Immigration and Naturalization Service. *Statistical Yearbook of the Immigration and Naturalization Service.* Washington DC: Department of Justice, Immigration and Naturalization Service, 1965–2000.

———. Office of Policy and Planning, "Estimates of the Unauthorized Immigrant Population Residing in the United States: 1990 to 2000," 2001.

U.S. President. "Executive Order 12711—Policy Implementation with Respect to Nationals of the People's Republic of China." *Weekly Compilation of Presidential Documents* 1–26, 558–559, April 11, 1990.

U.S. Senate. *Report of the Joint Special Committee to Investigate Chinese Immigration.* Washington: Government Printing Office, 1877.

United States Statutes

INS Act of 1965, Public Law 89–236.

Public Law 99–803, Act of November 6, 1986.

Public Law 104–208, 110 Statute, 3009–546, Act of September 20, 1996.

Newspapers, Periodicals, and Regional Directories

Chengshi kuaibao (Metro Express), 2004.

Chicago Chinese Yellow Pages, 2006.

Chinese Yellow Pages, Boston and Philadelphia edition, 2005.

Chinese Yellow Pages, Houston edition, 2000–2002, 2007.

Chinese Yellow Pages or *Chinese Consumer Yellow Pages*, New York edition, 1990, 1993, 2000; New York-New Jersey edition, 2001–2007.

Chinese Yellow Pages or *Chinese Consumer Yellow Pages*, northern California edition, 2002–2007.

Chinese Yellow Pages or *Chinese Consumer Yellow Pages*, southern California edition, 2000–2007.

Chinese Yellow Pages or *Chinese Consumer Yellow Pages*, southern California San Diego/Las Vegas edition, 2006–2007.

Chinese Yellow Pages, Washington, D.C. edition, 2005.

Jiushi niandai, 1995.

Ming bao, 2004.

Seattle Chinese Directory, 2006–2008.

Seattle Chinese Phonebook, 2007–2008.

Seattle Chinese Yellow Pages, 2007–2008.

Shijie ribao (*Chinese Daily News* or *World Journal*), 2002–2008.

Shijie zhoukan (weekly magazine of the *Shijie ribao*), 2002–2008.

SECONDARY SOURCES

Abelmann, Nancy, and John Lie. *Blue Dreams: Korean Americans and the Los Angeles Riots.* Cambridge: Harvard University Press, 1995.

Aldrich, Howard, and Roger Waldinger. "Ethnicity and Entrepreneurship." *Annual Review of Sociology* 16 (1990): 111–135.

Bao, Xiaolan. *Holding up More Than Half the Sky: Chinese Women Garment Workers in New York City, 1948–1992.* Urbana: University of Illinois Press, 2001.

Belden, Elionne L. W. *Claiming Chinese Identity.* New York: Garland, 1997.

Cao Guiling. *Beijingren zai nieyue* (The Beijingers in New York). China: Beijing Television Production, 1993. Television series directed by Zheng Xiaolong.

Cao Yang Qinmin. "Fenbie miantan: ceshi hunyin zhenshixiang de miantan" (Separate interviews: interviews that test whether a marriage claim is genuine." In *Shijie zhoukan*, October 19, 2008, 52–53.

Caughey, John W. *Their Majesties the Mob.* Chicago: University of Chicago Press, 1960.

Chan, Sucheng. *Asian Americans: An Interpretive History.* New York: Twayne, 1991.

———. "The Exclusion of Chinese Women." In *Entry Denied: Exclusion and the Chinese Community in America, 1882–1943*, edited by Sucheng Chan, 94–146. Philadelphia: Temple University Press, 1991.

Chang, Shenglin. *The Global Silicon Valley Home: Lives and Landscapes within Taiwanese American Trans-Pacific Culture.* Stanford: Stanford University Press, 2006.

Changle American Association. *Changle American Association, Inc.* New York, Changle American Association, 2001, 2002, 2003.

Chen Chao. *Jindai liuxueshen* (History of students studying abroad during the recent period). Shanghai: Shanghai guji chubanshe, 1998.

Chen, Hsiang-shui. *Chinatown No More: Taiwanese Immigrants in Contemporary New York.* Ithaca: Cornell University Press, 1992.

Chen, Shehong. *Being Chinese, Becoming Chinese American.* Urbana: University of Illinois Press, 2002.

Cheng, Lucie, and Edna Bonacich, eds. *Labor Migration under Capitalism: Asian Workers in the United States before World War II.* Berkeley: University of California Press, 1984.

Cheng, Lucie, and Philip Q. Yang. "Asians: The 'Model Minority' Deconstructed." In *Ethnic Los Angeles,* edited by Roger Waldinger and Mehdi Bozorgmehr, 305–344. New York: Russell Sage Foundation, 1996.

Cheng, Nien. *Life and Death in Shanghai.* New York: Grove, 1986.

Chin, James K. "Reducing Irregular Migration from China." *International Migration* 41 no. 3 (2003): 49–72.

Chin, Ko-lin. *Chinatown Gangs.* New York: Oxford University Press, 1996.

———. *Smuggled Chinese: Clandestine Immigration to the United States.* Philadelphia: Temple University Press, 1999.

Chun, Gloria Heyung. *Of Orphans and Warriors: Inventing Chinese American Culture and Identities during the Exclusion Era.* Philadelphia: Temple University Press, 1998.

Daniels, Roger, ed. *Anti-Chinese Violence in North America.* New York: Arno Press, 1978.

———. *Guarding the Golden Door: American Immigration Policy and Immigrants since 1882.* New York: Hill and Wang, 2004.

Dawley, Alan. *Class and Community: The Industrial Revolution in Lynn.* Cambridge: Harvard University Press, 1976.

Dirks, Nicholas B., Geoff Eley, and Sherry B. Ortner. "Introduction." In *Culture/Power/History,* edited by Dirks, Eley, and Ortner, 3–46. Princeton: Princeton University Press, 1994.

Eisler, Benita. *Class Acts: America's Last Dirty Secret.* New York: Franklin Watts, 1983.

Featherman, David L., and Robert M. Hauser. *Opportunity and Change.* New York: Academic Press, 1978.

Fong, Timothy. *The First Suburban Chinatown: The Remaking of Monterey Park, California.* Philadelphia: Temple University Press, 1994.

Glasgow, Douglas G. *The Black Underclass: Unemployment and Entrapment of Ghetto Youth.* New York: Random House, 1980.

Glazer, Nathan. "Concluding Observations." In *Debating Immigration,* edited by Carol M Swain, 265. New York: Cambridge University Press, 2007, 257–268.

Gordon, Milton M. *Assimilation in American Life: The Role of Race, Religion, and National Origins.* New York: Oxford University Press, 1964.

Gregory, James N. *American Exodus: The Dust Bowl Migration and Okie Culture in California.* Berkeley: University of California Press, 1989.

Gregory, Peter. *The Determinants of International Migration and Policy Options for Influencing the Size of Population Flows.* Washington, D.C.: Commission for the Study of International Migration and Cooperative Economic Development, 1989. Working paper no. 2.

Gutman, Herbert G. *Work Culture, and Society in Industrializing America.* New York: Knopf, 1976.

Han Jie. "Xun meimeng, shenfang yimin gongsi zhapian" (In search of American dreams, one should be careful not to be swindled by immigration firms). *Shijie Zhoukan*, March 25, 2007, 30–36.

Heer, David M. *Undocumented Mexicans in the United States*. Cambridge: Cambridge University Press, 1990.

Hollon, Eugene. *Frontier Violence: Another Look*. New York: William Morrow, 1982.

Horton, John. *The Politics of Diversity: Immigration, Resistance, and Change in Monterey Park, California*. Philadelphia: Temple University Press, 1995.

Hsu, Madeline Y. *Dreaming of Gold, Dreaming of Home: Transnationalism and Migration between the United States and South China, 1882–1943*. Stanford: Stanford University Press, 2000.

Ji Chaozhu. *Cong 'yangwawa' dao waijiaoguan* (From foreign doll to diplomat). Beijing: Peking University Press, 2000.

Katz, Michael B., ed. *The "Underclass" Debate: Views from History*. Princeton: Princeton University Press, 1993.

Keefe, Patrick Radeen. "The Snakehead: The Criminal Odyssey of Chinatown's Sister Ping." *New Yorker*, April 24, 2004, 68–85.

Kibria, Nazli. *Family Tightrope: The Changing Lives of Vietnamese Americans*. Princeton: Princeton University Press, 1993.

Kwong, Peter. *Forbidden Workers: Illegal Chinese Immigrants and American Labor*. New York: New Press, 1997.

———. *The New Chinatown*. New York: Hill and Wang, 1987.

Kwong, Peter, and Dušanka Miščević. *Chinese America: The Untold Story of America's Oldest New Community*. New York: New Press, 2005.

Kyle, David, and Rey Koslowski, eds. *Global Human Smuggling: Comparative Perspectives*. Baltimore: Johns Hopkins University Press, 2001.

Lai, Eric, and Dennis Arguelles, eds. *The New Face of Asian Pacific America: Numbers, Diversity and Change in the 21st Century*. San Francisco: AsianWeek, 2003.

Lai, Him Mark. "To Bring Forth a New China, to Build a Better America: The Chinese Marxist Left in America to the 1960s." In *Chinese Americans: History and Perspectives*, 1992, 3–82.

———. "The United States." In *The Encyclopedia of the Chinese Overseas*, edited by Lynn Pan, 267. Cambridge: Harvard University Press, 1999.

_____. *Cong huaqiao dao huaren: ershi shiji meiguo huaren shehui fazhanzhi* (From overseas Chinese to Chinese Americans: A history of twentieth-century Chinese America). Hong Kong: Sanlian, 1992.

Lai, Him Mark, and Russell Jeung. "Guilds, Unions, and Garment Factories: Notes on Chinese in the Apparel Industry." In *Chinese Americans: History and Perspectives*, 2008, 1–12.

Lee, Jennifer. *Civility in the City: Blacks, Jews, and Koreans in Urban America*. Cambridge: Harvard University Press, 2002.

Lee, Rose Hum. *The Growth and Decline of Chinese Communities in the Rocky Mountain Region*. New York: Arno, 1978.

Li, Wei. "Anatomy of a New Ethnic Settlement: Chinese Ethnoburbs in Los Angeles." In *Urban Studies* 35 no. 3 (1998): 479–501.

————."Spatial Transformation of an Urban Ethnic Community: From China-town to Chinese Ethnoburb in Los Angeles." Ph.D. dissertation, University of Southern California, 1997.

Li, Wei, Gary Dymski, et al. "Chinese-American Banking and Community Development in Los Angeles County." In *Annals of the Association of American Geographers* 92 no. 4 (2002): 777–796.

Liang, Zai. "Demography of Illicit Emigration from China: A Sending Country's Perspective." *Sociological Forum* 16 no. 4 (2001): 677–701.

Liang, Zai, and Hideki Morooka. "Recent Trends of Emigration from China: 1982–2000." *International Migration* 42 no. 3 (2004): 145–164.

Liang, Zai, and Wenzhen Ye. "From Fujian to New York: Understanding the New Chinese Immigration." In *Global Human Smuggling: Comparative Perspective,* edited by David Kyle and Rey Koslowski, 187–215. Baltimore: Johns Hopkins University Press, 2001.

Light, Ivan. *Deflecting Immigration: Networks, Markets, and Regulation in Los Angeles.* New York: Russell Sage Foundation, 2006.

Light, Ivan, Parminder Bhachu, and Stavros Karageorgis. "Migration Networks and Immigrant Entrepreneurship." In *Immigration and Entrepreneurship: Culture, Capital, and Ethnic Network,* edited by Ivan Light and Paraminder Bhachu, 25–49. New Brunswick, N.J.: Transaction, 1993.

Light, Ivan, and Steven J. Gold. *Ethnic Economics.* San Diego, Cal.: Academic Press, 2000.

Light, Ivan, and Carolyn Rosenstein. *Race, Ethnicity, and Entrepreneurship in Urban America.* New York: Aldine de Gruyter, 1995.

Lin, Jan. *Reconstructing Chinatown: Ethnic Enclave, Global Change.* Minneapolis: University of Minnesota Press, 1998.

Lipsitz, George. "Abolition Democracy and Global Justice." Unpublished manu-script, 2006.

Liu, Pei Chi. *Meiguo huaqiaoshi shubian* (A history of the Chinese in the United States of America II). Taibei: Liming wenhua youxian gongsi, 1981.

Mar, Donald. "Chinese Immigrant Women and the Ethnic Labor Market." *Critical Perspectives of Third World America* 2 (1984): 62–74.

Massey, Douglass S., Jorge Durand, and Nolan J. Malone. *Beyond Smoke and Mirrors: Mexican Immigration in an Era of Economic Integration.* New York: Russell Sage Foundation, 2002.

Meyers, Willard H. "Emerging Threat of Transnational Organized Crime From the East." In *Crime, Law and Social Change* 24 no. 3 (1996): 181–222.

————. "Of Qinqing, Qinshu, Guanxi, and *Shetou*: The Dynamic Elements of Chinese Irregular Population Movement." In *Human Smuggling: Chinese Migrant Trafficking and the Challenge to America's Immigration Tradition,* edited by Paul J. Smith, 93–133. Washington, D.C.: Center for Strategic and International Studies, 1997.

Miller, M. J. "Illegal Migration." In *The Cambridge Survey of World Migration,* edited by Robin Cohen, 537–540. Cambridge: Cambridge University Press, 1995.

Mills, Nicolaus, ed. *Arguing Immigration:* The Debate over the Changing Face of America. New York: Touchstone, 1994.

Nee, Victor G., and Brett de Bary Nee. *Longtime Californ': A Documentary Study of an American Chinatown.* New York: Pantheon Books, 1973.

Ong, Paul. "Chinatown Unemployment and the Ethnic Labor Market." *Amerasia Journal* 11 (1984): 35–54.

Ortner, Sherry B. "Identities: The Hidden Life of Class." *Journal of Anthropological Research* 54 no. 1 (1998): 1–17.

———. *New Jersey Dreaming: Capital, Culture, and the Class of '58*. Durham: Duke University Press, 2003.

Oxford, Connie G. "Protectors and Victims in the Gender Regime of Asylum." *NWSA Journal* 17 no. 3 (2005): 18–38.

Park, Edward, and John Park. *Probationary Americans: Contemporary Immigration Policies and the Shaping of Asian American Communities*. New York: Routledge, 2005.

Parrent, Ann. *Asylum Program: Representing Asylum Applicants, An Attorney's Guide to Law and Procedure*. New York: Lawyers Committee for Human Rights, 1995.

Passel, Jeffrey S. *The Size and Characteristics of the Unauthorized Migrant Population in the U.S.: Estimates Based on the March 2005 Current Population Survey*. Washington, D.C.: Pew Hispanic Center, March 7, 2006.

Passel, Jeffrey S., and D'Vera Cohn. *Trends in Unauthorized Immigration: Undocumented Inflow Now Trails Legal Flow*. Washington, D.C.: Pew Hispanic Center, October 2, 2008.

Peffer, George Anthony. *If They Don't Bring Their Women Here: Chinese Female Migration before Exclusion*. Urbana: University of Illinois Press, 1999.

Pew Hispanic Center. *Modes of Entry for the Unauthorized Migrant Population*, Washington, D.C.: Pew Hispanic Center, March 22, 2006.

Pickus, Noah, and Peter Skerry. "Good Neighbors and Good Citizens: Beyond the Legal-Illegal Immigration Debate." In *Debating Immigration*, edited by Carol M. Swain, 95–113. New York: Cambridge University Press, 2008.

Portes, Alejandro, and Rebén G. Rumbaut. *Immigrant American: A Portrait*. Berkeley: University of California Press, 1996.

Qi Ming. "Zhongguo nuren tiyan yixiang jianxin" (Chinese woman experiencing hardships in a foreign land). In *Shijie ribao*, October 23, 2008, B6.

Razin, Eran. "Entrepreneurship among Foreign Immigrants in the Los Angeles and San Francisco Metropolitan Regions." *Urban Geography* 9 no. 3 (1988): 283–301.

Razin, Eran, and Ivan Light, "Ethnic Entrepreneurs in America's Largest Metropolitan Areas," *Urban Affairs Review* 33, no. 3 (1988): 332–360.

Sanders, Jimy J., and Victor Nee. "The Limits of Ethnic Solidarity in the Enclave Economy." *American Sociological Review* 52 (1987): 745–773.

Sandmeyer, Elmer C. *The Anti-Chinese Movement in California*. Urbana: University of Illinois Press, 1973.

Saxton, Alexander. *The Indispensable Enemy: Labor and the Anti-Chinese Movement in California*. Berkeley: University of California Press, 1971.

Scott, Joan. "On Language, Gender, and Working-Class History." In Scott, *Gender and the Politics of History*, 53–67. New York: Columbia University Press, 1988.

See, Lisa. *On Gold Mountain: The One-Hundred-Year Odyssey of My Chinese-American Family*. New York: Vintage, 1995.

Sennett, Richard, and Jonathan Cobb. *The Hidden Injury of Class*. New York: Vintage, 1972.

Skeldon, Ronald. *Myths and Realities of Chinese Irregular Migration*. Geneva: International Organization for Migration, 2000. IOM Migration Research Series no. 1.

Storti, Craig. *Incident at Bitter Creek: The Story of the Rock Springs Chinese Massacre*. Ames: Iowa State University Press, 1991.

Swain, Carol M. *Debating Immigration*. New York: Cambridge University Press, 2008.

Thernstrom, Stephan. *Poverty and Progress: Social Mobility in a Nineteenth Century City*. Cambridge, MA: Harvard University Press, 1964.

Thompson, E. P. *The Making of the English Working Class*. New York: Vintage, 1966.

Tsang Wai-Yin. "Changle ren zai meiguo" (Changle people in America). *Shijie zhoukan*, September 21, 2003, to October 5, 2003.

———. "Fangfan beiju zai fasheng, zi bao shouze laoji zai xin" (Preventing tragedy from happening again: Keep in mind rules of self-protection). *Shijie zhoukan*, March 7, 2004, 28–29.

———. "*Zhongcan waimailang, beige he shi liao?*" (When will the sad song of the delivery boys of Chinese restaurants end?). *Shijie zhoukan*, March 7, 2004, 24–26.

Van der Leun, Joanne. *Looking for Loopholes: Processes of Incorporation of Illegal Immigrants in the Netherlands*. Amsterdam: Amsterdam University Press, 2003.

Weber, Max. "The Economic Relationships of Organized Groups." In *Economy and Society*, 1. New York: Bedminster, 1968.

Wegars, Priscilla, ed. *Hidden Heritage: Historical Archaeology of the Overseas Chinese*. Amityville, N.Y.: Baywood, 1993.

Wilson, William Julius. "Social Theory and Public Agenda Research: The Challenge of Studying Inner-City Social Dislocations." Presidential address, annual meeting of the American Sociological Association, August 12, 1990.

———. *The Truly Disadvantaged: The Inner City, the Underclass, and Public Policy*. Chicago: University of Chicago Press, 1987.

Wong, Bernard P. *Patronage, Brokerage, Entrepreneurship and the Chinese Community of New York*. New York: AMS Press, 1988.

Wong, Jade Snow. *Fifth Chinese Daughter*. New York: Harper, 1950.

Wong, K. Scott. "Cultural Defenders and Brokers: Chinese Responses to the Anti-Chinese Movement." In *Claiming America: Constructing Chinese American Identities during the Exclusion Era*, edited by K. Scott Wong and Sucheng Chan, 3–40. Philadelphia: Temple University Press, 1998.

Wong, Marie Rose. *Sweet Cakes, Long Journey: The Chinatowns of Portland, Oregon*. Seattle: University of Washington Press, 2004.

Xinjing yi re san (Arai Hifumi), "*She zhi dao: Fuzhou–Xianggang-Niuyue*" (The snake road: Fuzhou–Hong Kong–New York). *Jiushi niandai*, July 1995, 34–40, 90–91.

Yang, Fenggang. *Chinese Christians in America: Conversion, Assimilation, and Adhesive Identities*. University Park: Pennsylvania State University Press, 1999.

Yee, Alfred. *Shopping at Giant Foods: Chinese American Supermarkets in Northern California*. Seattle: University of Washington Press, 2003.

Yeh, Chiou-Ling Yeh. *Making an American Festival: Chinese New Year in San Francisco's Chinatown*. Berkeley: University of California Press, 2008.

Yu, Renqiu. *To Save China, to Save Ourselves: The Chinese Hand Laundry Alliance of New York*. Philadelphia, Temple University Press, 1992.

Yu Renqiu. *Qing ke (Dinner parties)*. Beijing: People's Literature, 2007.

Zhao, Xiaojian. *Remaking Chinese America: Immigration, Family, and Community, 1940–1965*. New Brunswick: Rutgers University Press, 2002.

Zhou, Min. *Chinatown: The Socioeconomic Potential of an Urban Enclave*. Philadelphia: Temple University Press, 1992.

———. "Once Excluded, Now Ascendant." In *The New Face of Asian America: Numbers, Diversity and Change in the 21st Century*, edited by Eric Lai and Dennis Arguelles, 37–44. San Francisco: AsianWeek, 2003.

Zhou Min. *Meiguo huaren shehui de bianquian* (The Transformation of Chinese America). Shanghai: Sanlian Publishers, 2006.

Zhou, Min, and Rebecca Kim. "The Paradox of Ethnicization and Assimilation: The Development of Ethnic Organizations in the Chinese Immigrant Community in the United States." In *Voluntary Organizations in the Chinese Diaspora*, edited by Kuah-Pearce Khun Eng and Evelyn Hu-Dehart, 231–252. Hong Kong: Hong Kong University Press, 2006.

———. "Formation, Consolidation, and Diversification of the Ethnic Elite: The Case of the Chinese Immigrant Community in the United States." *Journal of International Migration and Integration* 2 no. 2 (2001): 227–247.

Zhou, Min, and Susan S. Kim. "Community Forces, Social Capital, and Educational Achievement: The Case of Supplementary Education in the Chinese and Korean Immigrant Communities." *Harvard Educational Review* 76 no. 1 (2006): 1–29.

Zhou, Min, and Mingang Lin. "Community Transformation and the Formation of Ethnic Capital: Immigrant Chinese Communities in the United States." *Journal of Chinese Overseas* 1 no. 2 (2005): 260–284.

Zhu, Liping. *A Chinaman's Chance: The Chinese of the Rocky Mountain Mining Frontier*. Niwot: University Press of Colorado, 1997.

Index

About the Author

Xiaojian Zhao is an associate professor in the Department of Asian American Studies at the University of California, Santa Barbara. She is the author of *Remaking Chinese America: Immigration, Family, and Community, 1940–1965* (2002), winner of the 2003 History Book Award from the Association of Asian American Studies.

CPSIA information can be obtained
at www.ICGtesting.com
Printed in the USA
LVHW040148230819
628638LV00001B/3